Magnificence at Work

John Dalla Costa

Magnificence at Work
Living Faith in Business

© 2005 Novalis, Saint Paul University, Ottawa, Canada
Cover: Eye-to-Eye Design
Layout: Caroline Galhidi

Business Office:
Novalis
49 Front Street East, 2nd Floor
Toronto, Ontario, Canada
M5E 1B3
Phone: 1-800-387-7164
Fax: 1-800-204-4140
E-mail: cservice@novalis-inc.com
www.novalis.ca

Library and Archives Canada Cataloguing in Publication

Dalla Costa, John
    Magnificence at work : living faith in business / John Dalla Costa.

Includes bibliographical references.
ISBN 2-89507-669-3

    1. Business–Religious aspects–Christianity. 2. Businesspeople–Religious life. I. Title.

HF5388.D34 2005   248.8'8   C2005-904708-9

Printed in Canada.

The Scripture quotations contained herein are from the New Revised Standard Version of the Bible, copyrighted 1989 by the Division of Christian Education of the National Council of the Churches of Christ in the United States of America, and are used by permission. All rights reserved.

All rights reserved. No part of this publication may be reproduced, stored in a retrieval system, or transmitted in any form, or by any means, electronic, mechanical, photocopying, recording, or otherwise, without the written permission of the publisher.

We acknowledge the financial support of the Government of Canada through the Book Publishing Industry Development Program (BPIDP) for our publishing activities.

5 4 3 2 1   09 08 07 06 05

In honour of Our Lady of Lourdes

With gratitude for blessings received

For my sisters Romana and Diana

Remembering and hoping, with love

Contents

Introduction
MAGNIFICENCE: *Attending to the Call* 11

PART I: *PREPARING TO SEE ANEW*
1. **PRESENCE:** Praying Towards Integrity 30
2. **BECOMING:** Uplifting Hope from Fear 54
3. **WRESTLING:** Acting from Understanding 85

PART II: *AWAKENING TO WISDOM*
4. **GRACE:** Needs Becoming Ideals 116
5. **BEAUTY:** Freedom in the Balance 143

PART III: *INTEGRITY FROM DOING IT*
6. **PERSPECTIVE:** Where Horizons Meet 172
7. **PROPORTION:** Fair Asymmetries 207
8. **PRACTICE:** Details of Devotion 237
9. **FAQs:** Frequently Avoided Questions 266
Notes 281
Bibliography 289
Index 297

Acknowledgments

Any creative act stands at a nexus of contributions, inputs, gifts and muses. This book is a prime example. While I am the author of the words, the content and flow would not have been possible without countless generosities from teachers, colleagues and friends. Their grace fills these pages, as their graciousness helped me write them.

Margaret Brennan IBVM introduced me to the writings and spirituality of Simone Weil while I was completing a Master of Divinity degree at Regis College. This is but one of many rich presents she bequeathed to me.

Ronald Mercier SJ led me through theology studies as Dean and teacher, inspiring scholarship as prayer. The attempt to fuse the disparate disciplines of business and theology grows in part from his example and encouragement.

Michael J. Naughton read an early draft of this manuscript and unlocked the premise of magnificence. His leadership in exploring business as a vocation is inspiring to all of us working at this deepening integration.

James MacKinnon has run five marathons with me. He too read an early version of the book, posing questions and inserting comments that helped make the material more relevant to business people. He also kept running with me.

Angela Brown provided a chapter-by-chapter critique. Largely from her careful reading I was able to re-conceive the final structure of the book. Her faithfulness and professionalism also helped raise relevance and readability.

Lela and Peter Lega opened their Tuscan home to me at a time when my wife was using our home as a retreat centre. It turned out that I wrote the most difficult chapter at the Legas's aptly named *Villa Santo Spirito* in Anghiari.

Michael Levine represented me to publishers, believing in the voice of the book before its tone and timbre were clear.

Gerald Rich read my final draft, catching dangling participles while also taking time to highlight insights.

Kevin Burns has been an enthusiastic supporter of this book since well before Novalis's decision to publish it. His care and humour made the work of bookmaking uplifting.

Managing Editor Anne Louise Mahoney kept all the moving parts together and coherent through edit and production, respecting content and collaboration as well as process.

Abramo Bettio never forgot to ask me about the work in progress, supplying peace and confidence at times when completion was anything but certain.

Lucinda Vardey walked with me, word-by-word, chapter-by-chapter, version-by-version, sharing my life in faith, hope and love.

Introduction

MAGNIFICENCE

Attending to the Call

Work has always been the locus of God's calling. It would be surprising if it were not, for work matters profoundly as a creative act, as a contribution to sustenance and community, as a mark of human dignity and personal identity. Hardly one to accept a "no-fly zone," God works with who we are, which means that God is persistently active and inviting within the work we do. David was called to become the anointed king of Israel while tending sheep. Similarly, the first disciples of Jesus Christ were invited to follow while repairing and cleaning their nets after a long night trying to catch fish. The stirring of souls for intimacy with the divine did not wait for after work or weekends, but instead came within the everyday reality of productivity. God's calling, like a BlackBerry, buzzes 24/7. "God has given us all a part," writes Dorothee Soelle in her *Theology for Skeptics*. "God comforts us, and we prepare God's way."[1]

Many business people are discovering this pattern in their own lives, feeling that spirituality must be a resource or flowering intrinsic to career rather than peripheral to it. Prayer groups are forming in workplaces or between peers – including among chief executive officers (CEOs). Busy managers are withdrawing during the workday to quiet rooms that companies have set aside for reflection and meditation. Many people are more informal and simply do what humans have always done: offer thanksgiving for blessings, petition for wisdom during difficult decisions, and plead for consolation in moments of trial or threat. While forms and motives vary, this movement of the soul at work occurs in the context of intractable impatience: God's impatience to be in relationship with human beings, and our human impatience to live integrated lives of moral meaning and creativity.

All too often, business people today experience the opposite of integration, having to self-divide moral judgment from managerial expertise to serve the overriding expediencies of efficiency. The management teacher Peter Drucker observes that many of his business students are in jobs without purpose that engage only a fraction of their skills or imagination.[2] As a friend explains, her role as a senior executive demands many things but not the chance to be her best. These divided hearts – these broken hearts – are fertile ground for God's call. The very real needs of the soul have fomented various spiritualities in the workplace. As Laura Nash and Scotty McLennan have found, much of this soul managing is ad hoc. There are moral as well as practical dangers to spiritual freelancing; however, what Nash and McLennan stress in their book *Church on Sunday, Work on Monday* is not the diversity or often ill-defined shape of the spiritual response, but rather the urgency of the common, underlying need.[3] Souls in business are hungry, sometimes agonizingly so, for models or guides to enmesh the interior desire to live in God's embrace with the exterior desire to make a successful contribution as professionals. Despite this craving for integrity, few people in the trenches of business resolved the disconnection – the dis-integrity – between what they pray for on Sunday and the work they do on Monday.

Paradoxically, the wisdom from religious imagination is very close to what business now acknowledges is needed for excellence. Corporate trust has been lost to scandals, but even without these improprieties, managers had been struggling to respond to the difficult moral claims of globalization and sustainability. The enmeshment will only get worse. C.K. Prahalad outlines the key challenges that are shaping managerial competencies for "future organizations." All of these – deploying new technology, creating mutual security, advancing knowledge work, protecting intellectual property, resolving labour issues, balancing public and private domains and infrastructure, and respecting intercultural differences[4] – have strategic implications that are inextricably moral, and moral claims that are of profound strategic value.

There has already been some progress on transparency and accountability; however, these largely imposed measures for default morality cannot realize the generative and substantive integrity companies need to confront what are now forces of history. Ultimately, managerial excellence must be reconceived on a higher plane as vocation – as calling "to work as collaborators of God" – with everyday decisions and actions not so much constrained by moral principle as inspired by it.[5] It is not enough to be merely consistently restrained, to simply deliver what is promised without impropriety. Integrity bespeaks a creative wholeness, the fusion of heart, mind and soul wrestling with the practicalities and dilemmas of life to achieve the most human and hopeful outcomes. While corporations are legal constructs with commercial aims, their functionality and effectiveness hinge on the very attributes of moral wholeness that constitute human integrity.

Investors depend on *truth*. Regulators expect *obedience* to the rule of law. Customers discern value through some calibration of *fairness*. Employees need a sense of animating *order* and belonging that comes from vision. Managers rely on *hierarchy* to apportion resources and multiply outcomes. Strategies aim to anticipate exigencies so as to secure operational *stability*. Renewal requires creative *risk* and innovation. Capital, to be *free*, needs, paradoxically, the regimen of a level playing field. Accountability, to be real, requires *responsibility*, with consequences commensurate to transgressions. These virtues, which managers recognize as the operational standards from best practices, and which society holds as normative for integrity, are corporate expressions of what the French philosopher and mystic Simone Weil named the "needs of the soul."[6]

Making Great Things

The correspondence between soul and corporate needs that is at the core of this book is not as surprising as it first may seem. Weil developed the idea of the needs of the soul as an exercise in restoring wholeness, seeking an intellectual and moral basis for reunifying France after the fissuring trauma of Nazi occupation. Hardly abstract, these needs serve both the universal and the particular, resonating with the demands of history while also addressing the practical realities of dislocated individuals within divided communities. As human beings cannot survive or be whole in isolation, the needs of the soul, and the integrity these confer, are inextricably personal and also corporate, as in the larger corpus or body of community. Weil envisioned these as the foundation of universal human rights – the obligations through which freedom, dignity and belonging would in fact be possible for all. To speak of needs implies deficiency, when quite the opposite is the case. These characteristics of the soul are actually the raw material for magnificence because they enable a wider healing of creation and history, and provide the roots for meaning and personal fulfillment. Hence, the inviting opportunity: what persons in business crave in their spirituality, the larger bodies of company, community, society or church also need to create and sustain.

Attuned to best practices and the search for excellence, managers and companies are already knee deep in a culture of "continuous improvement." Magnificence is excellence on moral steroids: achieving great things that are also good things. The medieval theologian St. Thomas Aquinas defined magnificence as a grand achievement that is shaped and motivated by "noble purpose." For Aquinas, the qualities of enterprise already engage courage, so the risk for moral impact is in natural continuity with what is already common in any business or innovation. Excellence aims for technical proficiency. Magnificence stretches further so that the impacts are not only just and ethical but also liberating and beautiful. There is attention to quality and craft in excellence. With magnificence, this technical commitment is motivated by heartfelt compassion as well as the desire for personal mastery. Business people recognize excellence as the joyful momentum and high-performance teamwork that generate superior results. Magnificence is part of the greater momentum of creation and human self-understanding, and touches what is both universal and transcendent. As Helen J. Alford and Michael J. Naughton explain, the virtue of magnificence does not diminish the importance of profit or return on investment, but makes "return on community" or "return on creation" integral to the risks and rewards of the company.[7]

Many businesses subscribe to some type of corporate social responsibility. This can be great but not necessarily magnificent. Rather than good deeds, the key is goodness itself. Courage is required not only when risking something new. It is also, more importantly, required when becoming someone new. Even small contributions can be magnificent when they give life to the aspirations of our souls. If it feels grandiose or abstract, magnificence is close to the urgent priority imposed by the new normal of our day-to-day commercial reality. Globalization is a much bigger opportunity for human consciousness and co-operation than merely the economies of scale for brands. We need imaginative new ways of doing business that create more transparency and accountability, and extend effective compassion to the two thirds of the global population still mired in poverty and excluded from hope. It will take grand enterprise and courage to meet the ever-steeper demands of sustainability. It will take highly developed integrity for managers to wrestle with the moral dilemmas posed by new technologies, such as biogenetics, or new efficiencies, such as outsourcing. Again the synchronicity: the longing in our souls to participate in magnificence corresponds to the most pressing needs and loftiest opportunities that define our time.

Peter Drucker argues that most of the management models still used in business are inadequate due to having been formulated in the industrial age and not for the knowledge economy. Companies misunderstood this wisdom when they adopted re-engineering, applying the metaphor and standards of machinery to people and, in the end, destroying wealth and human networks of creativity in the pursuit of efficiency. Drucker and others are probing the corrective skills and structures for management that are needed in the age of knowledge and innovation. But while trying to escape the gravitational pull of the past, we are already entering another stage of organizational upheaval defined by the imminent future. With the grave threats from environmental degradation and from growing imbalances in opportunity, we are by default passing from the information age to a moral one. There are no neutral decisions or actions in business. Every outcome expresses a set of values and presumes (or neglects) some ethical commitment. In most organizations, these moral dynamics are addenda to other, more pressing, management priorities. In the fast-emerging global reality, these are becoming primary competencies. Already, the new managerial job description is to create wealth with responsibility: to invest capital and focus innovations on opportunities that generate dignity and fairness as well as returns, and that secure the health of the natural ecosystem as well as competitive advantage. In its economic impacts, business is already doing great things. The challenge now is to transform this capacity for productivity towards magnificence.

EVOLVING NEW COMPETENCIES FOR A MORAL AGE

INDUSTRIAL PARADIGM	KNOWLEDGE PARADIGM	MORAL PARADIGM
• Use human muscle to manufacture wealth	• Use human intellect to create value from ideas	• Use human conscience to discipline value with values
• Extract wealth from natural resources	• Extract wealth from recycling and efficiency	• Extract wealth from protecting the ecosystem
• Implement systems for economies of scale	• Extend systems to allow for mass customization	• Open systems to maximize liberty
• Operate using top-down hierarchies	• Operate using circular teams of experts	• Operate using networks of wisdom
• Invest capital in bricks and mortar	• Invest capital in human skills and competencies	• Invest capital in moral imagination and relational development
• Be transactional	• Be interactive	• Be integrative
• Be autocratic in advancing the rights of shareholders	• Be democratic in considering the rights of stakeholders	• Be dialogic in accountability to human rights
• Be competitive, striving for independence	• Be collaborative, facing interdependence	• Be eucharistic, sharing dependence
• Maximize efficiency	• Maximize innovation	• Maximize accountability
• Focus marketing on fulfilling benefits	• Focus marketing on fulfilling image	• Focus marketing on fulfilling social responsibility
• Audit to determine profit or loss	• Audit for social and environmental impacts	• Audit worthiness resulting from contributions to beauty, hope and truth

The core challenge of this emerging moral age is not the problems, which are indisputable, but the quality, ingenuity and malleability of our responses. We need to bring every moral asset to the table to come close to matching expertise to task. The collaboration needs to be multidisciplinary and multicultural, breaking across silos of self-interest to unleash our best imagination for a shared purpose. Since morality is, for many people, rooted in religious experience or beliefs, we will need the courage and maturity to include spiritual wisdom in the discourse to frame issues and inspire solutions. More than tolerance, this approach is motivated by interdependence. No one view or expertise can alone solve problems that are now global and interconnected. From both believers and non-believers, we need contributions for understanding and shared action. From both we need their best talents and resources. From both, we also need integrity in its fullest form, with the whole person present, with all her or his emotional, intellectual and spiritual gifts. To be magnificent in a business world confronting serious moral issues and opportunities challenges us in two ways: to be open and respectful when engaging the beliefs of others, and to be open and respectful towards our own personal religious convictions.

Not all people turning to prayer at work are comfortable fusing profession with confession. This is only natural. The Hebrew and Christian scriptures overflow with resistance, with prophets unwilling to speak and disciples running away from the tasks of following. Magnificence always beckons as a tension. It seems impossibly demanding, except that it is what the soul naturally expects. It meets public resistance, except that it is exactly what society needs. It suffers from the stigma of being idealistic, except that it represents the essential practicality of what really needs to be done. Markets have a singular anthropology, reducing the worth of a person to measurable factors of consumption or production. None of us accepts these as the final determinants of human value, and much of the longing for spirituality at work is premised on countering this reduction. Honouring the needs of the soul in business stipulates a much richer humanity that has immeasurable capacity for realizing truth, creating beauty, imagining ideals and discovering holiness. Magnificence is variable. We may hear it, as many do, as the eternal within our own hearts clamouring for dignity. Or we may hear it, as the prophets have, as the eternal Source demanding presence and participation in justice. Either way, the movement is ultimately towards unleashing a latency that is both aspiration and necessity. The work of magnificence is our human vocation. Magnificence at work is the vocation of business.

The Christic Factor

In *Difficult Freedom*, the philosopher Emmanuel Levinas explains that morality as only a guide or control to behaviour "is thus already banished," leaving us in the shallow territory of kindness and good intentions.[8] In many companies, including those that have suffered ethical calamities, the investments for the moral age tend to be the thin ones of codes and compliance. Even businesses that have been shamefully caught in impropriety usually address the symptom rather than the cause. "Already banished," this superficial morality has not really changed the ethos of business; rather, it has only attempted to curtail its excesses. The magnified urgencies of the moral age will not be diffused as part-time priorities or with less than complete dedication. It will not be enough for business to be ethical. We need the ethical to be the business of companies. The reason for imagining work from the perspective of the needs of the soul is that the transformation required is not only in practice but more so in our person. In developmental terms, we can only achieve what is required in the moral age by who we become with our skills and hopes and within the limitations of our individual lives. For Christians, the model for this specific practice, and the measure for human integrity, is the person of Jesus Christ.

Just as we often forget what follows from being made in God's image and likeness, Christians often gloss over the implications for humanity of the Incarnation. What does it mean for God to have taken human form, if not that every human being is a temple for glory and transcendence? Christ personifies magnificence at work. Jesus started his adult life as a carpenter, a labourer. With prayerful attentiveness to his Jewish monotheism, he took on a larger calling, assuming a rabbinic role in building on God's scale a kingdom of beatitude and fellowship. Such a magnificent project sparked outrage, as it does anytime the status quo is challenged with truth. Jesus suffered the ignominy of death on the cross, but this emptying of self in service to calling became the vessel into which God poured infinite love and potentiality. By his humble obedience to the necessary tasks of justice and love, Jesus unleashed for all the triumph of divinizing communion with God (Philippians 2:6-12). These are not the usual reference points for a business book, but it is not an accident that the timber and nails of carpentry — the tools for productivity — were used for suffering and death, yet through Christ became the very symbols of healing, hope and harmony.

With our now global perspective and maturing sensibilities for diversity, it has become very awkward to speak publicly as a Christian. It is as if in our embrace of tolerance we have ironically ceased tolerating the voices and wisdom of our own tradition. Pope John Paul II taught an embrace of plurality that is neither passive nor proselytizing, stressing instead that "the truth about God the Creator and Christ the Redeemer is a powerful force which inspires a positive attitude towards creation and provides a consistent impetus to strive for its transformation and perfection."[9] My first (year-long) attempt to write this book was from a broader, interfaith perspective. A generalized spirituality seemed more appropriate to business people operating in a global economy, and more palatable to secular culture.

Three fallacies undermined this approach. First, how could I pursue this project for managerial integrity while denying or segregating the very belief systems that for me constitute healing and wholeness? More than authenticity was in jeopardy. As Richard McCormick explains, the risk is "neospiritualism," a private or imprecise spirituality "which ignores the concrete character of sin and virtue; a selective responsibility which collapses responsibility in one sphere to emphasize it in another; a narrow consequentialism which ignores the fact that neighbor is Every-person."[10] Being open to other faiths is an important acknowledgment of the mystery and ineffability of encountering God. But our spirituality cannot be a mere platform for observing life or taking refuge from its despair. It is what we practise, not what we preach, that the world especially needs from us. Christ's most passionate disciple is also the one who denied knowing him, not once but three times. When we do not embrace the truth and consequences of our own faith, we risk repeating what Peter uttered when it matters most: "I do not know him" (Matthew 26:69-75).

Second, as much as I wanted to be a global spiritual citizen, I could not seriously engage the wisdom of other religious traditions without first honouring my own. We desperately need dialogue: between religions, between diverging cultural perspectives and also, importantly, between the religious imagination and the managerial one. Such encounter, however, is not served by simplistic conflation. Serious transformation hinges on exchanges of depth, respecting the beliefs of others sufficiently to also represent the best of what we believe in our own hearts and souls. To see others as whole means standing in the truth of our own integrity, which for me means standing in discipleship to Christ.

Third, beyond coherence and consistency, Christian teaching is rich in relevance and beauty. Nash and McLennan found that many business people are removed from the treasure of their tradition, in part because of unfamiliarity, but also because of the antipathy that often seems to creep into Christian social teaching about economics.[11] The opportunity, now taken up by more and more theologians as well as business people, is to retrieve the significance of Christian faith, ending the estrangement between social justice and business practice to help embody a specific contribution to the tricky global quest for integrity in business. This relationship to tradition is important both to avoid the all-too-real tendency for idolatry – for reducing the transcendent to our own image and means – and to avoid robbing our toughest moral problems of their potential to engage our deepest creativity towards realizing what it means to be human.

The encounter of Christ at work goes back to the very beginning. In Luke's gospel, we are informed of the occupation of the first disciples before we are even told their names. Jesus walks into their midst while they are at labour, repairing and cleaning nets. He asks to be taken out on their boat, using this platform of entrepreneurial commerce to preach to the growing crowd pressing along the seashore. Here we have divine word proclaimed from a workplace, not displacing expertise but reframing its aim to serve the cosmic calling of divine relationship. Luke explains that the four followed Jesus and became "fishers of men" and women (Luke 5:1-11). This is the core challenge of this book: to receive Christ in our midst while we are at work; to take the challenge and allow Christ to speak from the platform of our own productivity; and to envision the cosmic potential that we as managers — whether as marketers, executives, bankers, researchers, CEOs, technologists or directors — share with first-century fishing industry entrepreneurs. The aim is not to affect a spiritual reverse takeover of companies, but to be taken over as a person by the claims of our soul and the call of our God. Rather than proselytize to others or impose dogmatic strictures of belief, our task is to live our work as managers in witness to the interior conversion of our hearts.

A Litany of Nots

- This is not easy work, but since the premise is needs of the soul, it is in fact necessary work.
- This is not therefore a conventional business book, but a book for business people who, in their longing for and relationship with God, seek to find transcendence in their everyday work as managers.
- This is not an exercise aimed at improving a skill set, but an exploration of our spiritual intuitions for goodness and wholeness as resources for reframing and managing integrity.
- This is not a "how-to" book, but rather a "why-to" exploration of the possibilities and power of business activity to promote human hope as well as development.
- This is not an attempt to build another business case for moral management, but rather a more experiential juxtaposition of theology with business, bringing these usually segregated disciplines together to focus on management as magnificent work.
- This is not a neutral, fact-based study, but a work of discipleship, using both strategic analysis and prayer to unsettle the unsatisfying status quo and imagine the holy potential of business.
- This is not an effort to exclude or in any way diminish those who do not believe in God, nor to make the fatal presumption that morality is somehow exclusive to spirituality, but to find the voice for faith in critically important discussions about the scope and responsibilities of companies.

- This is not an attack on managers or a dismissal of the largely beneficial role of management in human development. Rather, it is a challenge towards re-creation – a practice of continuous improvement applied literally and laterally to imagine renewal that is simultaneously effective and holistic.
- This is not a work of proselytizing, or in any way an imposition or judgment on other religious traditions, but a search by a Christian for a way to practise faithfulness in the demanding realm of business. As all spirituality struggles to unleash the sacred within the everyday, my hope is that any deepening of Christian authenticity may also serve as the basis for deeper exchange with other traditions.
- This is not a repudiation of secularism, but a claim within its freedoms to contribute from humanity's mystical resources to the re-imagining of managerial accountability.
- Finally, this is not another project, but a form of devotion, attempting to name the many blessings of business in order to appreciate the moral and ethical charge that is entrusted to those who participate in such gifts.

A Work in Three Movements

Growth in soul and magnificence in any sphere shares several dynamics. Neither is ordinary, yet both express something essential and natural about being human. We are somehow less than whole when soul is suppressed, and somehow less ourselves when denied the possibility to dream of grandeur. As we work on soul for personal completion, and pursue magnificence from this aspiration for human wholeness, we can see that both are integral to integrity. Another commonality is that neither soul growth nor magnificence is easy. This does not mean they are disposable, only that as with achievements in art, learning or athletics, they require diligence, discipline and devotion. Mystics speak of the work of the soul as a journey, as an ascent requiring perseverance and as a test involving a "dark night" of struggle or despair. Magnificence, too, requires a passionate commitment to the details of implementation, in service to a courageous cause or dream. The process for both is part of the outcome – *becoming* as verb and noun. We may think of magnificence as we do creativity, as a one-time event or epiphany moment in which a breakthrough leads to wholesale reinvention. In reality, the work of magnificence is more a slog through thickets of difficulty and doubt. This again relates to the excessiveness of what constitutes real integrity: not that human beings persist in doing great things, but that they persist despite obstacles, improbability and even seeming impossibility in trying to realize the fullness of what the soul needs in its magnificence.

The movements within spiritual growth and ascent have shaped the structure of this book. Saints and spiritual teachers point to three stages of soul work:
- seeing anew, which involves repentance or purification;
- awakening to understanding, which brings wisdom or illumination; and
- transcendence, which is experienced as communion or unification.

As the exercise of virtue, magnificence is something we embrace as purpose and yet grow into through practice. The story of calling in Luke's gospel unfolds in a very similar pattern. Jesus invites the fishermen to take him out on their boat so they can see the coastline anew through the perspective of the soul needs of the crowd clamouring on the shore. Floating free on their boat, surrounded by the tools of work but listening to the heart teachings of Jesus, the fishermen experience a profound, life-altering awakening of other possibilities. Before rising to magnificence, the fishermen's faith was then tested by Jesus' command to cast their net in what by hard-won experience they knew to be a barren bit of sea. By persisting through that professional doubt, by accepting grace as the complement to expertise, the fishermen ultimately harvested the net-straining catch from communion with transcendence. Unlike the usual prescriptions for personal mastery, with checklists or one-minute shortcuts, the soul's response to God is to experience magnificence as gift and potential. Such power can neither be accessed casually nor deployed without serious preparation through contemplation and prayer.

In keeping with this pattern of soul growth and development, the three themes of this book are set out in three parts. Part I: *Preparing to See Anew* deals with becoming open to the "in-breaking" of faith in business to reconceive what it means to become whole, and to manage with magnificence. Part II: *Awakening to Wisdom* explores becoming involved through grace and beauty in the possibilities for a greater entwining of soul and strategy. Part III: *Integrity from Doing It* outlines becoming expert in new roles and practical in the needs of the soul to help make magnificence operational. Simulating the devotional requirements for living faith at work, I have provided prayers throughout to serve as possible reflection points. More importantly, these are also intended to invite other prayers to make the language and precepts of spiritual practice as commonplace as spreadsheets in the work environment. The book ends with FAQs – in this case, the frequently *avoided* questions that I have sidestepped or have encountered with others at work or in conversation.

Part I: *Preparing to See Anew* unfolds in three chapters.

Chapter 1: **Presence** sets out the human potential that is implied and hoped for in prayer. At a time when the appreciation for integrity in business has grown more acute, there is a need to examine the moral competencies of managers, including their religious imagination and spiritual faith. Other important renewal initiatives, including business ethics, have all too often brought about only cosmetic change. The challenge with integrity is to get beyond "thin" prescriptions to engage complex problems with the "thick" moral commitment and creativity they deserve.

Chapter 2: **Becoming** tackles the great stress and frequent dissatisfaction that compress the horizons – professional and moral – of many managers. Long hours and unrealistic job descriptions are frequent complaints camouflaging the more existential fissuring of presence: companies demand passion but eschew compassion; they expect greater results but neglect greater meaning. Reversing this diminishment is essential for both the soul and the economy. Magnificence is an antidote for meanness. It is also the ambition that exercises and satisfies the needs of the soul identified by Simone Weil.

Chapter 3: **Wrestling** test-markets the business relevance of soul needs, establishing a specific principle from each to guide and inspire managerial renewal and business integrity. Magnificence is so compelling because it is simultaneously a moral ideal and a practical necessity.

Without exhausting the managerial possibilities of the needs of the soul, these principles are intended to raise our horizon of hopes, while helping us honestly face the struggle of intertwining the spiritual with the professional.

Having reconsidered our current assumptions and opened our hearts to see the imperatives of faith at work, we move from possibility to preparation.

Part II: *Awakening to Wisdom* comprises two chapters. While our instinct as managers is to get on with it, the soul learns and integrates at a different pace than what is required to achieve quarter-by-quarter results. Wisdom is not something we achieve, but something we receive. The task of preparation for the soul involves prayer and contemplation, learning to see the grace of God's presence in all things and understanding the gifts we have inherited for doing great things.

Chapter 4: **Grace** breaches the divide between holy things and profitable ones by positing money to be a form of grace. Several theologians have already made this leap. Fusing these usually opposing symbols is an important step in our reconsideration of management as a vocation. To again test relevance, the coherence of money as grace is explored through the respective dynamics of the needs of the soul.

Chapter 5: **Beauty** seeks to acclimatize us to magnificence and prepare us for its risks. Not only does beauty enthrall humanity, it, more importantly, changes us. This experience of being taken over by something greater than ourselves has profound implications for the artistry with which we carry out the projects, prayers and everyday responsibilities of life. The senses for apprehending beauty are in many ways those for enhancing integrity – for getting beyond bottom-line simplifications and restoring the managerial and moral possibilities of the balance sheet.

From Thomas Aquinas we learn that the key virtue for magnificence is courage. Obviously, there is no formula for fostering courageousness. We know that grace has a role, which artists often call "the muse" and saints call the "ecstasy of communion." Beauty, too, contributes to courage in that it always involves a risk that closely approximates the leap of faith for magnificence.

With the desire to integrate faith in business pushed by grace and pulled by beauty, we can move to a reconsideration of roles and responsibilities.

Part III: *Integrity from Doing It* is made up of four chapters, each dealing with possibilities of praxis.

Chapter 6: **Perspective** brings specific dimension to the prophetic role through three needs of the soul: order, which situates vision in God's creation and calling; hierarchism, which establishes context and priority for breaking the compartmentalization that stymies integrity; and responsibility, which relates to that "thick" accountability premised on both care and the commitment to achieve reintegration after mistakes or malfeasance. The prophetic needs of the soul strive for wholeness, to repair division or failure and participate in making real what ought to be. This is the often-neglected moral job of "creating creation" after "creative destruction."

Chapter 7: **Proportion** elaborates the priestly role. From experience, this section will most test users' expectations and expertise; however, this involves the vital task of making everyday work holy. Three needs of the soul are especially relevant to this: fairness, which recognizes the divine imprint on all human beings; risk, which connects the vital projects of innovation to the larger blessing of creation; and security, which provides the basis for belonging, in order both to mine wealth and to allow the flowering of magnificence. Many companies have adopted programs for "emotional intelligence." The priestly emphasis goes beyond the vagaries of values to express the moral clarity of the "thinking heart."

Chapter 8: **Practice** fashions the kingly role through the soul's need for obedience, which realizes effective governance from respecting limits and obligations; liberty, which keeps the human being as aim and end and not means; and truth, which is the principal responsibility of integrity and the primary basis for group integration. The Nobel laureate economist Amartya Sen has elaborated an economics in which the measure of development is not simply output but rather human freedom. There is a critical truth to making the data serve the human need rather than compelling humans to be subservient to the metrics of development and performance. To be free is an inalienable right, yet it has worth only if the choices available to us are for wholeness – for that integrity of dignity and creativity that include our soul as well as our capacities for production and consumption.

Chapter 9, as already noted, poses the **Frequently Avoided Questions** that allow us to evade responsibility for magnificence. All of us have reasons for opting out of living faith at work and remaining in the flow of business as usual. The concerns are real, as are the challenges. The questions – or, more precisely, their answers – are not really for persuasion, since the movement of the soul is affected only by conversion. The hope of this book is to support that soul growth, using the ideas, principles and questions to generate momentum on that blessed journey.

Invitation with Disclosure

Reciprocal disclosure between writer and reader is required before entering into the text that follows. The disclosure I make for – and in invitation to – readers is for suspending managerial impatience. We are in largely uncharted territory. As Laura Nash explains, "The greatest problem in the current religious and ethical dialogue about business" is that "there is no mediating language or framework that captures the special forms of meaning of religion and philosophy in such a way that the economic actor can integrate these meanings into the full complexity of his or her economic activities."[12] Forging links and interconnecting relevance requires deliberation and experimentation, eschewing the usual managerial core competence of "getting on with it" to seriously and creatively engage new possibilities. With truthful humour, rabbinic sources teach that the highest levels of heaven are reserved for ethical business people[13] – presumably because the temptations for wrongdoing are greatest, but also because the stakes for doing right are so critical for creation and for communities of the future.

Calling involves a process of spiritual transformation. We must give it time, especially time for prayerful hearing and attentive reflection. Again, it is helpful to reflect on Luke's story of the first disciples. Having worked all night, the fishermen had empty nets. Expertise and labour, in and of themselves, were merely exhausting. Only when the four paused to hear the word of God was work reconsecrated so that the sea yielded its full abundance. The demand from Jesus was not for outcomes, but for fidelity practised as hope, with nets tossed by hands trusting grace as well as technique. Social teaching and church building came later, after the spiritual need of the fishermen grew into spiritual competence, and eventually became spiritual trust. To let calling speak, to let it take hold, requires that we, too, surrender to this grace and cadence of becoming.

For my part, I could come to this material only with prayer, and I could finish this book only by praying. As a result, I have decided to include some of my prayers in the text of each chapter. Composing prayers has long been part of my spiritual practice. I have written prayers before and even during meetings, on airplanes, in lobbies, offices and boardrooms, waiting to begin projects, or bringing them to a close. St. Paul counselled continuous prayer, more rigorously when we encounter setbacks. He also instructed that praying be invisible, except through action. My reasons for transgressing this latter advice are twofold: to be faithful to the project, which could not have been completed without prayer; and to be faithful to the content, which is forever inadequate without grace. As Ian Mitroff and Elizabeth Denton have shown in their research, many people already pray at work.[14] While there are many benefits to such personal practice, our job in praying as managers is also to mark business as what the scientist and Jesuit Pierre Teilhard de Chardin called the "divine milieu."[15]

Part I

Preparing to See Anew

1

PRESENCE

Praying Towards Integrity

Woody Allen famously attributed 80 per cent of success to "showing up."[1] Magnificence takes a little more: showing up but with "presence" – with head, heart and soul integrated as a creative and conscious unity. To say "a little more" does not discount the difficulty. Success is hard work and magnificence harder still. What makes the effort relatively slight is that we are made for magnificence, the true vocation of human nature. Success usually involves an extreme interior drive to achieve some external ambition. Magnificence is a mark of dignity all humans already share for being in the "image and likeness" of God. Hard work and prayerful dedication are needed to enliven this latency, but as Jesus said, "My yoke is easy, and my burden is light" (Matthew 11:30). The stuff of our soul is already magnificent, already tuned to the eternal, already erupting with renewing possibilities.

Presence is not the same as being present. Many people have experienced the numbing diminishment of having only part of their person tolerated at work. For my father, a labourer, only his muscles and sweat were of value to his employer. Everything else was disposable. Surprisingly, knowledge and management work are not that much more expansive. While greater expertise is involved in creating wealth from information and innovation, the parameters of work have not necessarily been opened wider to include the creative urgencies of the heart or the moral priorities of the soul. As in my father's time, we have full-time jobs that employ only part-time humanity. Some companies acknowledge this fissuring of human presence with earnest programs for restoring "work–life balance." Many individuals pursue spiritual life at work in direct response to having their transcendence underutilized. The potential problem in both cases is that the corrective can very well perpetuate the cause. Balance will not be real if it takes the form of private restoration outside of work (as important as that may be). The key is to make work itself a balancing reality, a melting pot for all human needs and capacities, including those of the soul. The same applies to personal spirituality. Unless the encounter with transcendence infiltrates work – transforms its aims, outcomes and possibilities – we are not really integrating presence but only compensating for its disintegration.

Presence is the place to begin for four reasons.

First, as the ancient Greek philosophers insisted, the primary creative act for any human being is to "know thyself." To be busy with life without attending to presence risks the gnawing emptiness, chronic in our work and society, from not getting enough of what we need in our souls, even though we give more and more of ourselves in pursuit of career, money or ambition. Presence asks that we make explicit our answer to this question: What does it mean to be human? The answer has individual as well as universal implications, setting the criteria for personal growth and ethics while situating the priorities and practices of work.

Second, in business and public life there is an increasing hunger for integrity. The obvious impetus is to avoid the grave costs and consequences of scandal, but there is also the much greater opportunity of realizing within our economy and social systems the magnificent outcomes that are worthy of human dignity and potential. Integrity based on selective parts of our humanity is not really integrity at all. How can it be, since it disaggregates? To be real and complete, especially to imagine the most human possibilities, integrity must proceed from integration of all those capacities – intellectual, emotional and moral – that comprise our wisdom.

Third, many of the smartest management inventions, and many of our most stubborn business problems, are rooted in a misunderstanding of human presence. For example, memorable customer service usually means that a person has been seen, heard and respected, requiring expertise, imagination and relationship. This is full-time work engaging the full scope of human care, creativity and conscience. Conversely, lapses in accountability are often examples of absence, as with directors who fail to exercise their moral presence in board meetings or with employees who witness impropriety and choose not to blow the whistle. This squelched humanity, which business professor Rosabeth Moss Kanter calls "anonymity,"[2] perpetuates bureaucracy, impedes organizational renewal and dilutes accountability.

Fourth, presence is what sparks spiritual longing and ignites religious imagination. Before any understanding takes shape, before creed gets professed, prayer is a simple act of presence.

I'm here, God. Are You?

I'm here, God. Awed by You.

I'm here, God. Grateful to You.

I'm here, God. In need of You.

I'm here, God. To be attentive to You.

I'm here, God. To be made anew by You.

I'm here, God. Please, let's talk.

The human encounter with the divine presence usually leaves us at a loss for words. In ancient Israel, which established the monotheistic tradition that flows through Judaism, Christianity and Islam, the one inexhaustible deity was called "I AM WHO AM." Forever ambiguous and incomplete, the essential insight of this name is of God as "Presence Personified." The mysterious and awesome source of creation is at once incomprehensible yet accessible: transcendent, and therefore completely unlike our temporal human reality, yet immanent, and therefore present within it. Karl Rahner, a twentieth-century theologian, explained this immanence as God's "self-communication" within all of creation.[3] At every moment, in every experience, this originating and sustaining presence is palpable; it is the reason we feel our souls and quest for spirituality. Living in an age of wondrous advances in human knowledge, there is a tendency to keep God on the bench, using the divine presence as the occasional designated hitter for cleaning up what remains unexplainable. But it is not just the mysterious that is mystical. The ordinary, too, is latent with holiness. Israel's experience as a people chosen by God was immediate and urgent, so much so that, before the grand temple was built, the "indwelling presence of God" or *Shekinah* travelled with the Israelites in a tent. Ineffable, God is a presence neither to be grasped nor to be evaded.

With Jesus, the mystery of God becomes literally present among us, what Christians call the Incarnation. Everything in life already has the potential to make God near and call us to relationship. As the embodied presence of God, Jesus shows us the lengths to which God will go to deepen this relationship. Even death could not thwart the inexhaustibility of life within divine love. Theologian David Ford calls the Incarnation a "God-sized event of overwhelming joy" that is "parallel with creation by the Creator."[4] All religions have many variations within their core trajectory of beliefs; Christians, too, have diverse Christologies – different ways of describing, discovering and relating to Jesus. However, the central and shared descriptor for Christian discipleship is following, attaching our presence to Jesus, conforming our person and present reality to the potential he modelled and fulfilled. Jesus is one of us, and the ultimate one of us. Through him the presence of God becomes the familial one of parent. Through Jesus, our true human destiny for magnificence – making present God's realm in the everyday – becomes clear.

Made to Be "More"

We managers are usually impatient to know "what to do" to improve results. Carrying the soul to work and responding to possibilities for magnificence require that we ask a different question: Who are we to become? This involves defining the assumptions we have about the nature of humanity, recognizing the universal rights and claims that reside in that definition and linking work to the project of human history. Tough assignment. Even the best market research tends to skate on the surface of such existential questions. As a society, we have general norms for human rights, but as managers, the source and significance of these rights are usually recognized only indirectly. If anything, the calculus for human worth in business is often brutal, with a one-dimensional focus on either value created as a worker or value consumed as a customer. Concepts such as "human capital" and "knowledge worker" suggest that a more holistic valuation of human presence is emerging, and in some companies this is so. Despite the recognition that wealth and advantage increasingly depend on intelligence and creativity, most organizations have left their perspective of what it means to be human to be defined by markets, which means it has become ever more reductive.

Since we do not spend a lot of time at board meetings or strategy sessions defining the worth of human beings, we need signifiers to reveal our underlying operating assumptions. One is "outsourcing." Think about what the word means: feel for a moment what it would be like to be "sourced out." First, competence, commitment and contribution are eliminated as factors of worth, squashing any pretext of merit, fairness or belonging. Second, sourcing without presence is literally productivity by absence, making the person doing the work faceless because he or she is distant and outside the network of usual company relationships. Employment has always had migrations, but we must not kid ourselves that there is a direct correspondence in human dignity. Working conditions for the new workers are hardly ever more humane or expansive than they were for those displaced. If anything, these persons will be even more anonymous, doing the work but forever "out," contributing productivity for years without ever gaining the status of being "in."

Outsourcing is not just a practice, it is also an attitude. Many people who have jobs feel like they have already been outsourced, doing the work yet counting less and less as people. Some companies outsource customer service, which makes even customers feel like outsiders, as with airlines that make you buy your own lunch and then have you clean up the seat pocket in front of you. These may be small discourtesies, but they accumulate into the outright indignity that lays bare the operating perspective companies assume towards the people they hire and serve. In the 1980s we closed factories. In the 1990s we downsized middle management. Now it is professionals and executives, including CEOs and board directors, who are facing the buzz saw of disposability.[5] This is part of the paradox of expertise that the philosopher and theologian Paul Ricoeur calls *techné*:[6] racing to embrace new expertise to solve problems that expertise has created, investing hope that new technologies will undo damage from earlier technology. The more we value knowledge and competence, the greater our tendency to give professionalism priority over the person. The more we invest in systems and process, the more likely we are to listen to experts than our own emotions.

Hear my cry, Lord.

Running faster, I fall farther behind

Doing more only earns me more to do

I don't have time to think

I don't have time to pray

There must be more

But more I do not have to give

Hear my cry, Lord.

Dishonouring dignity is hardly new. What is original are the stakes. Although more and more businesses depend on smarts, few have become wiser about their human assets and obligations. This very thin bottom-line valuation of human presence is entrenched at a time when companies are commercializing innovations with very serious consequences. As Francis Fukuyama describes in *Our Posthuman Future*, advances in biotechnology pose radical possibilities for genetic engineering.[7] There are enormous potential benefits, with urgent and commensurate risks. At this point, public understanding of and debate about complex moral problems are only in the very preliminary stages. We are beginning to know what is possible, we are beginning to see what is profitable, but we are far from knowing for certain what is right and wrong. As Fukuyama points out, there are no direct lines within science or philosophy to our concept of human dignity.[8] In secular society, we have expectations of human rights, but the infrastructure for this morality is built on quicksand once we remove recognition of the soul or focus only on utility. Boards make bets about human destiny using mostly commercial or competitive criteria without having defined the moral terms or stakes for human dignity. Business people make investment decisions about human worth without having their own human presence clearly seen and cherished. When companies operate from a less-than-whole perspective – a less-than-complete respect for the human person – it takes a leap of faith to assume enterprises have the moral imagination and integrity to make all the right calls on such challenging issues.

If most managers face less consequential decisions, none are exempt from moral choices or ethical responsibilities. These cannot be defined adequately, cannot be managed coherently, without grounding in some definition of human worth. While the mystery of human nature will not resolve itself like some metaphysical Rubik's cube, the challenge of advancing humanity is nevertheless fulfilling because it is the basic work of the soul. Fukuyama argues that the human essence, what he calls Factor X, "cannot be reduced to the possession of moral choice, or reason, or language, or sociability, or sentience, or emotions, or consciousness or any other quality that has been put forth as the ground for human dignity. It is all of these qualities coming together in a whole human being that make up Factor X."[9] Most of us feel and decide as people, not factors, but Fukuyama is trying to make a neutral space with his "X" to allow science and religion to meet at the point where they both agree about human nature: something at the core of the person is ethereal yet essential, indescribable yet indispensable.

Even without the sacred fuel injection from theology, "Factor X" begins to reveal the moving parts that comprise presence. By recognizing a complex of qualities, we are challenged to see the breadth of human needs and possibilities in every interaction. By recognizing that these come together, we are challenged to engage each person from her or his wholeness. Reduction or denial of these effusive qualities dehumanizes, while slicing or dicing that wholeness injures and wounds. A third component, which Fukuyama implies but I think needs to be explicit, is that human beings are an integrated whole that is more than the sum of their complex qualities. Factor X for me is the "more factor." Whatever we learn in genetics or psychology or economics, the human person as presence remains "more" and a mystery. "More" reminds us to be open to surprise and always to remain humble before what we do not know. Importantly for this work, considering the "moreness" of human nature makes it natural to expect magnificence. Part of doing great things is expecting them; part of achievement is nurturing its potential. In Chapter 3, we will meet the saint whose name is a homonym for this premise, and who models both its possibilities and stakes. St. Thomas More was an administrator of the realm during the reign of Henry VIII. He wrote *Utopia* as a satire, not to disparage idealism but to expose the hypocrisy of making ideals disposable in pursuit of expediency or pragmatism. He was martyred for standing on principle. This latency for "more" is both powerful and ambiguous. We must be clear that our human excessiveness can easily yield the tragedies and inhumanities that mark so much of our history. The mystery at the heart of human nature is the capacity for either good or evil. It does not take a religious leap of faith to see both these traits, not only in history and holocaust, but also in the blood and despair that flow so freely in our own time. We are constituted to be more than the sum of our qualities, yet the choice is freely ours whether to aim for the stars or ground zero.

If we do not attend to this "more factor" with the seriousness human nature deserves, we end up suppressing something essential, which means it usually emerges as a distortion. Our personal struggles with obesity and addiction are like our corporate problems with greed and fraud: they are rooted in an insatiability that is ultimately self-destructive. The medieval mystic Richard St. Victor made the point that we humans are forever trying to fill up the eternal within ourselves with things that only leave us empty and longing for more. Only divine presence satisfies this transcendent craving; only God has the effusiveness to fulfill human excessiveness. Faith does not resolve the mystery of human nature, but only resituates it within the larger mystery of creation and source. This wiring for "more" is our inheritance of our being in God's image and likeness. The great challenge of faith is not to believe, but to be "more," because anything less is less human, less than God imprinted, less than what makes us whole.

As with freedom or art, the difficulty of attaining more wholeness is part of its essential worthiness, and not a reason for assuming it to be optional. The presence of Jesus puts God with us in this struggle. Through the Incarnation, the "moreness" of God is poured into human form, and in Christ the "moreness" of the human person realizes its zenith in God. Two aspects to Jesus' excessiveness are especially noteworthy:

extravagant love and extravagant forgiveness. Love is hard to define, but we do recognize it as an ache for "more" than we are alone, and thrive in its flow from becoming somehow "more" in its giving and receiving. Since part of being human is that we often fail in the stretch to become more whole, we need, along with love, reservoirs of forgiveness. To be forgiven is to be restored or made anew. Neither love nor forgiveness is possible alone. What Jesus reveals through teaching, example and healing is that we become wholly ourselves by being "more" for others. It takes grit and grace, but this is the reversal that corrects the diminution of human worth and completes presence: not outsourcing but out*pouring*.

To summarize: if we in business avoid defining human worth we have a proven tendency to underestimate it. All our knowledge only takes us so far in understanding the source or scope of our humanity, which is why clear-cut priorities such as efficiency often seem more rational and compelling. Although unfathomable, we know from our own experience – and from the hard-won lessons of history – that there are numerous qualities to such nature, none of which exhausts what it means to be human but in composite reside to some degree in all people. The imperative of presence is not simply to cease lessening what we assume humanity means, but to constantly expect, and respect, "more." For better and also for worse, every human being exists as a dynamic complex of capacities. Even the most secular view of society recognizes this basic dignity as the premise for universal human rights. While the aim has the purity of truth, the reality is a lot messier. The world is an imperfect place, and, to paraphrase the theologian Reinhold Niebuhr, the equality we share as human beings includes sharing equally in that imperfection.[10] Things get especially frantic in business. Short time horizons compress everything. Charged to do "more with less," managers have for a variety of reasons become experts at the "with less" part: less workers, less wages, less benefits, less regulation, less ethics, less security, less time off, less risky creativity, less service, less civility, less taxes, less responsibility to the long term, and less dignity overall. God's calling, which is not necessarily convenient, is to be "more" than the minimum – whole, not less, and holy by sharing in the overflowing surplus of divine relationship.

Holy God, Mighty God

Deliver me from the bottom line

Not to stop producing but to stop reducing

Not to eschew results but to escape their monopoly

Not to take it easy but to get the weekend off.

Holy God, Mighty God

Deliver me from the bottom line

Grant me the spleen to recognize what is essential

Open my eyes to not cut opportunity with costs

And help me be like Jack Welch, only nicer.

Amen

Beyond Part-time Integrity

Integrity is another critical quality that we all affirm yet rarely define. I recently interviewed more than 20 CEOs and found near unanimity among them on one issue. They believe that public confidence and organizational credibility hinge on personal integrity. Surprisingly, while almost all agreed on this as foundational to business, very few were able to explain what integrity means. There were some very interesting partial answers and some equally telling blanks. With few exceptions, the perceptions were more like platitudes: fuzzy, if heartfelt, generalizations that would defy serious management or measurement. These people were not being disingenuous. Rather, their vague responses attested to what one admitted: senior executives had risen through the ranks with plenty of operational experience but with little practice in personal or operational moral reflection. The call for integrity is coming directly from corporate boardrooms, but it is a fragile call undermined by the absence of familiarity with its fuller meaning, terms and demands.[11]

How do you define integrity? In its etymology, integrity connotes wholeness – a full and functioning unity or *integer*.[12] We mostly mean it as a validation of character: someone with integrity is someone to trust. In business, the shorthand is "keeping one's word." While we know integrity by its absence – by scandal, fraud or impropriety – we are much less sure about its presence. In crisis, when politicians, CEOs and even church leaders talk of restoring integrity, they mostly mean setting up rules or supervisory systems to prevent further breaches of the public trust. This is important, but confidence cannot be repaired or renewed simply by eliminating offence. This is the faulty presumption undermining most governance renewal. In promising more independent directors and more rigorous due diligence of executive action, we are simply reinstating what should have been done all along. After paying their fines of several hundred million dollars each for aiding and abetting Enron's corporate fraud, both Merrill Lynch and CIBC promised not to knowingly do so again. The implicit presumption in such a promise is that what we all must do – follow the law – satisfies the qualifications for what we ought to do.

Mitigating the causes for suspicion is not at all the same thing as nurturing and creating trust. Something "more" is needed for integrity, especially to heal fissures and restore wholeness. Integrity is valued as an asset but is actually an outcome, the end result of what I call "presence in action." If we recognize the human person as a complex of qualities, then integrity grows from the proper and respectful exercise of that totality. Choices in life and business are rarely clear and without moral entanglements. Bringing head, heart and soul as a unity to these decisions does not mean we will always be right, only that we will have done our best to be as whole as possible. Because we ascribe integrity to character, we assume it is personal. In fact, integrity is like trust, defined and earned in relationship. Certainly there are times when the harsh price of integrity – acting with consistency to principle and conscience – forces us to stand alone. But this courage, to qualify as integrity, serves not self-interest but some greater good, such as truth, freedom or justice. As Dorothee Soelle explains, the integration is not simply interior but also one of connectedness, a "dynamic holism" that "experiences the implicit enfolded order and lives according to it."[13]

Again, this is why anthropology is important. How we define human presence frames the norms of and expectations for integrity. To aspire to the latter without reflection about the former achieves only limited integrity, like that of blueblood, blue-chip banks promising not to do their worst, as if that were enough. This is confusing norms with minimums: forgetting aspirations to simply minimize exposure; forsaking principles to simply deliver what is minimally acceptable; forcing compliance to evade the deeper responsibility of contributing to relationship and social wholeness. The danger from this minimalism is that we will render integrity as impotent and formulaic as most business ethics programs. By their structures and policies, companies adopt business ethics as little more than a system of compliance, with a focus on rules, procedures and standards. In research on social capital, many executives surveyed evaluated their companies as ethical simply for not breaking any laws. The same survey found very few boards applying formal ethical screens for setting corporate direction or policy, and none that had created any mechanism or committee for ongoing ethical audits.[14] Many companies have adopted codes of conduct. Most large corporations have set up ethics offices; however, while there is undoubted intelligence and competence in such initiatives, most are without any real responsibility or operational teeth. Very few ethics officers report directly to CEOs or boards. Only very rarely are ethics operational to the degree of shaping strategy, performance reviews or financial audits. To add insult to injury, business ethics have suffered fad fatigue, with the buzz of topicality tipping to programs for corporate social responsibility.

 I report this with sadness. Most of us working in this field recognized that ethics were being used somewhat superficially, as an imprimatur still awaiting serious management engagement or deliberation. Of course, there has been progress. Just speaking the language of ethics, rich in moral implication and humanity, represented a hopeful alternative to the usual stuff of productivity improvement. After the workplace disrespect and diminishment from re-engineering, it seemed as though business ethics heralded the "re-humanizing" of business. These real gains in acceptability camouflaged the widening gap between codes of conduct and ethical efficacy. Thinking that the challenge was again the binary one of "yes" or "no" to ethics, we did not recognize, or honestly admit, that there was a reverse takeover underway in which ethics became a subset of efficiency. We worked so hard to make a business case for ethics that, in the end, what is "right" often became conditional on that business case. It is common knowledge that Enron was being touted as a model of business ethics best practices at the exact same time as its executives were defrauding employees and shareholders. This situation is far from being the exception: a recent survey (by Pricewaterhouse-Coopers and Wilmer, Cuttler & Pickering) reveals that up to one third of large companies have been "struck" by "fraud and other kinds of economic crime."[15] Since the vast majority of these companies have ethics functions or offices, one inescapable implication is that the current approach to business ethics is not working.

So far, much of the diagnostic about integrity failures is from the same problem-solving perspective that submerged business ethics in the first place. In their very useful book about organizational integrity, Muel Kaptein and Johan Wempe identify three clusters of pressures that undermine moral coherence. The first involves the distorting imperatives of efficiency. The second relates to the narrowing, often silo-creating, priorities of expertise. The third involves "dirty hands" – not just intentional duplicity but also intentionally ambiguous goals, such as promising both results and integrity without providing the principles or commitments for resolving their inevitable conflict.[16] While serious and perplexing, this list of pressures misses the more complex reality of human presence. Partial integrity is an oxymoron. Integrity requires the fullness of human nature to be involved in discernment, including the senses of the heart and the needs of the soul. Hard as they might try to disprove it, even fundamentalist economists admit that market and business decisions are not completely rational. In ethical or moral matters, the rational head lags behind the heart even more. As the Jesuit theologian Ron Mercier explains, "the ethical moment" is usually something we recognize viscerally first – a wrenching of the heart or an instinct in the gut that calls us to be attentive to the larger consequences of a situation. When our analysis of integrity misses the realm of intuition, we lack a quality essential to being whole, one that is indispensable to seeing holistically.

Missing the soul is equally problematic to integrity. Kaptein and Wempe do emphasize the need for corporate integrity to be "grounded in the social function" of the organization.[17] This seems to be their "Factor X" – neutral sounding, yet alluding to the various vectors, including religion, that inform society's moral understanding. Generalizing poorly serves what is essential. Perceptions of morality are closely interconnected to religious feeling, experience and imagination. It does not take faith to be moral, but it is almost impossible to dismiss the sacred inspiration for rights, obligations and rules that undergird secular society. Positing integrity without encompassing this spiritual capacity results in two basic suppressions and one distortion. Suppressed are memory, which links us to the founding religious stories of right and wrong, and participation, which keeps the soul sequestered from issues affecting the whole human person. The distortion is that denying this numinous aspect of human nature again underestimates its ability to choose intentional harm and perpetrate evil.

Simone Weil conceived the needs of the soul not as deficiencies but as obligations, leaving us with the exquisite tension that lies at the heart of all spirituality. Our giving fulfills that which we need most. Mystics teach that to be heard by God, we must listen. The twentieth-century philosopher John Macmurray argued that the positive dimensions of our personhood only emerge in relation to others, with our dignity and integrity springing from mutual interdependence.[18] Emmanuel Levinas, another twentieth-century philosopher, posited that finding acceptance and belonging depends completely on our extending invitation and welcome. Weil's needs of the soul similarly always couple aspiration with action, providing a workable framework for integrity that realizes the wholeness of the person by satisfying that which is incomplete in others or in society. Here are some examples:

- People of integrity contribute to *order*, advancing justice, healing exclusions and righting wrongs, thereby continuing God's work of creation by pushing back chaos and its dehumanizing disorder.
- People of integrity are consistent in their *obedience* to moral law, earning credibility and respect by taking public decisions and actions that align with beliefs professed in private.
- People of integrity respect the *hierarchism* of creation, giving proper priority to principles that respect our interdependence within nature and within society and its economy.

- People of integrity insist on *fairness*, not only in the basic dignity of each individual, but more importantly in helping make real and concrete the equities that are warranted by universal rights.
- People of integrity do not take the safe or proven way, instead embracing and exercising *risk*, practising creative thinking to penetrate the problems of the status quo, and using moral and practical imagination to bring forth solutions of wisdom.
- People of integrity serve *stability*, renewing in the face of change principles and practices that sustain hope as well as dignity, that sustain belonging and social memory as well as the natural habitat.
- People of integrity act to advance real *freedom*, liberating others as well as themselves from the constraints of prejudice or presumption.
- People of integrity care enough to insist on accountability, accepting and inflating *responsibility* in correspondence to rights for free choice and in the hope for reconciliation.
- People of integrity represent the *truth*, embodying in word and deed what matters most by respecting many voices, including those of the past, and denying ambiguity the power to rob any moment of its meaning.

Since human beings are intrinsically formed to be more than a complex of qualities, it is only logical and right that integrity manifest this expansiveness. Just as there can be no part-time integrity, there cannot be a partial integrity (such as preserving order by suppressing freedom, or taking risks without being truthful). Integrity grounded in human presence opts to make the most human possibility emerge from every situation. Facing difficulty, even seemingly intractable no-win situations, people with integrity, such as Gandhi, opt for enflaming magnificence.

Working Whole with Presence

Management stripped bare is the exercise of presence through other means; extending one's self through decisions, resources, measures and accountability. The reality, however, is often the opposite. In the harsh busyness of modern corporate life, the idea of presence gets sliced and diced, as in multi-tasking, into ever more frenzied fragments of productivity. BlackBerrys and their ilk have become like boomerangs, extending presence in outflow but often creating havoc or imbalance from unceasing, indiscriminate inflow. With 24/7 tools, we are more and more present to the challenges of work and less and less able to balance our essential human presence. E-mail is another proof of this simultaneously awesome and awful magnification of presence. As never before, we can reach out to one another, with remarkable possibilities for learning and exchange. Yet as never before, we are smothered in spam, invaded, inconvenienced and often left isolated, just for being electronically present.

The disintegration of presence has not been one of the diagnostic models for corporate renewal. There is no "total presence program" as there is a "total quality program." Nevertheless, absence is at the heart of many of our most intractable business problems. The now-tired call for transparency is actually a claim for information to be present, a growing intolerance of truth being absent. New laws prescribing executive accountability are themselves aimed at thwarting the exemption of presence by which many senior managers have evaded the consequences of their decisions. Management by *not* walking around is management by absence. Customer or employee dissatisfaction is often at root an experience of disrespect, which means being taken for granted – not seen, not heard, not responded to – as a living human presence. When access to service is frustrating or demeaning, it is the dignity of presence that is being besmirched. I always feel a pang of diminishment when the electronic voice on hold warns that "the call may be monitored for quality assurance reasons." First, I would prefer the quality of a human being answering and therefore respecting my time. Second, I feel for the employee who is forever being checked up on by this invisible presence – a policing by absence that is the supervisory equivalent of outsourcing.

O God, Hey God

You call. I run.

You create. I market.

You invite. I pass.

You give. I mark up.

You illumine. I wear UV protection.

You forgive. I forget.

You heal. I hurt.

You know. I learn.

You transcend. I rescind.

You protect. I deflect.

You expect. I consult.

You portend. I pretend.

You reveal. I retreat.

You command. I qualify.

You prototype. I beta-test.

You invest. I manage.

You multiply. I consume.

O God, Hey God

We make a great team.

Amen

It is the project for the rest of this book to define the needs and opportunities that result from the integration of soul and strategy. The opening to such radical possibilities requires a conceptual reframing and an interior one. On the macro level we need to reclaim the moral dimensions to that vast presence that markets call "the invisible hand." As a moral philosopher, Adam Smith assumed that part of the rationality of self-interest would include moral judgment, since no self-interest can be sustained in an environment of immorality or that disregards the law. Theologian Harvey Cox has pointed out that many business people bow to "the invisible hand" with near-religious zeal, sacrificing other human priorities for what is perceived to be the near-omniscience of market rationality.[19] We know markets can be wrong and reactionary, as with the dot.com boom and crash. The job of managers is not to accede to the market's whim, but to learn from it, surf with it and often bet against the predominant trend in order to create companies that mine advantage and continuously renew. It is our choice as free and creative individuals to either expect more of the economy as a human construct, or become less for expecting it to be without compassion or conscience. Either we co-create an "invisible hand up" or we co-succumb to an "invisible handcuff." Since the market is the whole comprised of millions of parts, we all have a role in its possibilities and responsibilities.

Reframing external possibilities will come to naught if we do not take the personal responsibility to reframe interior ones, seeking consistency between principles and action. We no doubt recognize this aspiration, which is why so many people are turning to spirituality at work. However, while admitting we need more from work personally, we have not yet made the work of business or management enabling of "more." Sociologist Douglas Porpora references several studies that expose the conundrum. While the great majority of people profess belief in God – in divine Presence – the majority of this majority also claims that its belief does not influence or affect day-to-day decisions or actions.[20] Before encountering the destabilizing pressures of work, we are already breaking up wholeness from within.

I have lived on both sides of this disintegration. In some ways, believers have simply incorporated – brought into our own bodies and being – the Enlightenment's separation of church and state. We avoid bringing the spiritual into the public space on principle, respecting diversity and exercising justifiable suspicion towards institutional religions that often fail to walk their talk. Not all the reasons for adhering to this split are so heroic. In many ways, it is just easier to keep the spheres separate, for expediency, but also to avoid what Rabbi David Rosen calls "not a clash of civilizations but a clash of expectations."[21] Our part-time absence from this part-time spirituality relates to the part-time place of the heart – to our overuse of facts, to our great suspicion of emotions, to our devaluing of wisdom's basic tenderness. The marketplace is indeed a harsh place, yet much of the harshness is self-inflicted by our readiness to separate what we need for the soul from what we do for a living.

The point is not to blame but to understand that absence cuts both ways, not only as a fractured mode of being at work but also as a fractured mode of practising spirituality. The signs of our times point to this as a rare, likely very fragile, moment in which the needs of business and the needs of the soul actually converge. Management excellence as perhaps never before depends on moral excellence. This claim is not, as some management consultants inveigle it, turning business into a religion complete with rituals and an all-encompassing structure of meaning.[22] Nor is it a theocratic reverse takeover to impose some religious doctrine or dogma on managers. Rather, it is an attempt to pray as if prayer actually matters, and at the same time to manage with the fiduciary responsibility that effectively and productively lives up to its task of engendering and sustaining trust.

God of judgment: Heart of mercy

I confess to irrational exuberance

To investing myself in a new economy

Even though I knew there could be no free lunch

I confess to keeping You in my pocket like a divine Palm Pilot

Seeking grace on demand

Wanting more and more access to Your wisdom

Without being present to Your call and claims

I confess to habitual absence

Substituting compliance for ethical deliberation

Offering transparency instead of honesty

Voicing silence in witness to aggressive transgression

I confess to excellence

Practising productivity when the world needed healing

Offering FAQs when customers needed service

And mastering "just-in-time" grace

Amen

Called to Presence

As in the speaking forth of creation, the initiative for calling is God's. In Luke's gospel, Jesus walks towards the fishermen cleaning their nets, and despite the crowd already trailing him, calls them. St. Ignatius described his ecstatic experience of sacramental communion as being swept up in the dance of the Trinity,[23] the effusive and overflowing relationality that early Christian theologians named *perichoresis*. Calling is the "dance" coming to us, a gift of being seen and wanted before being invited to reciprocate and swing. It is sublimely precious to be called, yet not so unusual, for it is in the relational nature of God to reach out and in the nature of humans created in God's image to respond. "We do not have to go very far to catch echoes of that game, and of that dancing," wrote the poetic monk Thomas Merton. "When we are alone on a starlit night; when by chance we see the migrating birds in autumn descending on a grove of junipers to rest and eat; when we see children in a moment when they are really children; when we know we love in our own hearts; or when like the Japanese poet Bashō, we hear an old frog land in a quiet pond with a solitary splash – at such times the awakening, the turning inside out of all values, the 'newness,' the emptiness and the purity of vision that make themselves evident, provide a glimpse of the cosmic dance."[24]

For the four fishermen stooped in their work, calling materialized from the uninvited presence of Jesus. With the Incarnation, God walking among us is forever near, forever approaching uninvited and forever choosing us to participate in divine life.

The nature and implications of calling to presence do not come into instant focus. The first thing Jesus asks is to be taken out on the fishermen's boat, to use this platform of work to speak about sacred possibilities. What Luke seems to say in this story is that for discipleship, the spiritual movement is founded on intimacy rather than understanding. We need to retreat, to cast off, to float free, not necessarily forsaking the tools and environ of our work, but creating time and space within that productivity to encounter the divine. This pause is essential for what theologian John Haughey calls "receivement": awakening through grace to the transcendence that our knowledge or expertise alone cannot reach.[25] While the crowd wanted to be near Jesus, only the fishermen had the "backstage passes" to see Jesus close up and, importantly, to see the impact of Jesus refracted in the faces of the people on shore. Receivement is part of the embrace from God that we feel personally, yet that is not ours – that is, in fact, inherent to all creation and extends to every face when we take the pause to see them. It is this instantaneous intimacy and solidarity that, even before the Beatitudes were spoken, created the substance of Christian ethics. The calling to be on the boat with Jesus cannot be segregated from the obligations to attend to the clamouring needs of those standing on the beach.

What did the crowd need that made Jesus so compelling? What did the fishermen experience about Jesus' presence that made them want to conform themselves to him? There are many ways to envision the Messiah or formulate Christology, but the common themes for understanding Jesus as the anointed are what John Paul II called "the threefold mission of Christ as Priest, Prophet and King."[26] In his priestly role, Jesus broke the monopoly of institutions, making holiness accessible to all, creating sacrament around the simple fellowship of meals and teaching prayer of radical intimacy to God. Especially with his healing, which often violated religious rules, Jesus consecrated as holy, as grace-filled, the personal moments of need transformed by faith. Priesthood flowed as compassion: ritual released the cosmic in the mundane.

As prophet, Jesus challenged the presumptions of how humans expected God to be. The Messiah was for sinners, not for the righteous. The feasting was for the prodigal son, not the steadfast one. Wages paid to part-time labourers were equal to those of full-time workers. Jesus drove money-changers from the Temple, chastised hypocrites and demanded self-renunciation for discipleship, yet he also wept over the impending suffering of Jerusalem, taught forgiveness on a scale greater than judgment, and remembered, after miraculously bringing the little girl back to life, to have her fed. This is prophecy envisioning wondrous possibilities of life with God, while at the same time serving the urgency and coherence of practicality.

Much of what Jesus taught had to do with the kingdom of God, but as Walter Wink explains, his model for realm and royalty was "a counter-assertion" against domination. "Jesus does not condemn ambition or aspiration; he merely changes the values to which they are attached: 'Whoever wants to be first must be last of all and servant of all.' He does not reject power, but only its use to dominate others. He does not reject greatness, but finds it in identification and solidarity with the needy at the bottom of society."[27]

Not all of this could have been clear to the sleep-deprived boat owners, but being so close to him, for seeing his ministry to the crowd, they could hardly escape the messianic qualities of his person. Indeed, for being with him on the boat, the four fishermen eventually became like him. This is our charge, too: as Christians, we must be present to the living presence of Jesus and *become* the living presence of Jesus. This is the essential construct for what follows. The needs of the soul help define what it means to be wholly human. The priestly, prophetic and kingly roles help define how we orient that wholeness to holiness, to the magnificence that is both the human birthright and destiny. Business consultants David Specht and Richard Broholm have been doing groundbreaking work translating these scriptural roles into managerial job descriptions. All our work and efforts hold possibilities for priestly enactment of communion, for offering sacrifice and extending the whole-making healing of compassion. All our tasks and projects also offer occasion to expose contradictions, to prophetically critique systems that perpetuate brokenness and project the alternative order of healing life with God. All our roles and titles have as a latent responsibility the charge to restore creation, to exercise kingly administration for justice and charity.[28]

Priestly, *prophetic* and *kingly* are terms laden with historical baggage, including gender exclusion, that muffles their resonance. I have chosen to invoke these scriptural terms for two reasons: to rehabilitate language that links us to a wealth of spiritual tradition; and to affect a purposeful intervention to demand that we see work for what it is, which is holy.

The demands of business are already calling forth the moral skills that correspond, in content if not image, with priestly, prophetic and kingly roles. For example, the expanding literature on "emotional intelligence"[29] aims for more compassion in operations and more dignity in interactions, which is a priestly orientation. Strategic planning and visioning exercises are attempts to scan the horizon for opportunity and renewal, which is inherently prophetic. As business professor Joseph Badaracco Jr. explores in *Leading Quietly*, there is a growing appreciation for power exercised with "modesty, restraint and tenacity," which is kingly.[30] These projects for business renewal all hint as well at larger eschatological themes: the richness of the whole human being, sustainability within creation, and the ethical obligations of stewardship. Profoundly valuable, this emerging managerial orientation still presumes that the problems of dehumanization, limited vision and faulty governance can be almost exclusively resolved with more expertise – with technique trying to correct technique in an enclosed spiral of more techné. The risk, if we do not enrich these management competencies with moral imagination, is for more exhaustion, for creating even greater futility by having invoked holy associations without their sacred depth and aim.

This is the challenge, and prayer, for the chapters that follow: without leaving the world of business to plunge into God, without leaving the world of management to plunge into the "moral grandeur"[31] of presence. Business is already a precious human asset, providing work, channelling resources, actualizing innovations that improve health and wealth. It is also an adolescent asset, not yet mature in its moral responsibilities, prone to hormone-induced excesses and capable of inflicting great damage on itself as well as others. We cannot expect a more human economy if we ourselves do not mature and invest our presence in it. We cannot reverse the diminishment of dignity at work if we ourselves do not insist that human beings, as creatures and souls, deserve more.

Holy Lord, Jesus Christ

My head doubts

But my heart prays

My head divides

But my heart heals

My head wants to be smart

But my heart wants to be wise

My head thinks

But my heart sees

My head defines "I"

But my heart beholds "we"

My head seeks facts

But my heart seeks faces

My head wants progress

But my heart wants peace

My head needs to hear

But my soul longs to speak.

Lord God,

Help me to live in the presence of "but."

Amen

2

BECOMING

Uplifting Hope from Fear

To be constituted for "more" precipitates temptations as well as possibilities. One temptation is to succumb to more without limits. Another is to settle for less. Ambition without limits displaces transcendence, making our personal priorities or corporate measures bigger than those of eternity. Conversely, ambition without aspiration for transcendence confines us to what is pragmatic, affordable or doable, stunting dignity by stifling potentiality. Surrendering to wanting without discernment of higher needs expresses what J. Krishnamurti called "the acquisitive instinct, the possessive pursuit of more."[1] This is when the soul's journey of longing for perfectibility gets detoured onto the ever more heavily travelled tracks of insatiability, including addiction and greed. The opposite temptation is to give up on the possibilities for more without even trying, a suppression of interior resources for goodness that Thomas Aquinas called "meanness."[2] This is when we are less than we can be, turning away from excellence by underusing the practical and moral capabilities we have at our disposal.

Wanting to be more than we are is a completely human aspiration, driving much of what we understand as social progress and economic development. It is also the restlessness to be expected among the children of God. This option for magnificence does not deny or condemn the natural impulse for more, but instead channels understanding and achievement to the underlying needs of the soul. Chapter 1 defined the terms of presence, inviting managers and companies to imagine an integrity that respects the whole *worth* of human beings, including souls. Chapter 2 now explores the corresponding opportunities for *worthiness*, shifting the horizons for what we do to create wealth so we can also serve the inner restlessness for becoming. As the previous chapter set up a more radical anthropology, the current chapter begins to shape the aim – the eschatology – for that humanity created by, and called to relationship with, divinity. This will be developed in three stages: a more elaborate and practical definition of magnificence through a dialogue between business and theological sources; a review of some of the widely held yet faulty managerial assumptions that thwart the soul's desire for this higher form of output; and an introduction to the needs of the soul, which are the resources for achieving what the Jewish theologian Abraham Joshua Heschel called "moral grandeur and spiritual audacity."[3]

Magnificence Calling

Thomas Aquinas wrote that "the soul is known by its actions." So, too, the character of a company is known by the totality – that is, by the integrity – of its outcomes. Microsoft is perhaps one of the best examples of a company striving ceaselessly for more yet missing magnificence. Whether you admire it as a competitive force or decry it as a monopolist, there is no denying Microsoft's significance as one of the defining companies of our time. With its ubiquity, talent, profitability and cash hoard, Microsoft has the leverage to change the world. For all its power, the company inspires little trust or appreciation. Critics note that Microsoft is most often an imitator rather than an innovator. There are also the less-than-laudatory business practices that have earned the company legal condemnation and penalties from anti-trust regulators around the world.[4] While hardly exemplary, Microsoft's magnificence deficit relates to a deeper squandering – that of treasure and potential – by investing its human and financial capital in frivolous ventures such as the XBox. Certainly, the market for games is huge – bigger in revenue than Hollywood's box-office take, and, yes, many expect the appliances that play computer games to become the smart hub for the wired home. But here again is the crux: while there is no disputing the worth of this market for Microsoft, the measure against which it comes up short is worthiness. Is Microsoft really at its best – is it making the most of the skills and aspirations of its people, and adding most to the possibilities of its hundreds of millions of customers – by co-developing and selling games entitled "Dungeon Siege," "Brute Force," "Full Spectrum Warrior" and "Crimson Skies: High Road to Revenge"?

As with all other companies, Microsoft has the right to pursue any strategy it chooses within the law. Such choices, however, have not incidental consequences since they express, and condition, the horizon of managerial imagination, the priorities of culture, the comprehensiveness of company values and the depth of accountability for the investments being made. It is important to acknowledge and applaud the groundbreaking work being done through the foundation endowed by Microsoft's founder, Bill Gates. Many business people will argue that this is the proper forum for philanthropy, and that companies will only become inefficient if moral or social expectations are imposed on what are commercial operations. The problem with this view is twofold. First, it perpetuates the dangerous segregation between managerial profession and spirituality, keeping that which stirs for magnificence sequestered in the private realm, away from that which strives for day-to-day public results. Second, it underestimates the moral environment in which companies operate. Business does big damage in many ways, and carries even bigger obligations for the well-being of our planet, global society, communities and human equality, freedom and dignity. Historically, philanthropy has been an outcome made affordable by excess productivity. In our time, it is increasingly becoming the aim and motivation for correcting productivity's excesses.

Magnificence is not an alternative to results. It is the practice of managerial rigour and innovation applied towards success with attentiveness and commitment to what is also good and right. It is the call to create worth, with its attendant risks, challenges, skills and rewards, while also respecting the criteria of worthiness, with its moral, human and aesthetic dimensions. There is no one recipe for magnificence. As with art, we can train for it and use our acumen and discipline, but as with art the realization of magnificence is utterly original. For St. Thomas Aquinas, such achievement represented not a singular virtue but a harmony of many highly developed habits and traits for doing good. "There cannot be magnanimity," he wrote, "without the other virtues. Hence it is compared to the other virtues like an embellishment of them."[5] Practising justice is good; practising justice with courage releases magnificence. We need prudence to sift through issues and decipher what is really worthy. We need fortitude to persist even when the odds against us seem long or impossible. With the mindfulness from presence, all of our talents and capacities are engaged so that the striving for good represents all that we can be. We have debased good in business, either as mediocrity for being "good enough," or for being fuzzy as with corporate social responsibility. Goodness is the outcome that attests to magnificence, the highest excellence for being intellectually, emotionally and morally excellent.

This is a high standard, but not a grandiose one. Jesus' teaching about magnificence was implicit in his descriptions of the true kingdom of God. The majesty in this realm is in small things done with great love. In one story, he explains that while people often call attention to how much they give to charity or to the Temple, it is the offering of "two small copper coins" by a poor woman that is exemplary. Such magnificence "out of her poverty" teaches that greatness is not a quantity from achievement but from generosity in sensibility (Luke 21:1-4). Humble words or tiny acts seem as inconsequential as the "smallest seed," yet in another parable Jesus insists that these grow into solid and stubborn mustard bushes (Matthew 13:31) that are notorious for taking over entire ecosystems.[6] With Jesus, the kingdom of God is a splendour of multiple virtues, albeit the ones of presence and dependence: "Be merciful, just as your Father is merciful. Do not judge and you will not be judged; do not condemn and you will not be condemned. Forgive, and you will be forgiven; give and it will be given to you." This magnificence is an inverse reciprocity, being great for having been greatly given to by God. Rather than a leap outwards for what is exceptional, magnificence is a dive inwards to retrieve what we already have. This innate giftedness is why Jesus adds, "The measure you give will be the measure you get back" (Luke 6:36-38).

To aim for such high virtue suggests the burden of another "stretch target." Again, this is not so much an imposition as liberation – not another particularity of performance but a recalibration of professionalism to include the needs and assets of the soul. Business people tend to identify themselves with what they do, often excessively, deriving not just status but purpose and meaning from work, career and company relationships. Many worry about this for the obvious reason that it diminishes a "human being" into a unit of "human doing." I think we must indeed be cautious of how and where we invest our human transcendence. We must especially be watchful of work's tendency towards addictiveness or exploitation. In principle, however, the fusion of identity with work is an opportunity for practising and deepening presence. What we do to make a living is latent with possibilities, including for expressing our wholeness and growing our holiness. Work in this context can be prayer brought to life, a form of worship – of doxology – that reflects and respects the interior relationship we experience with divine Presence. This was the integration – the practical integrity – demanded by the prophet Ezekiel. If we accept the invitation to be present to God, if we receive "the new hearts" from being in transcendent relationship, then the everyday striving of magnificence is the basic norm and right of our human becoming.

Glory to God

What am I making to honour You today?

Glory to God

How can I raise what I do to Your standard of graciousness?

Glory to God

I'm a brick in the wall of history's Temple to you

Glory to God

Receive this day's work in praise

Glory to God

Receive this day's strivings in thanksgiving

Glory to God

Keep me open to Your grandeur

Glory to God

Keep me true to the possibilities of hope

Amen

Magnificence as "Double And"

Jim Collins has had a hand in two of the best business books written in the last decade. With Jerry Porras, he defined the key attributes for companies that had achieved endurance as well as excellence, and were therefore *Built to Last*. More recently, he published an exhaustive study as a "prequel" to that work, tracking the leadership and managerial skills that stepped up company performance *From Good to Great*. Substantive and accessible, these works pivot on an insight that is as relevant to spiritual wisdom as it is to operational greatness. Collins and Porras called this "the genius of AND," which is the imagination and flexibility to "embrace both extremes on a number of dimensions at the same time. Instead of choosing A OR B, figure out how to have A AND B – purpose AND profit, continuity AND change, freedom AND responsibility."[7]

Profit and trust, or share price and integrity, seem harder to achieve as co-objectives than as alternatives. However, the evidence from Collins and Porras is not that people worked more, only that they worked differently in ways that raised both results and what I have been calling presence. In effect, managers employ more of their human faculties to engage more of the complexities of business, not only building companies that last – such as Hewlett-Packard, Johnson & Johnson, and Procter & Gamble – but also achieving much more personal satisfaction from a greater sense of purpose or vision. Not surprisingly, workers whose wisdom is respected and used tend to feel much more loyalty to their company and deeper ethical commitment to customers, shareholders and other stakeholders. The word *and* does not instantly dissolve paradox. Rather, it acknowledges the full weight of options with a respect for competing values, an honest questioning and appreciation that often leads to creative decisions with more nuance, understanding and responsibility. The outcome is simple if rare: better results from better work, resulting in more satisfaction from more responsibility.

Hinting at the wisdom roots of their managerial precept, Collins and Porras use the yin and yang symbol to visualize the dynamic integration unleashed by *AND* thinking and practices. What seem like competitive interests are actually complementary. In his subsequent book, Collins shows that this pairing of opposites is paradigmatic for greatness. Debunking the myths surrounding celebrity CEOs, Collins identifies "level 5" leaders as combining professional "willfulness" with personal "humility."[8] Similarly, organizations that elevate performance and sustain greatness have the uncanny ability to both rigorously debate options and unite with intense commitment on the chosen course of action. Other dialectically opposed attributes are similarly combined, such as strategic freedom with responsibility for consequences. The key is having the human depth – the presence – to wrestle operational wisdom from what others see as contradictions. "AND-thinking" is wisdom in action, a commitment to a more broadly defined excellence that charges management not with the easy pickings of cutting costs, but with the more demanding but ambiguous task of increasing efficiencies *and* raising innovation, or achieving higher productivity *and* liberating more integration for employees.

And is an important managerial idea. Although Collins stays true to his academic roots as a management professor, this concept – as with the concepts of vision or mission – involves discernment skills that spiritual traditions have mined in the experience of paradox. Magnificence reconsecrates this capacity, agitating the existential equivalent of a "double and" – the personal need to work *and* the soul's need to work towards the larger purpose latent in the capacities of our human presence; the need to grow more professional competence *and* to grow more holy and Godlike; the obligation to manage in service of shareholders *and* to obligate managerial excellence as worship; the creative risk to innovate for results *and* the creative collaboration that comes from appreciating work and business as divine milieu. Aquinas defined magnificence as "the discussing and administering of great and lofty undertakings, with a certain broad and noble purpose of mind." Aquinas, too, envisioned multiple *and*-factors:

- great execution or implementation *and* "greatness of purpose";
- "making" great things as "quantity" *and* making "dignity"; and
- "doing" with craft and quality *and* being transformed as subject by the effort, artistry and beauty.

For Aquinas, magnificence was a synonym for or extension of courage. Since he regarded this as the principal virtue for founding and administering any enterprise, he believed that moral greatness was in direct alignment with what we call management.[9] To be effective in creating worth requires taking risks; to be proficient in what is also worthy requires risking on the "double and" scale of practical achievement and human fulfillment as a spiritual creature.

Simone Weil was a mystic as well as a philosopher. In her spiritual reflections, entitled *Waiting on God*, she wrote that "the beauty of the world is the mouth of a labyrinth."[10] Naming and understanding God has always been an exercise in disorientation and getting lost. As with beauty and truth, magnificence also defies easy directions. Jesus used parables for teaching about the kingdom because the essence could not be reduced to facts or rationale. Instead, people were invited to participate in the promise, experiencing magnificence by becoming magnificent themselves: "like children" in their wondering; like "lilies in the field" in their radiance; like "salt" giving life flavour and tang. With death not having the final word, Jesus modelled the glory available to all human beings who risked self-emptying in service of goodness. In the mystery and joy of their encounter with the resurrection, early Christians formulated the ultimate "double and" that recognized Jesus as fully human and fully divine. Over centuries, this experience of God Incarnated in human history led to the "double and" of Trinity. Christians pray in the name of the one God, and the Son, Jesus Christ, and the Holy Spirit. St. Augustine explained this relational unity of distinct "persons" as "freedom, and will, and love." God is transcendent Creator, immanent Redeemer and actualizing Sanctifier. Incomplete and un-whole through the prism of either/or, the Trinity is a mystery, which speaks to the spiritual, liturgical and mystical magnificence of meeting God in human history. Spirituality as participation in divine life follows this "double and" imprinting. Morality inspired from faith involves the human person in the rights and obligations from relationship to God and to one another.

Aquinas explained magnificum as "proficiency in virtue," meaning that it is not excellence in faith or hope or love, but a culmination of the interwoven combination.[11] Importantly, these are not "acquired" in some personal feat of discipline or discipleship. Rather, virtues are "perfected in relationship" with God, supported by grace and gifts from that encounter, and made real and relevant by "serving what is due" to another, or others. Virtues have different characteristics, but their vector is loving action to repair injustice. "Blessed are they who long and thirst for justice, for they shall be filled" (Matthew 5:6). Since human beings are constituted to be more, to become whole and holy, we have innate personal gifts and capacities to contribute to creation. Spiritual life needs to be more than withdrawing to consoling wisdom. Instead of being a receptor or conduit for magnificence, we must live up to the soul's DNA and become its magnifier. St. Paul, in his letter to Timothy, admonishes followers "to be rich in good works." St. Ignatius of Loyola likewise stipulates "generosity towards God" as a criterion for entering into his Spiritual Exercises.[12] Magnificence is an outcome of excessiveness; we, by virtue of our capabilities and capacities, are already made to magnify, to share the richness of our talents, to offer generosity as well as gratitude to God. We need grace and prayer to rise to the challenge of magnificence, but we begin as children of God with the innate wisdom for ending the tyranny of "or," and multiplying the possibilities of "double and."

It is hard to imagine a unanimous envisioning of business as a divine milieu. But as happens with faith, our readiness or openness may be secondary to the movements of grace that are already posing answers to what we have yet to learn to ask. In many ways, the latent holiness in business is already calling forth the spiritual imagination, hopes and prayers of more and more business people. It is the already sacred potential of what we create as human beings, including systems of trade, innovation and wealth, that implicate our souls in discerning and enacting meaning. It is obviously also brokenness, or sinful disregard for the transcendent within what we do as managers, that obligates us to restore integrity and wholeness. In other words, we are not so much inventing "double and" thinking or applications as catching up to what holiness, dignity and history are laying out before us as a challenge to our wisdom and becoming.

"Double and" creep is already emerging as a business best practice. Think about Intel's driving precept for innovation and manufacturing excellence. Recognizing the exponential nature of technical development, the company committed to doubling the computing power of its chips, and halving the price, and doing both every two years. Known as "Moore's Law," for the founding partner who coined the dictate, Intel thrived for more than two decades by focusing its resources and imagination on the seemingly impossible "double and" task. Management itself is being reshaped to continuously reshape this doubling stretch. With typical prescience, Peter Drucker argues that corporate leadership cannot be reduced to one bottom-line measure, that responsibility to shareholders cannot be discharged without growing as co-equal priorities capital in financial and human and social dimensions. So convinced is he about this "double and" performance that he sees the need for co-CEOs: teams of leaders that discharge excellence while the board discerns and balances overarching priorities. Research in Motion (the company behind BlackBerry) and Nike are two high-profile companies that have already adopted co-CEOS. While still exceptional, this "double and" performance is becoming a new standard for excellence, with corporate results increasingly scrutinized through what John Elkington coined the "triple bottom line," which measures profits, social impacts, and environmental sustainability.[13]

Some of the most the successful companies of the new millennium have mastered their own version of "double and." Southwest Airlines, for example, manages a unique, competitive and successful trifecta, offering warm, personalized service and low prices and a liberated humanity that creates belonging for employees and a sense of welcome for passengers. Breaking the dehumanizing juggernaut model of Wal-Mart, Costco has used scale and efficiencies to produce low prices and high profits and fair wages that create hopeful and satisfying working conditions for employees.[14] Conflating usually disparate disciplines, Toyota attends to the small details of quality, winning top slots in annual product satisfaction surveys. And it embraces the big risks of innovation, leading the world with its hybrid Prius. And it bravely experiments with its social obligations, including creating a pharmacy to help dispense healthcare to employees. Admittedly, these doublings are for efficiencies and profits rather than outright altruism; however, the lesson is that for an "or" business culture, profits and human priorities are seen as competitive. From an "and" perspective, there are opportunities in the creative difficulties posed by contradictory objectives. With "double and," managers are naturally progressing to the operational excellence that creates value for people rather than through them.

"Double and" is also emerging as a corrective to those thin ethical practices based on codes or rules. In their important study on the practicalities of ethical excellence, professors Howard Gardner, Mihaly Csikszentmihalyi and William Damon frame "good work" (good results doing good) as dynamic, multi-faceted and inclusive. Again, "double and" is evident. In this case, the moral convictions of the practitioner and the ethical standards of the professional domain or field and the expectations of stakeholders in society at large need to be in some working congruence. Any break in this chain risks relativism, specialist silos or breakdown in moral relevance and authority. The authors observe that the process for ethical discernment itself operates as a "double and," with equilibrium requiring the constant vigilance and renewal through dialogue and tension and alignment.[15] Any truthful assessment of the current reality in which business operates will recognize that the ethical challenges we face as managers will require ever-greater agility enmeshing opposing requirements from society, the economy and the natural environment. It does not take a prophet of strategic planning to acknowledge that we need globalization that creates shareholder value, and opportunities for more equitable social development, and protects and sustains the life-supporting ecosystem. Nor does it take a particularly enlightened human resource policy to acknowledge that managers and employees need to make a living, and make a contribution to their company and derive meaning and dignity from the work that consumes ever more time, creativity and identity.

God in Heaven

You Are Who Are

We be to become

You create by calling forth

We create in response

You are infinite in mystery

We are infinite in curiosity

You are Source and Aim

We are work-in-progress

You gift Yourself within life

We live to glimpse and grasp You

You pull us towards Your heart of love

We walk ever aimlessly on this gravity

You are inexhaustible

We exhaust even despair towards You

You are inexpressible

We sometimes cease naming You for running out of hope

You are Beyond

We are made to stretch up for You

You are Being

We are made to find you within

You are Becoming

We are made to unfold, evolving churning imagining pushing coming – coming

Amen

In summary, to make great things requires leveraging the great talents, longings and wisdom from presence. Several things flow from this approach:
- Magnificence is a birthright as well as a challenge.
- Magnificence at work requires melding managerial expertise and moral imagination to strive for worth and worthiness simultaneously.

- As with any enterprise or strategy, magnificence is based on risk, with stakes of success and failure part of a larger calculus that also includes right and wrong.
- The inspiration to innovate and the fortitude to succeed partake of the same courage needed for magnificence, so the issue is not suppressing managerial expertise but liberating it to also serve human and moral aims.
- What magnificence we strive for or achieve portends possibilities we recognize and inherit because we are the children of God. More than work, magnificence is work as prayer and praise – the cathedrals we erect to signify the depth of devotion from the heights of expertise.
- As with art or wisdom, magnificence is rarely an instantaneous achievement but rather something we grow into by developing mastery, expressing passion, and investing head, heart and soul.
- "And" is the key to unlocking personal and operational greatness. "Double and" springs open magnificence, which includes but is not exhausted by greatness.
- We are not spiritually deficient in managing magnificence but must instead, with clarity and generosity, invest the transcendence within us to magnify the gifts and graces we have received.
- The test and criterion for magnificence is justice: undoing its aberrations, renewing its living relevance and extending beatitude.
- As we are transformed both by the journey towards magnificence as well as its outcome, we need to attend to both what we strive for and how we get there.

Lost Horizons from Lowered Hopes

Those of us aching for integrity at work implicitly envision our own "double and." We strive to grow as managers, and want to fulfill the performance targets of our companies, and expect to do what also nurtures and satisfies our spiritual longing for transcendence. Unfortunately, the widespread experience of work is actually of a corporate culture retreating from wisdom, ever more narrowly disregarding humanity, sacrificing dignity and any iota of holiness in pursuit of a single "or," such as shareholder value or this week's sales. Even as economic priorities have assumed more importance in society, even as companies have become more powerful in local and global communities, managers have become far more disposable and paradoxically powerless. Several recent surveys paint a stark picture of the human consequences of this dispiriting trend. All over the world, but especially in North America, the stress from work is becoming chronic. According to the *New York Times*, "Sixty-two percent of workers say their workload has increased over the last six months; 53 percent say work leaves them overtired and overwhelmed"; and more than half expect this pressure to only get worse. In addition to the financial burden to companies (over $300 billion a year in lost productivity in the U.S. alone), the cost for workers is the grave one of health and hope. While advertising has made it seem sexy and smart to have a laptop on a beach, the intrusiveness of this technology has meant that more and more people "are always on the job." For sociologist Arlie Hochschild, this conflation in which "home became work, and work became home" has induced a splintering (or disintegration) of self – "a constant state of distraction, doing one thing and expecting another."[16]

Another study that focused on workers in high finance – what novelist Tom Wolfe once called "masters of the universe" – concluded that 23 per cent of male brokers and traders at seven of the largest firms on Wall Street "suffered from clinical depression," a rate more than three times the national average. This was "before the market fell by one third from its record high, before Wall Street firms shed 30,000 jobs and before an explosion of investor lawsuits and arbitration cases."[17] The people most in tune with markets, often those who earn its greatest rewards, are among those suffering most in human and health terms. Alden M. Cass, the clinical psychologist who authored this study, attributes this magnification of illness to "a form of 'learned helplessness'" – the loss of choice or control that makes even the rich or powerful feel they are "in a prison with no way out."[18] Stress is widely acknowledged as a health problem; however, we are only beginning to acknowledge its ethical and moral determinants. What hurts people is the compression or disregard for presence: not just the pressure of dehumanizing expectations, but also the underlying loss of freedom, dignity and hope. Despair is one of the fuels feeding depression. While not all managers succumb to depression, most implicitly or explicitly operate with some despair, decrying imbalance yet accepting it, feeling they have no choice. Less time with families or for reflection, unused vacation days and logged-on weekends seem to confirm managerial indispensability, yet the truth is actually one of frenzy: grasping for more to resist the pressure of being made less.

British sociologist Keith Glint argues that management has become an almost endless exercise in "firefighting." Even essential responsibilities for strategy, leadership or accounting have been hollowed out by the continuous claim of day-to-day practicalities. We try very hard to time-manage the endless meetings, cellphone calls and e-mails that yank us out of our priorities to put out fires. We have generally become far less visionary and innovative for being used as problem-solving plumbers. As Glint sees it, this compression of role and possibility is at once imposed by circumstances and self-inflicted, creating what he sardonically calls "mimetic pyrophobes."[19] He notes that companies now routinely delegate the jobs with greatest scope and involving the most creativity to consultants, condemning most managers to the stressful firefights of implementation. Often these interventions by outside experts are intended to catch a company up to excellence pioneered elsewhere (hence mimetic), so that we are forever chasing best practices without nurturing, developing or risking our own innate magnificence.

Wisdom corroborates Jim Collins's assertion that great leaders manage to combine "humility" with "willfulness." For a growing number of managers and employees, the experience of work is quite different – what could be characterized as "willfulness" with "humiliation." Goals are the focus of what is willed, superseding morals. Individuals matter less and less. Many companies now follow GE's model of firing the bottom quintile of managers, whether the yearly business results warrant it or not. As described in the literature about the implosion at Enron, personnel performance appraisals have become notorious "rank and yank" sessions, knocking off people of worth and with histories of accomplishment simply to make the statistical quotas.[20] People are needlessly traumatized by such arbitrary and disrespectful processes. Impossible to isolate, such hard-heartedness inevitably ricochets and contaminates the culture, twisting judgment and impeding moral perspective. The exemplar for training managers, GE is itself a victim of this dysfunctional approach to disposability. For all its purported greatness, GE has been plagued by recurrent ethics violations across many of its divisions. Its environmental record lags behind that of even several oil companies. For all its managerial training, the truth is that many of its top performers leave when passed over for promotion. That ex-GE executives lead a host of big companies is a compliment to the company's training, but what is the cost to GE of having lost such valuable talent? Is it really smart to be so hard-nosed towards people that it actually repels the most talented? Is it really state-of-the-art thinking in a knowledge economy to so vehemently abuse the empathy or solidarity of collaboration? The Jewish prophet Ezekiel condemned the "stone heart" for making us impervious to truth and numb to injustice (Ezekiel 11:19). Humiliation may get some results over the short term – even over the entire tenure of a CEO – but these will be hollow, fleeting and sad because they miss magnificence.

Every prayer, O Lord, is a sigh of hope

A crack in the certainty of what I must do

To feel in my heart what I might be

Every prayer, O Lord, is a song of hope

A turning to create another possibility

Living in the embrace of flowing grace

Every prayer, O Lord, is a claim of hope

Because the world I aspire for

Interdepends on me

Every prayer, O Lord, is an act of hope

Silence and words penetrating to see

The promise in the gift of expectancy

Amen

The Wrong Mean Has Become Average

Many factors contribute to this harsher business environment. Two of these are needlessly self-created or self-perpetuated. One is the now largely institutionalized conventional wisdom of "lean and mean" business process renewal. The other is the willing participation by many managers in what I call "the despair from pragmatism."

First: mistaking meanness for excellence. Aquinas's pre-PowerPoint medieval methodology defined virtues by also explaining their contrasting vice. As magnificence is to literally "make great things," the reverse is "doing smaller things" than the opportunity, resources or needs warrant. As noted earlier, this is what Aquinas called "meanness." As Michael Naughton explains, this is "not so much in terms of doing wicked things, but in terms of doing small things when one should be doing great things."[21] This is a vice because the diminishment is by choice, doing what is needed without approaching what is possible, leaving unused the stirrings and skills that flower as becoming. By osmosis or strategy, business has adopted "mean" as the natural complement to "lean," and as a norm for competitive excellence. I remember how "lean and mean" emerged as a shocking indictment of the status quo in the early 1990s. Some companies needed dramatic shaking up to restore focus on productivity and shareholder value. Very quickly, this tactic for emergency restructuring became a substitute for serious strategy. For many less imaginative companies, meanness became the primary driver of organizational vision. Even as some of its most famous promulgators, such as "Chainsaw Al Dunlop," became discredited, "lean and mean" inveigled itself into practices and cultures of business at large. So embedded is this orientation that much of the meanness is now invisible to us, like the facile disrespect from most auto-attendant call systems. Like magnificence, meanness is not self-enclosed but becomes contagious. Lean and mean companies value lean and mean employees who take lean and mean actions to deliver lean and mean results. The result is small things done minimally while things that matter for sustainability, innovation and human enrichment atrophy from neglect. I believe strongly that new rules or laws are inadequate for addressing our numerous corporate failures because there has been so little serious undoing of the root meanness.

"Lean" is actually an imperative rather than strategy, the commitment to ever-higher efficiency required not only by markets but also by environmental pressures to reduce waste and preserve depleted resources. "Mean" is always an option, a choice about the attitude and sensibility brought to the pursuit of operational leanness. Companies heavily invested in knowledge could fashion prophetic strategy by striving for "lean and smart," which would focus on the values that lead to creating value from compassion and intelligence. Those involved in resource extraction could lead with a kingly vision by aiming for "lean and green," committing to the corporate renewal that must go hand-in-hand with renewable strategies for raw materials. For service companies, "mean" actually breeds practices and attitudes that undermine engagement, co-operation and relationship. The nuance in this case could be "lean and caring," a Collins-like pairing of opposites that sparks creative expansion of possibilities by rooting value in the human qualities of need, respect and dignity.

Aquinas recognized that meanness was not only an outcome, but also an interior state. He called this pusillanimity – the "pettiness of mind" that shrinks meaning as well as consequences.[22] Some business school teachers now concede that narrow-mindedness is bred into many MBA programs, with economic parameters "hi-jacking" any "sense of moral responsibility."[23] Without necessarily intending it, much of our spirituality at work has caught this "lean and mean" bug. We pray leanly, mostly alone, without investment in community or tradition or Sabbath. We pray efficiently, within stress, or to alleviate it, expecting the relationship with transcendence to shape itself to our personal constraints or priorities. And we pray productively, often for goals of personal development, including balance or inner peace. We also pray meanly, to recover from diminishment without embracing the larger gifts and possibilities orienting us to transcendence. We pray at work, but apart from investing our roles, projects and responsibilities with the aims of the sacredness we so long for. And we pray mostly without daring for the grace and hope to realize the significance of the petitions and praise we offer.

The Despair from Pragmatism

We used to believe progress had an inevitability, that technology and knowledge would solve even those problems progress created, that human well-being and culture would rise in parallel. Now we are not so sure. The environment is a mess, thousands of scientists support the claims about human-accelerated global warming, yet pragmatism supposedly dictates that the U.S. exempt 17,000 power plants and industrial polluters from previously mandated clean-air laws. "Our hands are tied," say the advocates. "The economy requires cheap energy and we have no choice but to supply it." There is no room in this discussion for ideals. Alternatives are too "impractical" for requiring innovation and investment. These are "must-do's" dictated by the iron aims of practicality and affordability. This is the disclaimer I hear again and again. "We'd like to be more ethical, but we can't afford to be so nice." Or, "We need to grow our relationship with customers, but it is not practical to be generous." Such automatic elimination of alternatives is presumed to be an imposition of logic, but it is only a synonym for despair.

Companies are in a self-constricting trap of logic and practicality. William Ford III is the chairman of the company founded by his great-grandfather. A committed environmentalist and passionate outdoorsman, William made headlines several years ago decrying the pollution and poor gas mileage of the large pick-ups and SUVs that are Ford's bread and butter even in times of low-fat profits. By all accounts, Ford the person is sincere about his concern, even if under his watch the fleet gas mileage of Ford the company is lower than during the heyday of the Model T. To be fair, Ford has brought some smart advances to manufacturing and plant design, winning international awards from environmentalists for the radical overhaul of the Rouge River facility, which even boasts a grass roof. However, the overall impact in efficiency and waste reduction relative to untamed vehicle emissions and gas consumption is marginal. My argument is that pragmatism thrusts despair upon even the most privileged managers with the most sincere hopes. If Ford's idealistic arm has been twisted by practicalities, how much more pressure is felt by average managers or employees?

This is not to disparage practicality, which expresses part of our human ingenuity and has been an asset of saints. The problem is scope. When the "doable" becomes the hard and fast standard for imagination, what gets most constrained are aspirations, including those for magnificence. We have embraced practicality as the remedy for excess or wastefulness, but are now so tightly in its grip that we are being squeezed of hope. Many agree that the spate of fraud and scandal in business points to a moral deficit. I think the problem is also a hope deficit. By and large, people know the difference between right and wrong. When they do not act on that understanding, it is because they have little hope that any intervention will make a difference. Many companies espouse values, but few accept or invite the intervention of hope that would make them vibrant resources for ethical aspiration. Practicality trumps even ethics, which explains why so many "good" people at Enron and Citibank remained silent despite witnessing practices that were illegal as well as immoral. Not only have ethics antennae been blunted by the overruling criteria of pragmatism, those for strategy, innovation and long-term planning have also been bent out of shape. Decisions that are not fact-based are automatically not supportable. Since few hopes have a trail of facts leading in a straight line to their realization, and even fewer ideals live up to business-case scrutiny, little that is not scalable or doable or consultant-certified ever gets on many corporate "to-do" lists. Again, pragmatism can be valuable, but as it serves practicality more than possibility, its outcomes are less than we can be, especially when meanness substitutes for magnificence. Trust and suspicion are antonyms but not antidotes: to grow and sustain trust, we must undo the meanness of fear and re-enchant the possibilities of hope.

Lord God

I sometimes confuse coveting for hoping

Measuring dreams by the yardstick of things

I sometimes mistake optimism for hope

Wanting the glass to be half full instead of imagining bottles and rivers

I sometimes synonym wishful thinking for hope

Making it easier to dismiss for being a daydream

I sometimes interpose expectations for hope

Conditioning outcomes by pre-set norms for what's doable

I sometimes want assurances for hope

Demanding more security to muffle ever-smaller risks

In the times left over, I sometimes know that hope is more

In the times in between, I sometimes feel what this hope can be

In the times in the gaps, I sometimes glimpse the hope of the cross.

Lord God, I believe. Help my cheap belief.

Lord God, I hope. Help my autopilot despair.

Amen

My experience is that the diminished expectations from pragmatism have also reformed our spirituality. Sometimes we do not ask much of God because in our bottom-line way we do not expect much. Sometimes, when the firefighting is particularly difficult, we use spirituality as a firehose, dousing despair, cooling diminishment. There is more widespread spirituality at work, yet it may be more realistic to see this as spirituality practised *as* work, with "just-in-time" prayers and meditation for "continuous improvement." We buy business books, seminars and prescriptions from celebrity CEOs. For spirituality, we increasingly manage the same way, buying soul advice from late-night marketers who sell shortcuts to enlightenment as if they were quick-cooking George Foreman grills. Just as retailers are growing profits and customer loyalty by launching an ever-expanding range of store brands, our spirituality too has gone generic, the no-name brand of interiority that gets advertised as "I'm spiritual but not religious." As a merely personal preference, this generic spirituality extends the easy tolerance of accepting any other point of view, without rigorously contesting what is really right or wrong. It is private and therefore exempt from public discourse. And it is customized and therefore free from any responsibility to history or community.

Many companies are now involved in programs of strategic philanthropy, which, besides managing giving as an asset for reputation, fulfills social responsibility by outsourcing. So, too, the Jack Nicholson character in the movie *About Schmidt* realizes a moral epiphany – after neglecting family and enduring the loneliness of a life consumed by productivity – by adopting an as-seen-on-TV foster child. There is pathos in the experience of self-realization, but what seems like a great moral awakening for Schmidt is only a fractional expansion of his human potential for relationship and responsibility. The movie perhaps was intended to show that only a little hope goes a long way, but it also mirrors a spreading couch-potato spirituality that downloads grief in between *Seinfeld* reruns, and outsources charity via 1-800 call centres. It is not hope that has grown huge in our practical spirituality, but the minimalism conditioned by despair.

Lord of Light

What do I fear

Other than to draw near?

What do I flee

Other than to see?

Why do I pant and run

Other than delaying what needs be done?

Where comes this sense of loss

Other than dread for my own cross?

Lord of Night

What truth do I evade

Other than what the facts have made?

What beginning remains stillborn

Other than hopes already shorn?

What goal am I seeking

Other than cost-keeping?

What limit do I transcend

Other than to You pretend?

The Needs of the Soul

Before human work becomes God's, the human heart must become God's. The mindful undoing of meanness and the willing consecration to magnificence proceed from within as the external response to our interior experience of divine life. Psalm 17 reads, "In my justice I shall see your face, O Lord; when your glory appears, my joy will be full." In this work, it is the soul that is being challenged, not the skill set. It is the soul that is being expanded, not competence. Writing during the social and moral upheavals of the Second World War, Simone Weil envisioned human reconciliation from within the lived experience of hatred and displacement. She predicated human and social integrity on the needs of the soul because while she was an elite expert – one of the great thinkers of the French intellectual system – she gave precedence to the movement in her heart for being in God's embrace. Weil has been described as one of the first postmodern saints. Just as appropriately, we could see her as the prototype for postmodern calling. Although she did not overtly espouse the threefold mission outlined in Chapter 1, her discipleship seems to have spontaneously assumed that pattern, writing prophetic theories, priestly prayers and kingly constructs for healing the traumatized social order.

A bundle of contradictions, Weil was that rare intellectual with a heart as developed as her mind. She loved the great ideas of her volatile time between world wars, but not more than people. A protected daughter of a privileged household, Weil studied at elite French schools, yet threw herself with abandon into quixotic work adventures to experience the reality of the proletariat and poor. Of frail disposition, she worked for a time as a labourer in a grubby Renault plant, and later as a boat hand in a fishing village. She matriculated to teach, but left France in 1936 to join the Republic forces in the Spanish Civil War, where she was wounded. Weil disparaged both ideologies that were then tearing apart France and threatening Europe with war. However, so passionate were her human ideals, and so urgent her soul's needs, that she risked sickness, injury and even death to practise principle.

Weil had the unwavering faith and therefore compulsions of saints. She was described as having a "soul incomparably superior to her genius." Leaving behind prayers and mystical musings as well as tracts for philosophy, theology and political science, Weil was a Jew who embraced Christianity, enigmatically devoted to the Holy Eucharist yet refusing baptism, intensely Jewish except in prayer and relationship to Jesus Christ. Some regard her inexplicability as neurotic. I love her for it. T.S. Eliot believed it was "because she had a very great soul to grow up to."[24] Weil died young, at 33, in England. She was in exile there from the Nazi occupation, and died, it seems, because of iron-willed desire for solidarity, taking only the food and calories that corresponded to the "official rations of ordinary people in France." Like St. Ignatius, Weil prayed with the intensity of tears, fuelling passions and focusing talents from her immersion in sacramental mystery. Like St. Catherine of Siena, who withdrew in mystical ecstasy, Weil puzzled and confounded her contemporaries by finding herself among the power brokers at the epicentre of the political, religious and social conflicts of her day. Like St. Pio of Pietralcina, who suffered stigmata and suspicion, she practised self-mortification as a means of drawing forth hope from fear. Weil had an over-developed heart, like that of religious writer and activist Dorothy Day, who stood in solidarity with the lowest rung of workers and labourers. Like St. Maximilian Kolbe, who offered himself as a substitute for another prisoner condemned to execution in Auschwitz, Weil died in solidarity with an ideal that compelled her to live with integrity.

So great was her mind that during her exile in England, she was commissioned by then-General Charles de Gaulle to write a philosophical charter for post-war France – thoughts and principles for bridging the wounding divide between Vichy-era collaborators and the free-France resistance. Intermixing politics with faith and spirituality with ethics,

Weil drew from the prayers, observations, questions, experiences and movements of her own spiritual journey to write *The Need for Roots*. Audaciously for a political tract, the start and heart of her book defined what she called "the needs of the soul." Before exploring this material, we need to recall that Weil was defining these needs in relation to a larger concept of place – to a France of history with memory, now broken and split by betrayals, seeking within geography and culture to again become whole. With this particularity of time and place, with the utter pragmatism resulting from the scars of her social reality, Weil believed that the ethical claims on politics, commerce or one another sprung from the physical and spiritual integrity of the whole human being. This sounds obvious, but for Weil this priority for human wholeness had revolutionary implications, undoing almost 200 years of French self-understanding and political theory to assert that obligations, not rights, are fundamental to social organization.

Ideals are neither abstract nor optional in this model. Rather, ideals are simply the necessary aims that fulfill essential needs. For most of us, rights are basic in our lives, but these in fact are conventions conferred by history, and are still not universally recognized or applied. Needs are not a historical reality but a human one, not awaiting to be acknowledged and protected but already owned and urgently felt by all persons. Think about freedom. Whether or not the law recognizes the right for free speech or free expressions of religious belief, these needs are already there. Too often in history the right has been absent, yet the need has never been optional. By starting with needs, we constantly refer to what we cannot do without. Once rooted in needs, ideals become the only valid standard for pragmatism. Coming out of the Second World War, the United Nations established the landmark International Declaration of Human Rights. Five years before that, Weil had written *The Need for Roots* as a "Prelude to a Declaration of Duties Towards Mankind." Importantly, as we will see in outline below, the needs that invoke duty to one another are those of presence – of head, heart and soul as a unity. While covering a range of possibilities, Weil also recognized these needs as a unified totality, meaning that each to a degree enabled, enriched and participated in all the others.

Weil's list of needs includes nine that are especially important to the work of managers:
- *Order* – the "first" need that situates belonging and morality, and incorporates all the other needs;
- *Liberty* – the ability from head, heart and soul "to choose";
- *Obedience* – the accountability to which we "consent" to realize order and serve liberty;
- *Responsibility* – the "initiative" we owe for being connected to the "whole" to which we belong;
- *Equality* – the "same amount of respect and consideration" that is due to every person simply for being human;
- *Hierarchism* – the symbols and interdependencies that relate us to our mutual, moral obligations;
- *Security* – the mitigation of "fear and terror," including from unemployment or continuous threats to personal displacement;
- *Risk* – the restlessness that seeks to escape boredom and exercises courage towards becoming; and
- *Truth* – the most "sacred" need linked to both our capacities for beauty and love, and for magnificence.[25]

There is a lot here. Much of the rest of this book will organize these needs into categories to unpack implications and possibilities. Applying these needs of the soul to business may seem a stretch, but it is consistent with what Weil intended as she tried to make her work of practical benefit to the agrarian and industrial reality of pre- and post-war France. Although she did not use the word, the needs she enunciated very much involved fusing work with magnificence. In *Waiting on God* she wrote, "The order of the world constitutes a certain contact with the beauty of the world." Often more so than prayer, "physical work is a specific contact with the beauty of the world, and can even be, in its best moments, a contact so full that no equivalent can be found elsewhere."[26] Not only is there no divide between soul and work, for Weil work was the exercise by which the soul encounters the beauty of the world and participates in creation's inherent magnificence.

How many gifts, O Lord, will it take me to see

That what I aim for is what You hope me to be?

How many prophets, O Lord, will I need to hear

To break free from shackles of hopes that I fear?

How many faces, O Lord, will I need to evade

To encounter one that will test of what I'm made?

How many hopes, O Lord, will I need to receive

To live the becoming You in me perceive?

How many histories, O Lord, will I need to consume

Before hoping like Mazda and going "zoom, zoom."

Amen

The Heart of the Challenge

The joy of life and much of its ache come from its mystery. It takes commitment to prayer and contemplation to develop the spiritual agility to embrace the grace of "double and." It requires serious investment in relationship with the Divine to grow the expertise and confidence to bring the beauty of the soul to presence at work. As with a marathon, we must train consistently and add distance to our regimen, setting and passing intermediate goals on our way to the ultimate distance. Rather than a single race, a marathon is the culmination of many shorter runs. The significance of the achievement often also includes having developed the mental will and emotional fortitude to get through that dark night of depleted electrolytes that marathoners call the "wall." We dishonour magnificence if we shortchange the preparation needed to go its distance.

Saints and mystics in many traditions have established a training regimen for the soul, usually as a progressive movement through stages of purification, illumination and unification. Purifying in this case calls us to shed meanness, recognizing the injuries to our own dignity and liberty, while also owning our complicity. How have we become meaner? How have the incessant pressures in our own lives bred invisible acts of meanness? How has our spirituality been mean towards God? The aim of these questions is not guilt but humility – seeing anew to see clearly where greatness is foiled, as well as where it is possible. This is the prerequisite that both Aquinas and Collins stress, where the managerial and mystical correspond, cohere and combine.

Purification sets three tests for Christian managers: conversation, cross and courage. Conversation relates to upholding the sacred in corporate discourse, not as a hammer for righteousness or proselytizing, but as a voice in discerning the moral impact of choices. Respect for diversity invites tolerance, and for managers that may well mean first tolerating their own voice of religious consciousness. Markets and shareholders, as well as employees and communities, would have been well served had managers of faith at any number of companies said, "It's against my religion to lie, cheat or steal." More constructive for the long term is drawing without apology from religious imagination to grapple with the material problems facing companies. Engagement between religion and business leaders has already begun at the Davos Economic Forum, the Caux Roundtable, and many business and theology schools. The charge for managers is to take this conversation about soul needs into the trenches of business. This means creating pause for the Spirit, learning the language of the heart, humbly hearing others and respecting difficult problems enough to bring our whole and best humanity to them.

Again, it is important to stress that generic spirituality is a "house built on sand" that will not stand up to hurricane winds of market greed or typhoon floods of personal ambition. The foundation for building moral management must be on rock, which for Christians is inescapably the cross. As has always been the case, this is the big test. For all its familiarity as an icon, the scandal of the cross has never abated. No single theology exhausts or satisfies the meaning of this mystery, yet there is no way to be in the boat with Jesus – to be in a relationship of calling – without personally embracing the cross. J. Krishnamurti wrote that "Truth cannot be brought down: rather, the individual must ascend to it."[27] Holding the cross, bearing it, is really the only devotion for accessing its truth. Jesus stipulated "taking up your cross" not as a possibility of following him, but as a precondition (Luke 14:27). Bearing the cross makes us, and marks us, as Christians. Yet Jesus also stressed that the yoke of the cross is easy, that its burden is light. Something about the cross is as natural and whole-making to the human heart as love. In the parable of the "talents," Jesus hints further at the uplifting potential latent in crosses we are to bear (Luke 18:11-27). Each of us has been given gifts – talents of expertise, skill and imagination – that are of indispensable value to God's kingdom. Our burden is to exercise these capacities to their fullest, investing for a return on God's investment as well as our own. This risk is light, this burden of talents easy, because it is in this creative relationship with God that we are most fully ourselves. To carry the cross every day at work need not be a Mel Gibson mega-production; it means carrying all our human talents with creativity and integrity into work decisions and activities.

Lord of the Cross

Bad logo

Sends the wrong message

A God who fails won't cut it

No one likes to stare suffering in the face unless it's on CNN

Why can't we go straight to the happy ending?

Forgiveness and eternal life, no wrinkles or need for Viagra

Lord of the Cross

Messy marketing

Son of God should be a model

Aspirational like BMW

This is not the way to compete for conversion of the heart

Why can't we relaunch with more miracles and special effects?

The second coming, but not with Jim Carrey

Lord of the Cross

Broken brand

Not very user friendly

There's enough pain in life without contemplating Yours

Too little cache even with diamonds as a hip-hop fashion accessory

Why can't we move beyond evil?

Focus on innocence that's street smart instead of bloodied and dead

Lord of the Cross

Irritating icon

Makes me turn away

Yet puzzling every beat of my heart

Outrageous scandal where life death fear hope past future heaven earth intersect interconnect fuse mutate merge out of into love unfathomable

Why can't I turn away?

And get back to work so Sunday I can watch Tiger Woods?

Amen

The third test of courage is precisely that faced by the four fishermen in their first encounter with Jesus. In every life, in every job, there will be moments that require the leap of faith to fish when it seems impossible to catch anything. One senior banker asked me to develop a business case for a more robust, company-wide ethics program. There exists such a case, but it is flawed for again applying a model of productivity to correct productivity's excesses. While the correspondence between needs of the soul and those of business is considerable, there are inevitably situations in which the priority of the moral claim must stand in opposition to the overriding conventions of competitiveness and the bottom line. Sometimes the right moral action has no business case. Sometimes what is good requires outright obedience to principle rather than calibration of payback. Sometimes magnificence is no more than insisting on integrity and exposing invisible meanness.

Spiritual purification serves several purposes. To sincerely cleanse the soul requires the "seeing anew of repentance." Not for guilt or self-diminishment, this purifying is to shed the broken assumptions that impede our growth and thwart the real needs of the soul. By this shedding we make space for the illumination of grace and the reception of wisdom. And through purification we prepare ourselves for the zenith encounter of communion. This chapter explored magnificence as well as its opposite meanness. It introduced the management device of "double and." Finally, it identified the needs of the soul as the criteria and enablers for realizing beauty and goodness. With details of purification considered, we can now turn our souls to the beginning of illumination – in this case, in the next chapter, casting light on possibilities inspired by the soul's needs for magnificence.

3

Wrestling

Acting from Understanding

What would it look like to manage from the needs of the soul? Is it even possible to live faith so coherently at work? I would nominate Jacob as the biblical model for what is possible in the struggle to hear God's call while doing the dirty work of getting ahead. No goody two-shoes, Jacob personified self-interest, using charm and hustle to usurp his own brother's inheritance. While Cain took to violence in an earlier biblical story, Jacob leveraged competitive advantage. With cunning that we would recognize as smart marketing, he wrapped his arms in lambskins to convince his blind father that he was in fact his hairy, firstborn brother, Esau. Whatever slick persuasion it took to sate ambition, Jacob earned the blessing that anointed him as the king of the roost. A smooth operator, Jacob presold the concept to his mother, who supported him in the bait-and-switch swindle that deceived his father and defrauded his brother. We know that Jacob was competent because his clan grew in numbers and prosperity during his tenure as patriarch and CEO. What is really interesting is that neither Jacob's ambitions nor his obvious ethical shortcuts disqualified him from service to creation and salvation. God favoured Jacob despite his entrepreneurial zeal, going so far as to reward him by changing his name to Israel (Genesis 27:1-29). The implication seems outrageous yet is typical of God: even our ambitions and competitiveness have seeds for serving the divine purpose, and even our excesses and failures are not necessarily the final legacy of aggressive self-interest. We may subscribe to a Darwinian business reality, or a Machiavellian management model, but, like Jacob, we find that God's love breaks through even our foibles to animate possibilities for relationship and becoming.

Wanting to get ahead and wanting to get to God are neither perfectly aligned nor diametrically opposed. Everyone, including and especially "sinners," are invited to feast at the table of God's friendship (Luke 15:2). The issue is not saintliness, but engagement. God takes us as we are, but we must be at least somewhat willing to give ourselves over to God. In his famous dream, Jacob spent the night wrestling with a stranger, not giving up his humanity and personality, yet not releasing his adversary until he had won from him a blessing. Jacob awoke to realize he had been wrestling with God. He came out of the dream with a physical impediment because the blessing for having wrestled with the divine was a stone smashed into Jacob's hip socket (Genesis 32:22-32).

In our entertainment culture, wrestling has become a big-business pantomime of violence. Its image from scripture is instead outrageously hopeful: we wrestle, simultaneously resisting and clutching the Presence that simultaneously invites and demands encounter. We do not necessarily win or lose in this struggle, nor necessarily emerge with clear moral options and action plans, but we are inevitably left with a limp. More than marking inadequacy or checking the swagger of pride, the limp as experienced by Jacob actually slows us down: we still move forward, but with more deliberation; we still advance, but with the humility from having God's drag on our every step; we still work and apply ourselves to progress, but with a slower gait for knowing that winning and losing are amorphous rather than binary. Jacob is the perfect patron saint of managers because he had the ambition to climb ladders and earned a limp for having wrestled with God, and because even his burning self-interest morphed through openness and grace into a legacy that founded a nation and changed the course of salvation history.

Most of us have job descriptions that are already chock-a-block with targets, performance measures and accountabilities. The added criteria of integrity compound this busyness, demanding that we work out the ethical and legal obligations of decisions and actions. As important as it is to do the right thing as well as the strategic one, the obligation for Christians does not stop here. Since our experience of God is through the person and presence of Christ, our understanding of the moral claims in our work comes from wrestling with the cross. If the right thing is to speak honestly to investors, the cross demands that the truth also be wrestled with to serve the freedom and dignity of those most poor and powerless affected by the organization. If the ethical option is respect for customers, the cross demands that we also wrestle with questions pertaining to justice and peace that dignify respectfulness.

Spiritual development aims at growth in goodness, but we need not wait – cannot wait – to be saints to take on this daily wrestling match. Like Jacob, we must clutch and grab as who we are, feeling in our hearts the desperation from not wanting to be taken over, and yet not wanting to let go. We cannot be clear about which, if any, blessings will come from such a struggle. Yet we can trust that limping into boardrooms and feeling the hip ache while sitting through PowerPoint presentations will keep us alert to the grace that is forever striving to break through our imperviousness. Wrestling is an admittedly strange form of discipleship. We would hope for something more straightforward and quantitative, such as the race metaphor that St. Paul uses to convey perseverance and faithfulness (2 Timothy 4:7). While speed and skill have their place, the key is that God is just as willing to roll in the dirt with us, even on business trips for competitive advantage like Jacob's. If it seems primitive, we must remember that wrestling is a test of strength that in its physical intimacy, sweat and groans closely resembles lovemaking. We cannot wrestle alone, and whatever the outcome, it is a sport only played in relationship. As Jacob found, the object is indeed not simply winning or losing, but self-discovery and encounter with another.

When we wrestle with the pointed moral dilemmas of our work or life, we are simultaneously strong and vulnerable, on our own yet in the embrace of the challenge, striving to win while not being lost. Form and strategy are needed, but wrestling more than many other sports involves restlessness – improvising, responding and almost dancing with moves that use the motion and momentum of the adversary to pivot or pin. Resetting business priorities to serve creation or reworking management as a holy vocation cannot anticipate every exigency, but wrestling with the demands tests our character, fortitude and perseverance. Wisdom is often won in such struggle so it can hardly be surprising that it could leave us limping. If we, too, dream, then every day and project will thrust forth possibilities for grappling with the needs of the soul. There will be times when these will require tag teams of faithful managers, groups of minds and hearts struggling with pressures such as environmental degradation or destabilizing cost-cutting. Other times, the struggle will be within our personal journey, as ambitions confront the claims of obligation. However much we train, we cannot tangle without improvising, which is why discipleship is active, generative and immediate rather than imitative.

Jacob proves that spirituality is a contact sport. It is confrontation rather than ballet, a twisting exertion that borders on violence. Such are the stakes facing the soul. For Jesus the struggle led to death. Scriptures and mystics teach that spirituality begins with fear of the Lord. This is not to intimidate but to demand the respect and effort warranted by good and posed by evil. Much greater violence breaks out when we avoid the wrestling. Many will regard so much attention to moral issues as a distraction to the real work of economics. But the truth is that the issues to be contested will not be placated or held back by facile distinctions of ideology or priority. Global warming is a giant that will take all our commercial resources and organizational strengths to wrestle to a life-sustaining draw. The monster of persisting poverty will likewise require every sinew of managerial muscle to keep the global economy from being pinned down by destructive despair. Poor countries are getting poorer.[1] Paradoxically, during the unprecedented liberalization of trade we have witnessed the stark re-emergence of slavery – not just the degradation of sweatshops but also actual exploitation of millions of indentured workers and illegal immigrants. Data from the International Organization for Migration in Geneva estimates that by yearly count, "more than 700,000 women and children were victims of human trafficking networks worldwide."[2] It will again require countless hands and hearts to wrangle the ogre of slavery to the floor. Rich countries have their own threats. In North America, 24 per cent of the workforce is stuck in such low-paying jobs that even households with two incomes are often below the poverty line.[3] More than widening, this gap between rich and poor is also hardening, with class distinctions "calcifying," and social mobility disappearing in the very home of the "American dream."[4] Businesses are embroiled in these issues either as contributors to many of the problems or because they are affected by them. Managers may opt not to wrestle, but that will not prevent companies from being bloodied and beaten by the unavoidable fray.

If we cannot run away from the match, we need to begin imagining the skills for not getting clobbered by our generation's Behemoth and Leviathan. As happens with good and evil, the heroic qualities required to wrestle with what matters most are also those required for magnificence. Working with Simone Weil's needs of the soul, I have formulated nine principles for attacking the issues we can no longer evade, and for managing to the higher calling imposed by historical circumstances. While these principles seem audacious, they are based on the moral trajectories of existing best practices. While they seem far-fetched, they are only as extreme as I imagine the need to be.

O God my God

Help me see

With anguish for what is and impatience for what can be

Open me to seethe

Towards dehumanizing complacencies around and within me

Guide me to seed

Hopes and possibilities

Pull me to seek

The healing pattern of Your love

O God my God

Strengthen me to seize

The moral moments which await my response

Prepare me to receive

Inspiration and motivation from Your grace

Amen

1. Order: The Principle of "ROI"[2]

Disorder destabilizes the soul and destroys economic value. The greatest threat to order is from business practised without the moral temperance to match our growing interdependence. Rather than play continuous catch-up with skimpy codes for business ethics, we need a reframing in which performance and results are measured to the "double and" criteria of integrity. The principle for creating wealth by contributing to this enriching social and natural order is for squaring the return on the investment (ROI^2). Beyond return on investment, it is economically smart and socially imperative for companies to generate return also on *dependence*.

Every organization does not so much create value as unleash it. Oil companies, for example, find, extract, process and sell fuel that they did not create. Banks do not make money from scratch but earn value from deploying savings and assets of customers to finance opportunities and investments for others. Software companies similarly attract and deploy intellectual capacities that have been developed by communities that have created infrastructures for education and funded far-reaching university research. Of course, companies add value through expertise and innovation, but the benefits from any operation are never realized free from society's charter to operate, or free from some inescapable interdependence. Some companies have patented certain gene sequences, setting themselves up as proprietary gatekeepers of information on, for example, diagnostics for breast cancer. Smart companies obviously deserve fair return for their investment in knowledge; however, the data being used in this last case is precious beyond any economic valuation, and has existed as a shared human asset for millennia prior to any corporate discovery. Companies such as Myriad Genetics have sued healthcare jurisdictions that have used the "copyrighted" genetic sequence as a diagnostic screen for disease or to identify those at high risk. This aggressive assertion of property rights often plays fast and loose with both morality and legality. Not only are many people blocked from proactive treatment, by some studies as many as "73% of the patents" on "human genetic material related to nine diseases" contained "at least one such problematic claim" that undermines the legal requirement for asserting copyright.[5] As with speculators who claimed domain names in the early days of the dot.com boom, some medical companies seem to be making wide and sometimes wild claims about their genetic technologies and achievements. With life and death at stake, the usual terms for strategic advantage are inadequate. Any ROI is doubly dependent on capital from investors and on DNA from creation, so the proper benchmark for performance is benefit returned to both those who hold shares and those who share in the wealth-enabling humanity.

Through the lens of "double and" criteria, many of our biggest companies earning the biggest profits would have the most responsibility to address their underlying dependence. More than "triple-bottom-line" measures for environmental or social impacts, this expectation for ROI^2 would situate worth and managerial aptitude in the proper context of risk and wealth creation from what is precious and life-enabling. For every industry, we would redefine the terms of excellence and performance based on its own sphere of dependence. The global economy depends on shipping. Imagine container companies, now usually hiding behind the flags of least responsibility, investing in oceanic parks and protection structures to attend with rigour and commitment to the devastation of fish stocks. More and more manufacturing companies now depend on just-in-time logistics. One effect of putting warehouses on wheels has been to drastically increase congestion and the wear and tear on highways. Imagine transport companies investing in forestry planting to expand the lung capacity of the planet in some balance to its emissions and pollution. Imagine manufacturers taking responsibility for some proportion of road renewal that corresponds to the benefits of using public infrastructure. All of these "double and" initiatives would naturally add expense to operations, but these in fact are some of the real costs that simplistic ROI formulas ignore, and that our natural and social dependence cannot endlessly absorb.

There are hurdles for such vision, but investing in dependence recognizes that all companies extract value as a privilege, in the process inevitably draining some common asset or straining interdependence. The obligation is to invest back into that drain or strain, restoring health and shaping vision by doing more than the minimum. That obligation is also a great opportunity, often representing an evaded or unacknowledged strategic need that, for being ignored, will eventually impose some type of environmental or legal accounting. Such investment finally engages the imagination and skills of employees who long for purpose: core competence applied to core dependence.

ROI^2 situates our work within the larger reality of God's creation, and within the historical continuity of passing on to future generations the possibilities, opportunities and freedom that we have inherited. The strategic questions are simple, yet far-reaching:
- What natural or social asset is at the base of our wealth creation?
- How are these valued, invested and accounted for?
- What are the terms and stakes of our operational interdependence?
- How are these interdependencies respected or flouted? Advanced or neglected?
- What are we doing to wrestle with the moral demands from globalization and sustainability?
- What are we returning to global society and the earth that advances order and enhances hope?

2. Responsibility: The Principle of "Seven Sigma"

For the integrity of order, we need people to assume responsibility for their actions. As *The Economist* explains it, the pictures of CEOs being arrested do not so much satisfy vengeance as reaffirm the credibility of the system. Without consequences there is no basis for trust. While the working of justice demands some commitment to compliance or penalty for malfeasance, the social and moral need for responsibility is more inflationary and positive. As Weil explained, responsibility makes possible the deeper, more robust social confidence that includes honour as well as reconciliation, uplifting the common good as well as achieving forgiveness for our inevitable shortcomings. For the most part, our legal and governance remedies to broken integrity are aimed at the much narrower target of culpability. We need instead to break through this blame-throwing to recognize responsibility as a productive and catalytic factor in carefulness that I call Seven Sigma.

Six Sigma is the statistical methodology for improving quality that was pioneered by Motorola and adopted by such paradigm companies as GE and IBM. Initially undertaken as a discipline for maximizing efficiency by reducing defects, Six Sigma is now being used by some companies as a system for improving customer interactions and experience. Borrowing from total quality models of W. Edward Deming and Joseph M. Juran, Six Sigma has precise protocols for "defining, designing, measuring, analyzing, improving and controlling" processes and outcomes. Seven Sigma adds the overarching and all-infusing protocol for care, which is responsibility. The principle inspires and conditions the statistical dynamics of performance with those of human impact and interdependence.

Seven Sigma pivots on practical carefulness, such as when Jesus brought the little girl back to life and then had to remind her ecstatic parents and friends to give her something to eat (Mark 5:42). Six Sigma relies on statistical attention to every detail; Seven Sigma relies on the attention resulting from compassion and love. Wal-Mart is close to Six Sigma performance in its drive to amplify every one of its efficiencies and reduce every waste to deliver the lowest possible prices. It would go Seven Sigma when it cared about the quality of life of employees and the diversity of communities as much as it does about prices. The idea is not to diminish operational excellence, but to expand it with the human opportunities for dignity, creativity and hope that stem from authentic carefulness. In such a reality there would still be consequences for failure or misdeeds, but these would be framed as responsibility for living up to carefulness instead of only culpability for failures.

Seven Sigma demands that we account for institutional carefulness as a norm of integrity, and address moral carelessness as an operational failure equivalent to defective product quality. Using GE's framework for Six Sigma,[6] we can structure the governance and operational questions for the Seven Sigma dynamic:

- Have we defined the moral "attributes" that are important to integrity?
- Have we identified the "defects" in responsibility that undermine trust or violate the higher "quality" of moral excellence?
- Have managerial "processes" been established to deliver on ethical commitments?
- Are we measuring trustworthiness or "variance" from integrity from the perspective of customers, critics or the moral ideal?

- How are we "ensuring consistent, predictable processes" to embed moral discernment and imagination throughout "operations"?
- Have ethical and moral criteria been "designed" into products, experiences and innovations?

3. Hierarchy: The Principle of "More/Moore"

With the term "hierarchy," we acknowledge that not all values and value are equal: that persons are equal but not necessarily the same, and that structures and systems are essential for both operational and spiritual excellence. Abraham Maslow listed a now famous hierarchy of human needs. Research into high performance organizations shows that great results are not only the function of higher competence and expertise, but also of higher purpose.[7] From mystics it is clear that the soul is inexorably drawn to ascend through stages of awakening to the apex enlightenment that comes from communion. Business people view themselves as paragons of practicality, but the greatest innovations that most managers strive to emulate have come from ideas that are outrageous in their upward reach. Consider again "Moore's Law." This was at once a prophetic prediction and an ordering benchmark for performance. When Intel delivered against so steep a target (which it did amazingly frequently), it both prospered and delivered meaningful productivity to customers. It may be that the science of chips is reaching some threshold of discontinuity that will make it hard for the law to stand, but that this hyper-innovation has had a 20-year life cycle has generated indisputable wealth and benefits. Given the great challenges of our moral age, and given the great resources and imagination of managers, we now need a comparable law for multiplying the moral impacts of business within a prescribed time frame. Recalling St. Thomas More's *Utopia*, I call this principle More/Moore.

As noted in Chapter 1, Thomas More wrote his satire not "to attempt the impossible," but as "an appeal addressed to all of us, which allows of no refusal, that we should try and do each one his [or her] share to mend our own selves and ease the burden of our fellow [human beings]."[8] More/Moore would invite every company as a condition of its licence to operate to identify its "stretch target" for moral contribution to humanity and creation. What would this look like? Imagine car companies setting performance terms that have the utopian pull of ideals and the urgent push of Intel's "paranoia." The target-imperative of More/Moore could be something like halving emissions and doubling fuel efficiency every new product cycle. Of course there are engineering hurdles to such "double and" overreach, but the very difficulty posed by such a stretch creates skills and knowledge that are indispensable for the future. From realizing the targets set by its "law," Intel grew proprietary knowledge and systems that are now among its assets for dealing with the fast-coming post-PC reality.

Again, every company would fashion from within its own competencies, creativity and competitive reality its particular version of More/Moore. As nodes in the central nervous system for the global economy, banks could perhaps halve the interest rate and double the capital pool for micro-credit loans to help the poorest consumers and communities. Fast-food companies, confronting the social and legal obligations for illnesses from poor diet, could halve the calories and double the nutrient quality of foods they serve, or work with local health officials to double the marketing for exercise and nutrition education while aiming to halve the rates of childhood obesity. Urban developers could band together with equipment companies such as Caterpillar and supply companies such as Home Depot to halve homelessness and double low-cost housing units every two years. Boards that chronically underrepresent women or minorities could double non-traditional nominations of directors and halve the number of seats held by traditional "old boys' network" members. Many companies already have programs for corporate social responsibility, but the premise of More/Moore is for a more radical effort and alignment between what is doable and what is right. The objective or arithmetic will vary, but, as with Intel, the idea of being inspired by an almost impossible target is what unleashes the best of what managers can do. This risking for magnificence is exactly what the soul both most needs and most contributes to. Christ asked us not to hide our faith under a bushel basket but to use it to light up the dark corners of despair (Matthew 5:15). By his example and words, Christ instructed that it is possible to move mountains of possibilities with an iota of faith (Matthew 17:20).

More/Moore makes "double and" achievement the average rather than the exception, which it needs to be if we are to be excellent within the criteria of our moral age. Again the questions conflate the soul needs with the strategic:

- What are the "signs of the times"? What needs or opportunities cannot wait for average effort, but instead require heroic imagination and execution?
- What unused competencies or creativity are aching to be leveraged to give meaning to employees while delivering surprising value to customers?
- What are the assumptions, processes or measures that stunt magnificent performance and preserve uninspiring mediocrity?
- What are the social, environmental or moral risks of not risking a radical upgrade in objective or performance?
- What is the innovation arithmetic that best captures the relationship between the organization's core competence and its moral mission?

O God Our God

Our work is gratitude

For gifts and blessings we have not earned

Our work is repentance

For interdependencies we have not always attended to

Our work is offering

For prayerful scope awaiting our courage

Our work is holy

For magnificent possibilities latent in small acts

Our work is purifying

For discovering dignity within "creative destruction"

Our work is consecrating

For insisting to see Your presence in mundane duties

Our work is communion

For linking us to the mystical body of human hope

Our work is blessing

For living Your freedom and wishing Your peace

4. Equality: The Principle of "Global-we-zation"

By law and moral principle, most of us are committed to equality. The conundrum is that despite our acceptance of human rights, societies, systems and human hearts accommodate varying degrees of injustice and unfairness as a cost of everyday functionality. When imbalance becomes unsustainable, we have revolutions or reformations. But mostly we settle for short-term remedies such as food banks or product rebates without attending to the long-term causes. In business, the gap between principle and practice is under the most pressure from globalization. Protestors have usually been dismissed for being idealistic, impractical or too shrill in their opposition, but the truth at the heart of their concerns has forced companies and regulators to rethink their assumptions and reform practices. The greening of business – through organizations such as the Forest Stewardship Council, debt relief for the most impoverished nations through such mechanisms as the Equator Principles, and sweatshop reform through certification with organizations such as the Fair Labor Association – has led to best practices that companies and regulators have adopted after protestors exposed systemic unfairness.[9]

Companies are responding from public pressure but also, in some cases, from conscience. To be fair, we are still in the early days of a global mindset shift, and may yet realize what the French theologian and paleontologist Pierre Teilhard de Chardin envisioned as a unified global consciousness. Nevertheless, globalization remains primarily a commercial construct for expanding offerings and not yet a moral construct for embracing the shared obligations from this increasingly interdependent planetary reality. Managers driven by business case criteria still view globalization through the narcissistic lens of self-interest and personal advantage. Rather than undoing globalization, we need to reframe it as a fully shared equal possibility – not "global-I-zation" that primarily benefits the "I," but "Global-we-zation" that also serves the obligations for the "we."

Australian scientists now have evidence that the Great Barrier Reef will be dead within a generation. Self-interest multiplied by self-interest cannot catch up to the scale of such life-threatening global problems. It will take a "we" to serve and preserve the globe, a "we" composed of private as well as public sectors, of developed as well as developing countries, of governments and non-governmental organizations, and of citizens, consumers and investors. Many companies currently shield revenues in divisions that operate in less-regulated countries, or use labour or environmental loopholes in poorer jurisdictions to maximize short-term returns.[10] Global-we-zation would harmonize the regulatory and reporting structure, making protections and rigours constant, and giving investors a truer sense of worth by allowing them to judge the real operational creativity and integrity of their managers. Within Global-we-zation, managers may still find themselves forced to outsource production or merge operations, but with a consciousness and commitment to the larger "we" that includes governance for dignity and obligations to create wealth within the balancing human demands of security and freedom.

Global-we-zation situates business as an operation within the web of natural, social and moral systems from which the current presumption of exemption is an unsustainable aberration. It is the maturing of consciousness that unleashes both the full potential of our globe-connecting technology, and the full obligations of our shared, growing and ever-more-fragile interdependence. Even if it takes a while to get the macro systems up and running, companies can begin to address Global-we-zation by aggressively accelerating commitments and practices for diversity. More than deepening tolerance and facilitating the exchange of ideas, this hyper-diversity would have structural consequences: reconstituting boards to include cultural anthropologists, environmentalists, poets and theologians (among others); recalibrating performance measures to connect the explicit contributions from wealth creation to growing peace and easing the world's thirst for justice. Currently, managers are accountable to investors and regulators – individuals and groups that already have considerable power. Based on the principle of Global-we-zation, managers would also report on impacts and implications from the perspective of the least powerful, who are usually ignored or left unmourned.

The questions for this principle link our responsibility for equality not to the abstract average, but to the forgotten persons at the extremes of powerlessness, despair and participation:

- How are our organizational contributions to global development and sustainability on par with the benefits we derive from them?
- How much money and managerial imagination is being expended on evading legitimate tax obligations?
- What enslavements are we missing? What practices or policies injure human dignity or constrain freedom?
- How does organizational power serve stakeholders, especially those attending to the issues and needs for a more open, hopeful and just global reality?
- What commitments are we making as managers to the public, global infrastructure that serves and sustains commercial opportunity?
- How are we building the consciousness and capacities to effectively and honestly address sustainability?
- How are strategies and processes aligned with corporate social responsibility programs?
- What specific strategies and practices demonstrate our commitment to "think globally" in scope and "act locally" in ethical consequence?

5. Risk: The Principle of "Kenotic Creativity"

Creativity is an irrepressible characteristic of our humanity, part of our drive to discern and express truth, part of our pleasure in finding or making beauty, and part of the creational restlessness that we share with the Divine maker because we are made in God's image and likeness. Creativity is a sacred asset and, not surprisingly, a shared one. When we write, paint or invent we inevitably draw upon master disciplines inherited over centuries, and contributed to by peers in the present. It is often lonely work to achieve magnificence in any medium or discipline, but such creativity is almost always plural – from others, with others, for others.

In the Gospels we find that Jesus not only exemplified creative relationality, but also in mysterious ways depended on it for the full flowering of his healing power. We learn that he could not perform his usual ministry – "could do no deed of power" – when he was rejected by his fellow Nazareans (Mark 6:5-6). In another encounter, Jesus struggled and had to try a second time to bring sight to a man born blind (Mark 8:22-26). We are not told why this divine agency was thwarted, yet it implies that the energy of creative regeneration relies not solely on the application of power but also on its receivement. By contrast, one of the most startling moments in scripture – one that amazed even Jesus – was his encounter of faith with the Roman centurion, which led to the long-distance healing of the soldier's servant (Matthew 8:5-13). Where faith combines – when even strangers meet in prayerful belief – the creative and healing powers of grace leap both time and space.

Business people respect and usually relish the idea of risk. However, while we overappreciate the relationship of risk to reward, we tend to miss or severely underappreciate the relationality of risk. To foster the radical innovation to address our current human and natural challenges, and to restructure rewards to reflect responsibility for a wider complex of impacts, require a principle in the image and likeness of God's acts of creation and salvation. This giving over of self to enable the freedom and risk taking of others can be called Kenotic Creativity.

To be kenotic is to be an agent for change by offering oneself and one's talents for the transformation of others. Early Christians used the Greek word *kenosis* to fathom the mission and meaning of Christ, who by "self emptying" enabled the radical freeing of dignity and belonging that shattered even death. This imprint of self-emptying is a defining characteristic of Christian discipleship, and a feature of spiritual practice in many other traditions as well. As we empty ourselves of worry or attachment, we create the interior space to be filled by compassion and hope. As we empty ourselves of resentment with forgiveness, we enable healing and freedom. Conversely, the more we grasp or try to accumulate for ourselves, the less full or sated we become. By kenosis we personally give what the world needs so as to receive the communion we need with

God. The principle of Kenotic Creativity places us in direct continuity with Christ so that our work shares in the great risks needed by history and creation for healing and hopeful human development.

As business people, we are usually removed from the world's despair and agony by our positions of relative power and privilege. Doing our jobs with compassion and ethical clarity will help, but this alone will not fulfill the call of faith or the example of Christ. In any life, and in every job, there will also be moral moments that demand another level of risk from us, and that pose possibilities for effusive creativity. Walter Wink observes in his theology of power that thin, frayed threads of fear and complacency often hold up systems of injustice and annihilation. Exposing these undermines empty authority and unleashes pent-up hopes. This is what happened with the fall of communism and the fall of apartheid. However, this was not done theoretically or from a safe distance. Challenging destructive power requires the "embodiment" from our personal opposition and sacrifice, as happened with Jesus on the cross: taking the risk onto the self to enable the freeing risks of others.[11]

Kenotic Creativity is relational. Jesus taught that when a colleague asks us to walk with them one mile, we in fact go along for two (Matthew 5:41). This is a key pillar of Christian ethics, the everyday practice that translates profession of faith into action. The injunction is to go beyond obligation and give the considerations of support and friendship even to strangers. God loves us with superfluous abandon: this practice of everyday extravagance unifies us within this equal-opportunity outpouring. The beneficiaries of the "double and" become its mediators, which means that we are in the experience of God – step by step with what Christians call the Holy Spirit – when we gratuitously offer that extra mile. If there is service or comfort provided in this act of giving, the practical benefits far exceed that of charity. Since the accompaniment of the first mile was requested, the relationship until that point is lopsided due to the need of one and the generosity of the other. Once the obligation is expired, the walking together becomes a more genuine fellowship, freeing possibilities for human relationship and for the "where two or more are gathered" experience of the Eucharist.

The first mile we walk for the other; the second we walk for the holy possibilities of "we."

Spirituality at work needs to be spirituality for, with and through work. We pray to prepare the soul to be alert to the moral moments, and to be free and strong in taking the required risk to "walk the extra mile" or "bear the cross" that needs to be carried for the sake of what is right. Again, the burden from these obligations of discipleship is difficult, yet also easy to bear because these usually involve the talents and gifts that are most precious and fulfilling to us as individuals. Our risk in God is always our risk to be most authentically the person we are created to be. Kenotic Creativity is not another methodology for innovation. Instead, it sets a higher bar for managers to be like Christ: refusing to let indignity or fear have the final say; insisting with confidence and grace that better possibilities are close at hand; discovering new forms to bring God's love and hope into everyday reality; and aiming high to what is most ennobling and magnificent.

The questions for Kenotic Creativity are those of the Beatitudes applied to self-awareness:

- Have we freed ourselves from busyness and occupational preoccupations to recognize the "poor in spirit"?
- Are we willing to risk "business as usual" to be attentive and responsive to those mourning, or in agony?
- Do our "personal values" reflect Christ's creativity, including empathy for the meek and poor, for employees not in the managerial class, for those whom market research rarely bothers to survey or value?
- Have we blessed and supported those who have the confidence to "hunger and thirst for righteousness"?
- Do we have the confidence and imagination to be "merciful" and "pure in heart"?
- Do we have the audacity to be "peacemakers," and the self-emptying courage to face "persecution for righteousness' sake"?
- What do we risk to make hope real?

6. Stability: The "Simon of Cyrene" Principle

History teaches that stability is forever under stress and rarely taken seriously until a crisis hits. Even when galvanized by an urgent threat or catastrophe, the effort that secures stability is often only a small factor beyond those posed by chaos or destruction. Fine tolerances are at the heart of spirituality. Every word, indeed every breath, matters in Buddhism, for what is not relieving suffering is understood to be contributing to it. In Jewish theology, only one person performing the Torah (the Law) with a pure heart may hold the key for all creation and humanity. For Christ, the tolerances between good and evil were so fine that even the thought of robbery or exploitation or impropriety threatened to annihilate the soul and society (Matthew 5:17-48). Everything matters, and seemingly small acts often have huge consequences. On the road to Calvary, the completion of the mission for salvation relied on the reluctant contribution from an uninvolved busybody called Simon of Cyrene (Mark 15:21). He had other errands to run. Jesus' mission and sentence were not his business. However reluctantly Simon co-operated, the final destination for Jesus could not have been reached without this help for a few steps along the way. The decision of an empire, the destiny of a nation and the cosmic clash between forces of good and evil came to rest for a few moments on one man's shoulders. The Simon of Cyrene principle acknowledges that God, too, relies on us, that there are moments when our busyness or agendas are insufficient excuse for not taking the few strides necessary to make an infinity of difference.

Drug companies have practised philanthropy and community service. With AIDS in Africa, the Simon of Cyrene task is to take on the burden no one else can bear. This means suspending the exclusive busyness of market logic for a few steps to flood the market with free or the lowest-cost-possible drugs.

Many companies showed great heart responding to the 2004 tsunami disaster in Southeast Asia. The Simon of Cyrene imperative is to go the distance to the summit, shouldering relief aid and logistics support beyond the short attention span of the world's media to help re-establish normalcy and hope.

Many managers may have a heavy heart when circumstances force them to consider outsourcing or restructuring. The Simon of Cyrene requirement is to get out from behind the desk and walk with the displaced during the heavy trial of their job loss, or to walk with new workers to ensure that their jobs are dignifying and liberating.

Directors are more conscious today of the duty and care aspects of their fiduciary responsibility. The Simon of Cyrene secondment is to pose what theologian Bernard Lonergan called "the subversive question" – the enquiry that challenges the easy checklists behind most decisions to unlock the weight of ethical ambiguity or moral consequence that the decision and its makers must bear.

The Simon of Cyrene principle compels every one of us to lift up the contribution to human order and healing that no one else can do. However small, every hand has a role. However insignificant, every business plan or strategy has possibilities for also contributing to the freedom that the visionary economist Amartya Sen has made the criteria of economic development. However embroiled in competitive pressures, every project and product has potential impacts that are eternal for unfolding the moral story of human becoming. Every hand is also indispensable, every plan interwoven, every project and product complicit by default in the cosmic battle between good and evil. The lesson from Simon of Cyrene is that there are no neutral bystanders in this contest. Even when we seemingly have nothing to do with some injustice or humiliation, our humanity as constituted for relationship with God needs us to get involved, to break free from busyness to do the messy work that must be done. Like Simon, we may not have volunteered, but nor can we walk away. And like Simon, we may complete our small intervention without realizing that heaven and earth were to be changed forever by our begrudged bearing of responsibility. With the tolerances between good and evil so fine, we cannot know which exertion of effort or care will make the final difference. But we do know that the final difference would not be possible without every single effort.

The questions for this principle are about seemingly lost causes that must be borne anyway:
- When do we silence the call from our heart to challenge what is happening?

- When do we use busyness as the excuse for not getting involved in the messier moral implications of decisions or actions?
- When do we give in to the inevitability of systems and forsake the agency and obligations that give expression to our freedom?
- When have we turned away from what was clearly wrong, unfair or unjust to take comfort in business as usual?
- What inconveniences do we shoulder to make a difference to the healing qualities of our organizations?
- Who needs us to walk with them and share the weight of their loneliness, brokenness or disposability?
- When have we heard God's call to lend a helping hand? How did we respond?

Reverse takeover

Buy me out, O God

Float me shares in Your grace

Leverage the skills granted to me

Shift my options to pay out Your plan

Merge me to participate in Your economies of scale

Consolidate our bottom lines

Teach me Your best practices

And prepare me for the convergence being thrust upon us

Shape me with Your vision

Delegate to me the uplifting to-do list

Give me training in Your ways

Bank my risks in following the call

Extend me credit when I screw up

Integrate me in your grand operation

7. Obedience: The Principle of "Magnification"

Ultimately, obedience is not as simple as following the law or even staying within its spirit. For integrity, the obedience that makes us whole and holy is the action that brings faith to life. As we read in the letter from James, "Faith by itself, if it has no works, is dead" (James 2:14).

We obey to believe, to model the truth even when its words are not yet clear, and to practise the understanding from the heart that often stirs with truth before our thoughts. More than obeying God's will, we obey to become instruments of God, incarnating in our own person the fuller possibilities of what it means to be in God's image and likeness. In Luke's Gospel, Mary's consent to the call of the Holy Spirit to bear and raise Jesus Christ qualifies her as what many theologians call "co-redemptrix." She did not merely accede to what was needed. Instead, she responded to God's superfluous love with excessiveness of her own, taking the grace of burden and giving back poetry and passion. "My soul magnifies the Lord," she said, "and my spirit rejoices in God my saviour" (Luke 1:46). Her ebullient response to God's call inspires The Principle of Magnification.

Magnification is premised on doing more than is asked for, magnifying the actions and accountabilities beyond the minimums of propriety to the maximums of beauty and truth. Managers already have an orientation to continuous improvement. Indeed, one of the defining pressures of managerial excellence is to continuously grow profits and results versus a year ago. Magnification asks us to apply this spirit of continuous enlargement to moral discernment and ethical action. From this perspective, rules are not simply limits but springboards for poetic elaboration of their ideal. If laws demand transparency, Magnification means that we go beyond disclosure and with integrity become advocates and servants of the truth. If the competitive reality requires improving the service experience for customers, Magnification means that we look beyond processes of convenience to recognize this as an ethical responsibility: respecting people's time so as to enrich and not steal what is most precious to them; honouring human needs to enable what frees and creates dignity. Just as managers naturally do more to improve processes and results, Magnification involves us in doing more to strengthen relationships and account for interdependencies.

Such obedience is gracious – a commitment to more than compliance resulting from a response of heartfelt gratitude. Thankfulness makes obedience a means, not an end, a mode of co-generating possibilities, not a code. Having been given freedom as a gift, we obey graciously to help sustain the order that frees. This is what the pastor, theologian and courageous Nazi-objector Dietrich Bonhoeffer challenged us to understand when he wrote that our "freedom is freedom *for* others."[12] Obedience infiltrated by gratitude also melts isolation, because in the exuberance of thanksgiving, we are at once filled by what we have received and are involved in an energized, optimistic, circulating outreach. While obedience confirms that we have followed, gratitude affirms that we have been changed. This fuels organizational excellence focused on breaking rules and laws upwards – surpassing ever-higher standards for relational performance, doing always better than the minimum required.

Venting pent-up gratitude, car companies that drive on society's infrastructure and consume nature's combustible oxygen would be aggressively trying to out-do one another in voluntarily magnifying and surpassing gas mileage requirements. In gratitude for participating in the global economy, companies would be breaking all sorts of rules, codes and laws upwards – spontaneously increasing the minimum wage, aggressively spreading norms of human development to migrate sweatshops into "hope shops," serving customers with service that surprises and surpasses expectations, expressing the ordering grace of gratitude. For employees, codes would no longer simply be filters to ensure that decisions comply with laws. Rather, the ethical reality would be the basis for strategy: for breaking promises, upwards – to add to the stock of trust; for violating total quality expectation, upwards – as a contribution also to the quality of work-life, customer engagement and human relationships.

Mary's response was a beginning, and so it needs to be with companies, with the primary magnifiers sitting on the board. Theirs is the responsibility to set aims and purpose. Theirs also is the accountability for moral performance. Magnification accepts that while operational targets cascade from the top, principle delegates upward to those with the most power and authority. While bedevilling, it is at the board level that people have the most flexibility for exercising choice and honour, and it is this respected, privileged group that has the most resources for withstanding the pressures to not do the right thing. Magnification is serious, for it involves restoring humanity to health, yet, as Mary showed, it is also a cause for rejoicing, for it is in this work of rising up to challenge that the favour of God's grace flows with us. God is magnificent, and we become closer to God when we, too, become instruments for magnification.

Magnification questions are the restless ones of creativity unleashed through disciplines mastered:
- What are the business goals to elevate as offering and praise?
- What rules or codes are the springboards for realizing God-given human potential?
- What worthiness is latent and awaiting release from the worth we earn or offer?
- How are we creating total quality for the moral age?
  – Have we designed in the ethical reliability?
  – Have we expanded the quality circle to invite dialogue about freedom and dignity?
  – Are we measuring ethical defects as well as those diluting product or service satisfaction?
- How can we overdeliver when fulfilling contracts or transactions, adding gratitude and joy as well as value?
- Have we defined the variables for "carefulness" or "integrity"? Are we tracking these as part of performance and excellence?
- What moral magnification best leverages the competencies of the company, and makes the greatest contribution to human becoming?

8. Liberty: The Principle of "Just Time"

God sealed the liberation of Israel from slavery with the precious gift of Sabbath. To be free means having free time. Managers readily admit that pressures on time impede both strategic performance and prayer life. We lose the big picture. We react rather than reflect. We become exhausted by priorities that come at us that are often other than those that really matter. Paradoxically, we try to undo stress by taking on more projects, even when these are pleasurable, such as going to a spa or for a workout.

One of the most transformative innovations pioneered by Japanese managers, and now the standard among best-practice adherents, is "just-in-time." Conceived of as a logistics solution, "just-in-time" drives out the inefficiencies and costs of warehousing by literally driving supplies: carefully orchestrating the delivery of parts to coincide precisely with the moment when they are needed. Huge efficiencies have accrued to those who have mastered "just-in-time," and this innovation, enabled by information technology, has been the fuel for many of the paradigm companies of the new economy, including Dell, FedEx and Wal-Mart. As with any skill set applied too rigidly, the tight tolerances of "just-in-time" have sometimes snapped, such as when automotive plants in the U.S. had to close for lack of parts from Canadian suppliers during the border shutdown after 9/11. A valuable efficiency with some unacknowledged downsides, "just-in-time" is increasingly an ethos rather than simply a logistics solution. The trend by companies to part-time work is for "just-in-time" labour. In offices and plants, people have less and less time for interaction because beepers and BlackBerrys keep them continuously connected to "just-in-time" issues that need to be addressed urgently. All of this careful calibration for efficiency has compromised the time and space for relational encounter, strategic thoughtfulness and prayerful reflection.

As a principle, Just Time points to strategies that respect the absolute, soul-level preciousness of people's time. In this hyper-service, the value is created in more than convenience but in health sustenance, in more than fast food but in good food, in every sense of that word. Kraft has acknowledged the role of its many food products in global health problems such as obesity. With some fanfare, Kraft has promised to do better, reformulating ingredients and shrinking sizes to help people manage healthier eating. Some see this as a cynical move to pre-empt class action lawsuits (with which its parent cigarette company, Phillip Morris, has much experience). Others point out how difficult it will be to satisfy taste criteria, especially for products that are, for the most part, snacks or other non-essential foods. The real problem, though, is that the company again assumes that making some corresponding adjustment to its products will be enough to fulfill its relational responsibilities to its customers. The larger healing requires a much larger freeing, relieving among other things the time stress that compels so much bad eating (convenience) or overeating (comfort food). If Kraft wants to make a serious contribution to health, it will apply its corporate expertise and power to leverage reformulations not only for its products but also for its productivity practices. Kraft is the largest packaged foods company in the world, with reach and influence into countless other companies, so any initiative towards freedom would be far bigger than a "mustard seed," with domino-like implications throughout business.

To free people within companies, to liberate us from the shackles of ceaseless, uninterrupted productivity, we need something as simple as Just Time. This principle has, of course, a double meaning: "just time" to be free from obligations and pressures; and "just" time to apply ourselves to those contemplations and activities that serve the needs of justice – for ourselves and for others. Mother Teresa, echoing the wisdom of saints and mystics, made the observation that we are made most whole by giving from ourselves to others exactly what we need the most. If we are lonely, then the whole-making comes from giving companionship to those around us who are most isolated and alone. If we need to be heard, then the holy service is to hear individuals whose own cries have been dismissed. Just Time leverages a similar reversal. As time is our most stressed and precious commodity, we make it whole and healing by giving it away to nothing productive – only for rest and reflection, to play and pray.

The principle of Just Time would perhaps involve formal processes for personal and group deliberation. Just as more companies are creating prayer space, we would create prayer time – time apart from activities for serious contemplation, and within meetings and projects to free possibilities from the tyranny of exigencies. Just Time requires discipline, not simply perfunctory timeouts but reflection nurtured as a competence with skills and expertise. In addition to formal protocols for internal contemplativeness, Just Time would have companies make their employees available to serve social or moral needs of the community from within their workplace duties and job descriptions. Some companies, such as IBM, already offer this. Just Time elevates such ad hoc innovations to the status of a best practice: performance not as a social responsibility afterthought but intimately integrated with just outcomes, internally and externally.

Just Time has just two questions:
- What must I sacrifice for my own liberty, to free the time to be free to play and pray?
- What can I do at work that frees those around me and those whom we serve as customers, shareholders and stakeholders?

9. Truth: The Principle of "Trumpet Blowing"

One of the ways we managers inadvertently show our casualness about – perhaps our antipathy for – truth is by characterizing the person who stands up for moral principle as a whistle-blower. Where is the beauty in that designation? How does this bring honour to the risk of speaking honestly?

Truth has no substitute and needs truthfulness – more than disclosure, more than crossfire, more than accessibility to information. When we say "Truth will set you free," we mean truth smashes silos. The principle for this commitment to extreme honesty is Trumpet Blowing. It was not battering rams or strategy but the relationship of covenant heralded by a trumpet blast that brought down the walls of Jericho for the newly liberated Israelites (Joshua 6:1-22). We do not know the nature of the sonic force that reduced the walls to rubble, except that in the relationship between God and people it signified the power of truthfulness, of a promise met that wrested despair from hope and secured liberty after enslavement. With such potency, truth is not to be trifled with. It is the essence of what draws us to God, yet such is its power that in distortion or deception truth can become a terror that destroys, imprisons (en-silos) or dehumanizes. As with wisdom, we must seek rather than assume truth. We must co-create it in dialogue with other seekers, including those of history who can teach us truth's difficult hiding places or mystical combination locks.

For the privilege of truth and its gift of liberty, we owe more than simply to be its recipients and become its amplifiers. For managers, this means giving up the easy solace of unused whistles and becoming "trumpet blowers," not only challenging corruption (which ruptures order), but also blasting energy, ideas and skills to reach for beauty and gratitude (which are the raptures of order).

In addition to paying their fines for failing to blow any of their cobwebbed whistles, Merrill Lynch, CIBC and their not-very-truthful banking peers could help restore the health of the financial system by Trumpet Blowing. This could take the form of investing in new forms of corporate disclosure and accounting, including fully interactive electronic annual reports that allow investors to communicate directly with managers and employees of the company. Trumpet Blowing could start reporting on corporate lobbying expenses to create ratios and norms for evaluating governance and informing public scrutiny. This could also include software to decode the complex structures for CEO compensation, which are now so loaded and deceptively packaged that even sophisticated boards such as those at the New York Stock Exchange or Hollinger were unaware of the motherlodes they had sanctioned for their own chief executives. Trumpet Blowing would not only promise to not intentionally deceive investors (which is the extent of current practice), but take the morally fiduciary responsibility to warn them, exposing the ethical tricks and reporting loopholes that (like overused pro forma exceptions) destabilize balance sheets. Such norms for aggressive truthfulness will take time to fashion, but so did what are now generally accepted accounting principles. This is the price of progress, investing in moral accounting to keep up with aggressively evolving financial accounting.

In the Ken Burns documentary about jazz, Wynton Marsalis compares the sound coming from Louis Armstrong's trumpet to a brilliant flash of light. Truth involves us in making both beauty and meaning. Our goal, our vocation, and our God-given talents are to shine. Trumpet Blowing asks us to make as artists the "brilliant flash of light" that we most need for our own souls:
- What is the human story aching to be heard or questioned beneath the veneer PowerPoint slides?
- When have we spoken the truth at work in ways that changed the destiny of outcomes? When have regretted being silent?

- How is dialogue practised? Are executive town-hall meetings with staff real, or staged with pre-determined questions and answers?
- What is the underlying aim for disclosure? For reporting results and accounting for performance?
- What are the questions defining the scope of audits?
- How are balance sheet issues disclosed and experienced?
- What are the systems for intervention, for encouraging managers and employees to exercise moral judgment and ask the toughest questions?
- How is beauty served in the environments of work and in the experience of problem solving or service delivery?
- What is the poetic premise of the strategy?
- How are unknowns owned so as to make space for insight and wisdom?
- What sets you and the organization free?

I believe; help my unbelief

I hope; help my unhopeful doubts

I care; help my uncaring heart

I try; help my trying ambivalence

I see; help my cloudy bifocals

I long; help my shortened attention span

I weep; help my unshed tears

I pray; help my unspoken silence

The Gifts from Aiming High

Wired for transcendence, our humanity is designed to evolve towards what illuminates and unifies. Development that does not uplift our capacities for creativity sets too low a horizon. As Amartya Sen suggests, the proper measure of economic growth is growth in freedom, with its choices for dignity and self-actualization. Production and consumption are important factors in this process towards freedom, but these alone do not exhaust what it means to develop, grow and thrive. The needs of the soul point to possibilities for grounding the business of work and wealth-making in the true vocation for our presence and passion. We aim high because that is what the problems dictate. But we also aim high because that is the home most natural and comfortable for our exuberant souls. It is not known whether such soul efforts will realize these ambitions, especially those that seem most out of reach. We do know that the trying itself matters profoundly to the soul. In spiritual life, the risk more than the achievement yields the gold of wisdom. The more we stretch, the more comfortable we are in our own skins as God's children. The more we stretch, the more space we open for the mystery, efficacy and surprise of God's grace.

Having explored what is needed and possible, we now turn to the resources available to us for being souls in relationship with Divine Presence.

Part II
Awakening to Wisdom

4

GRACE

Needs Becoming Ideals

Whether explicitly formulated or not, every Christian assents to a Christology, a set of convictions, understanding and devotions that define Jesus as model and set the terms of personal relationship. As suggested earlier, Jesus taught, preached and embodied a "double and" theology. In every interaction or experience – for every decision or response – he insisted that binary exclusions be broken and that the intimate, loving presence of God be made near and dear. In his compassion, Jesus saw not only the illness or deformity of the individual, but also the disease within culture and society that doubled the burden of isolation, disposability and despair. Always the second "and" addressed this second sickness: the systems or assumptions that, by missing the magnificence of God's nearness, perpetuated and magnified meanness. Most of the provocative precepts that are essential to the Christian message have a "double and." We are charged to love God with our whole hearts, and love our neighbours as ourselves *and* love also our enemies. Knowing that humanity has capacities for intentional, sinful meanness, and recognizing that our competence for magnificence is "already but not yet," Jesus invited doubling, doubling and doubling again forgiveness (seventy times seven, in fact). In both of these foundational lessons, it is the second "and" that enables moral magnificence, ending cycles of exclusion, healing the inflationary reciprocity of meanness. Since injury, hate and scapegoating persist in our world and economy, this moral magnificence is not an abstract aspiration but is utterly practical.

Chapter 2 began the process of giving scope to this quest, preparing the ground for magnificence as an aim of life, including as an outcome of work. Small things matter because any company or person that settles for less than magnificence in effect collaborates with the opposing multiplication of meanness. Chapter 3 identified principles from the needs of the soul that take up the wrestling match. Moral imagination is a resource, not an impediment, to healthy productivity. In anguish as well as hope, the needs of the soul call us to recognize that doing better, doing good, doing more, is the minimum for fulfilling both hearts and history. Chapter 4 now tests the practicality of this "double and" orientation, stretching our perceptions to see money as grace. This analysis of embedded magnificence unfolds in two parts: first, through the prism of currency, which motivates and sustains commerce; and second, through a more detailed immersion in Simone Weil's list of needs, which motivate and sustain the soul.

The Real Value of Money

What do you think of money? Or, what do you think about when you think of money? We spend our working lives earning it. Most of what we do as managers involves decisions about spending money to make more in return. The living we do outside of work is closely linked to what we do with our earnings. Money is at the centre of career and corporate culture, but have we shaped a personal or organizational definition of its meaning? Money makes the world go round, so we presumably know its value. But without a philosophy or theology, can we really discern its values? Can we really measure return from its worth without also measuring the investments we make in money's worthiness? I did not realize how little I had thought about money until I heard Arturo Paoli speak about it at a business ethics conference in Florence in late 2001. Despite having grown up in a frugal immigrant household, I have been casual about money. I make a good living. As a CEO and consultant I have focused on growing opportunities to grow income and profits. I have taken care to do some financial planning. Although most of my daylight hours are in some way related to earning or enjoying money, I have given little thought to its essence.

Paoli is an unusual spokesperson for money because he is a Roman Catholic priest and a liberation theologian who has spent most of his life working with impoverished peasants in Latin America. Paoli calls money "grace"; not for him the dirty stuff of mammon. Money represents an exchange of potentialities that depends on trust and circulates hope. None of us create money. We may earn and grow it, but like grace it is a value that exists beyond any one of us – that we participate in without any particular merit, and that ultimately passes through us. Theology explains grace as a divine blessing that sustains, inspires and heals humanity, and empowers our souls to do more than we could otherwise do on our own. Economists, using other terms such as *opportunity* and *yields*, would ascribe very similar characteristics to money. Grace cannot be ridden like a horse or bicycle. It comes and flows with its own urgencies and mysterious priorities. Money, too, is mostly unpredictable, defying models and eventually humbling the achievements of even its most astute financial advisers. Aquinas's theology of virtues assumed grace as the indispensable and gifted resource for magnificence. Enterprise or professional magnificence similarly depends on the capacities and possibilities that are among the gifts from money.

The experience and use of grace brings us into relationship with presence: agitating to life parts of us numbed or wounded, awakening recognition of the profound gifts and joys of sacred reality, connecting to the "becoming" latent in every person we encounter. The experience and use of money places us in a similar web of transaction and interaction – not simply functional exchange but complexities involving presence, such as assurances of trust, commitments for service, hope for continuing relationship, and faith in a value to be realized at some future time. Although psychologists who have studied creativity call it "flow,"[1] we could just as easily name the surprising participation and intervention of inspiration as "grace." It has happened to me as both a writer and businessman, this sense of being lost in the task, struggling in some joyful, consuming way with difficulty, and then coming out the other end with the feeling that the solution or insight came from elsewhere. Prayer participates in this grace: transporting, penetrating, creating lift like that of sucking up an airplane wing or the easy momentum that comes when you are rowing gently down a stream. Money, too, is generative: sometimes as an aim that inspires its own fervour, but often as an outcome of someone's passionate pursuit that enables the aim to stretch higher or go farther, like the builders of New York's Chrysler Building.

Money can be destructive as an idol, as a distorting, dominant priority that John Haughey calls "mammonolotry." This is not so much an intrinsic flaw but a dysfunction we bring to it. As Haughey writes, "Our faith can be made sensitive to seeing even the medium of exchange, which money is, as God's graciousness concretizing itself to us."[2] The great Spanish mystic St. John of the Cross warned souls about the temptation for "spiritual gluttony," recognizing that we can be just as greedy – just as deforming and disproportionate – in our desire for grace as for greenbacks. To paraphrase the twentieth-century monk and ecumenist Thomas Merton, we do not need to detach ourselves from money to "attach ourselves to God," but rather to become detached from *ourselves* "in order to see and use all things in and for God."[3] Grace and money both represent value that must be treasured wisely. Both are currencies in circulation that represent real hopes. Both leave trails of despair when they are meanly hoarded or taken out of circulation.

Paoli considers money "sacramental," which means it can serve to mediate God to human beings. This idea is controversial but hardly sacrilegious. Both Paoli and Haughey argue that the holy potential of money is "eucharistic" for binding us together as a society and creating shared meaning and values. In the same way, Christians use sacramental ritual to experience the divine Presence and unity in the mystical body of Christ. This is not to say that money is sacrament, but that – as Haughey insists – it "can and should be." Part of healing, part of daring magnificence, is to imagine alternatives. This was what Jesus brought to his time and ours, a different way of imagining what is possible for seeing a different, closer relationship to God. Haughey explains, "Jesus encouraged subordinating money's use to human purposes, purposes that in turn were subordinated to God."[4] With this "double and" imagination, it is not just that money gets consecrated as holy. It is also that grace gets repositioned as utilitarian. What we work for deserves reverence. What we believe in deserves practice. The mutation is co-mutation. Not only can we expect more from both, we can also expect money to serve the holy aims of grace, and grace to make holy the mundane reality in which we make money.

There is some alchemy to this: more than giving money to a good cause, we see the money itself as good. Once we stop holding sacred and secular concepts in opposition, we find amazing possibilities for synthesis and synergy just beneath the surface. Once we engage them as worthy of co-consideration, we liberate not only their other meaning and potential, but also our assumptions and prejudices. This is holy work, the work of making wholeness, the integration practised by saints. For having been a Jesuit priest and passionate man of faith, Pierre Teilhard de Chardin was mostly dismissed by his scientific peers during his lifetime. For his cosmology melding God's creation with evolution, he was even more severely ostracized by the Catholic Church, which effectively silenced him and prevented publication of most of his writings until after his death. With a soul big enough to hold the still-contested "double and" of faith and science, Teilhard humbly yet bravely persisted in studying and praying on holy ground.

Where Charles Darwin saw in evolution mostly a harsh, driving instinct for "survival of the fittest," Teilhard recognized the same profusion, leaps and progressions in paleontology as proof of a grace that he called "zest for life." When the Vatican saw evolution as a threat to creation doctrine, Teilhard instead embraced the record of stone as fingerprints of an unimaginably creative, loving force. He made evolutionary science into prayer, and in the process envisioned possibilities for human becoming that included a global, interconnected and unifying consciousness. This insight, generations before the arrival of the Internet, prompted the founders of *Wired* to make Teilhard the spiritual patron of the magazine 40 years after his death. His refusal to separate faith from science became an important model for reform, presaging the Second Vatican Council, which commissioned the laity to exercise professions in the modern world in priestly, prophetic and kingly service.

Teilhard's seeing matter as sacred represents a reversal of convention similar to the reconsideration of money by Paoli and Haughey. Such magnificence is neither revealed nor worked upon without the preparation, repentance and conversion from deep prayer. As much as we may know or be expert, prayer opens us to see more and understand beyond the boundaries of expertise. As hard as it might be to envision the interconnection of what society assumes as opposites, prayer makes the imagination malleable to the unexpected possibilities that come from making space for transcendence. Teilhard left a written record of his spirituality. His prayers particularly reveal a mystical awakening that insisted on breaching the exclusions of faith from science. Despite rejection and ridicule for standing firmly in both worlds, in prayer and profession Teilhard recognized the magnificence of holiness drenching every atom of matter. The "and" conflating science and spirituality, which Teilhard bequeaths to us, was inspired and held together by the "double and" of prayer.

Ideals Camouflaging as Needs

Some would argue that the holiness of money is an ideal, and they would be right. As much as we are beholden to the gravity of pragmatism, the presence of faith is always an acknowledgment that something more is possible. Whether incrementally by private, part-time prayer, or by all-consuming leaps like Teilhard's, spirituality invites a progression towards transcendent completion. Ideals are the points we aim at that reveal our truest and most fulfilling potential. These ideals are not free. They cost something – an investment in hope or courage or persistence – by which we wrestle the possible from the practical. In business we tend to think of ideals as impractical, the not-very-relevant view from "30,000 feet." The truth is that all commerce stands on a vast infrastructure of dreams, hopes and imaginings of previous generations. Laws are formed and reformed to clarify and protect rights, which are nothing if not ideals. The free movement of capital – a freedom in progress – is similarly inspired by an ideal. The economy based on these laws and capital flow is evolving, always growing and adapting towards a more optimal balance of rights and responsibilities within risk and returns. This unending optimizing is how we deal practically with problems and opportunities in pursuit of an ideal.

Plato regarded ideals as the original and originating forms that we remember only vaguely, as if they are shadows on the walls of a cave, yet live towards in order to realize our full humanity. The ideal for Moses was a return to original wholeness as experienced in the Garden of Eden through the community's observance of the law. This law had to be given twice, after Moses, enraged by the Israelites' quick reversion to idolatry, smashed the original tablets. Some rabbinic teachers, respecting the underlying efficiency of the Hebrew Bible, believe that the second version of the Ten Commandments must have been given for a reason. One speculation is that the first set of rules was too heavenly and therefore too burdensome for human beings to fulfill. The version that we have inherited in scripture was the rewrite, less onerous by design to be more practical and doable. Jesus as a rabbi held the Mosaic Law in his heart, modelling the ideal as the divinizing potential of living the law with love in an even more intimate relation with God, whom in Aramaic he called "Parent." As Moses did before him, Jesus taught an ideal that was shared, lived by the community as a body with all the parts in mutual interdependence, nourishing and being nourished. The ideal is the thrust of living with God's presence. It is "we," not "me." Together, the broken aims to become whole, the wounded healed, loneliness ended. Together, the incomplete seeks to become fulfilled, creativity to find expression, potentiality realized.

O my Lord

Be my heart

Reduce my shadow

To make space for the light

Ideals frame what *can* be. For ethics, they inspire what *ought* to be. For the soul, ideals mark what we *need* to be. "In my justice," writes the Psalmist, "I shall see your face, O Lord." The market economy is a lot like a democracy, inspired and guided by ideals, yet shaped in day-to-day history by a host of less-than-perfect factors. Every once in a while, we must scrape away the practicalities and compromises and get back to first principles. As participants in a free-market culture, we know this tension exists between ideals and practice, without perhaps understanding it. The focus for most market analysts is to read the signs of the influencing factors, taking stock from innumerable measures of daily performance. Managers looking for strategic guidance will similarly scope the competitive environment, or pull quantitative data from instruments such as "usage and attitude" studies. Ideals are rarely invoked, rarely considered as "critical success factors," and rarely measured as a dynamic of performance. We do have criteria for yields, planned targets and standards for best practices, but these are pragmatic aims absent considerations of goodness, beauty and hopeful justice.

This is changing, not so much from managerial largesse towards ideals as from the irrepressible pressures exerted by the corresponding human need. Amartya Sen won a Nobel prize in economics, in part for arguing that the conventional measures of development are too primitive, contributing to distortions in wealth and opportunity, as well as environmental degradation. Rather than track progress simply by outputs such as gross national product or trade balances, Sen believes that the proper gauge for economic development is the resulting growth in freedom for the human person. Not simply facile choice, Sen defines this as the freedom to participate, develop and grow individual capacities and creativity.[5] He agrees with most economists about the advantages from free movement in capital, but because he takes this freedom seriously, Sen insists that the economy be held to the responsibilities, regulations and transparency that protect and enhance the freedom of persons within society. This attaches an ethical claim to money, stipulating the "double and" return of both dignity and development. Sen alludes to soul issues and wisdom in his writing, but his focus as an economist is on using systems of wealth creation to serve human becoming – an ideal that he recognizes as a basic, indispensable need.

Needs are transforming possibilities much faster than experts are converting to Sen's model for more humanly measured economic development. In his book *The Fortune at the Bottom of the Pyramid*, management professor C.K. Prahalad provides an eye-opening introduction to on-the-ground businesses that are transforming both the economies and the personal opportunities of the world's poor. Food, banking, information, consumer goods and appliances are being provided on a vast scale to the five billion people who are at "the bottom" of the world's economic pyramid. The market is working in exciting and innovative ways that respect the unique conditions of the poor, honour their aspirations, nurture trust and, as Prahalad writes, create "opportunities by offering them choice and encouraging self-esteem."[6] This is "double and" thinking in practice, activity furthering the ideal of human potentiality, but motivated and made practical by the urgent needs of average people. There are moral and well as managerial implications of Prahalad's study. Banks that have pioneered micro-credit have been forced to consider more human factors in assessing risk. Since applicants have no collateral or credit history, decisions for lending are based on personal qualities gleaned from relationship. With this more human basis for exchange, the trust extended with the loan elevates the dignity and pride of the recipient. So powerful is this trust that default levels are far lower among the poor than for corporate or personal lending in the so-called developed world.[7] Money serves the usual purpose of exchange, investment and return, but it also works like grace for elevating possibilities and serving basic needs.

Numerous and difficult problems befuddle this "double and" use of money for profits and people. The interesting paradox is that the management skills required for effectively and humanely serving the poor correspond to those that most business people are struggling to master as necessary for the future. First, the sheer size of this problem represents a big opportunity. As Prahalad explains, "The collaboration between the poor, civil society, governments and large firms can create the largest and fastest growing markets in the world." Importantly, sensibility is also a source of value. Reaching the poor – transforming despair into profitable opportunity – requires real managerial insight and imagination. Strategy matters, as does innovation, not only in processes or technologies, but also, more importantly, for assumptions, agility and measures. Companies must be leaner than ever because low cost is understandably of critical importance to the poor. Meanness, however, is not an option, since the conditions of poverty are oppressive enough. Instead, smart companies seek to meld all the expertise that goes into lean practices with human qualities that include generous engagement and relationship. Cemmex – the world's largest cement company – has an outreach program to women, providing credit and information support so they can add one room at a time to their homes. This creates impressive sales for the company, future customers who return for help to add more rooms, as well as new, highly competitive skills for growth. It creates equity for the homeowner, not only as leverage for future consumption but also in the form of dignity, expertise and confidence.

The payout, like the investment, is richer in many regards for including valuable knowledge about resource management, sustainability, packaging, user-friendly interfaces, logistics, biometric authentication and one-to-one relational trust building.[8]

The term Prahalad uses to describe this new managerial excellence is *co-create*, which is a business professor synonym for what Haughey and Paoli call "eucharistic." As with breaking and sharing bread, money conceived as co-creative involves breaking barriers and sharing opportunity. Co-creating is by definition a "double and": co-risking, co-trusting and collaborating to realize mutually enhancing possibilities. When money elevates dignity and serves justice, it qualifies as sacramental, for that is when we "see God's face." While theology and Christian social teaching are mostly ambiguous about capital, Haughey situates the potential holiness of money in the central mystery of the Incarnation. With the Divine in human form, the totality of human experiences, structures and possibilities are "assumed" through Christ, rendered whole and holy. Everything is already "lifted up" to God by this Christic event, what Haughey calls *sublation*. This means that everything we do and create allows us to glimpse God's presence and participate in God's intentions. We must pray to catch this glimpse. We must purify the prejudices that conceal holy intent. But the holiness is now intrinsic: not to be achieved but to be released. Haughey writes, "These intentions can be reduced to one, to bring that which He [God] has made to the perfection for which it was made. It should also be evident that God would do this through, not despite, human beings."[9] All of creation is sacramental for being "uplifted," and we access and participate in this holy latency when we recognize the gifts from God, use resources and skills for praise and worship, and share in community the meaning and significance for the soul. "In God we trust" indeed!

To summarize, as with our humanity, our money is constituted for more than utility. Honouring money is not the same as idolatry. Money can be holy, just as we can become holy. Here again, this involves double appreciation of both worth and worthiness. It takes different eyes seeing from the heart to unleash this second, transcendent potentiality. Yet this perspective is not namby-pamby wishful thinking, but the wise pragmatism that honestly attends to real human needs while passionately pursuing the ideals inspired by magnificence. When ideals and needs enmesh, what we do and what we can become cease being separate.

What does it mean, O God

That what I need, the world needs from me?

I need Sabbath. The world, too, needs a big day off.

I need fresh air. The world needs me to park my Mini.

I need work. The world needs help working.

I need to be seen. The world needs to be seen by me.

I need to be heard. The world needs to be heard by me.

I need to create. The world needs me to not destroy.

I need to succeed. The world needs not to fail.

I need to be strategic. The world needs to be valued.

I need ROI. The world needs return on creation's investment in me.

I need peace. The world needs me not to be complacent.

I need devotion. The world needs devotion from me.

I need hope. The world needs me not to despair.

I need home. The world needs not to be homeless.

I need honesty. The world needs truth from me.

What does it mean, O God

That what I master, the world needs me to learn?

The Real Value of Needs

Spirituality is regularly perceived as something we must add to business, or that stands in conflict or opposition to money. Certainly there are choices to be made, and different valuations to be considered through discernment. However, so rigid a duality only contributes to interior disintegration, forcing a destructive break between who we are as souls and what we do in life and work. The dangerous duality feeds not only the distortions of greed, but also the facile dismissal of the moral potential of money by spiritual or theological critics, perpetuating what I call a "co-dependence to poverty." Just as some people get carried away with the pursuit of accumulation or consumption, others – usually in the guise of spiritual correctness – are obsessive in their condemnation and rejection. Both excesses are diminishments: greed for ascribing overriding worth to a means, and dismissive spirituality for underestimating the potential magnificence as an end. We know that coveting money too much creates a form of enslavement; however, so does outright disparagement. Just as looking up to money can create self-absorption, looking down on it can lead to self-righteousness. Neither extreme is in balance with money's possibilities and obligations. Neither reflects the dexterity of thinking or imagining from within the holy "double and."

Hoarding money is the easy target for moral indignation because the damage is obvious. People's souls shrink as their greed grows – their moral judgment diminishes as ambition for more becomes the overriding value. Corporate corruption is overtly linked to this imbalance. Surprisingly, despising money affects a corresponding damage. Often the attitude that assumes superiority to financial worth also neglects the disciplines for fiduciary management and accountability. Many charitable, not-for-profit and religious organizations ironically suffer from poor governance and are well behind commercial enterprises in adopting transparency and accountability safeguards. The faulty assumption is that good intentions are somehow good enough. Beyond the systemic inefficiency, devaluing money also often means devaluing the contributions of people who add preciousness to art or spiritual imagination. The point is that the temptations for reduction are great on both sides of the ledger, which is why we must take care to grow the interior reflective capacities for managing this external integration of secular with sacred. In my own experience, this is not something we make happen through learning or willfulness, only by allowing grace, prayer and persistent wondering to happen to us and through us. This is not to say we can be passive or casual. Rather, with diligence and hope we must make space in our frenetic managerial lives for what really matters. When in our work is our personal worthiness "lifted up"? When in our work do we "lift up" projects by recognizing their concealed potential for worthiness?

Simone Weil's list of needs provides a framework for exposing the sacred within the practical. To attend to what the soul requires automatically engages ideals as a pragmatic, hopeful necessity. This also invokes a richer anthropology that recognizes the richness of grace – as a flow that is spiritual, yet not limited to spirituality. I know from my own struggles with faith lived at work that the synchronicities are also unsettling. With my respect for theology I worry about diminishing the power and majesty of grace by applying so commercial an interpretation. As a business person, I wrestle with the already difficult challenges of providing value without adding on the moral opportunities or encumbrances that money as grace imposes. Grace may be welcome and needed, but it is also uncomfortable and unsettling, as precious and dangerous as fire. As in any dialogue, the initial encounter that follows in the rest of this chapter is not to convince or provide exhaustive rationale, but to experience the surprising commonalities and overlaps that create a basis for mutual transformation.

God of Harmony,

I'm tired of dancing alone

God of Percussion

I'm sorry to keep missing the beat

God of Blues

I'm sad in my bones for wearing my iPod

And tuning out the cacophony of the world's pain

God of Second Movements

I am stirred by mercy

God of Rock

Maybe we are all born to run

God of Tango

Maybe we are all burning and sweating with love

God of Jazz

Maybe we must all improvise to the swing of being together

God of Groove

Awaken in us the pattern of creation

God of Chant

Order in us the grace for transformation

God of Rhapsody

Agitate in us the ecstasy of becoming

Amen

Enabling Mutuality from Order

The act of creation in the Hebrew Bible involved God calling forth order from chaos, which in every phase God saw as "good." Grace can be perceived as the reverberation of that calling forth, divine words of power and goodness calling forth the continuing work of ordering creation to the aim God intended and perfects. Human spirituality is a response to that calling forth, always an act of grace for inviting us to participate in, and contribute to, the goodness that mirrors divine order. Grace is helpful to us — what theologians call "efficacious" — because it illumines the interior understanding and fosters the personal conversion by which we come to presence and develop our souls. When we speak of graciousness we imply the fullness — the civility, generosity or beauty — that indicates the human aspiration for "more." Creation, like relationship, is dynamic, so the equilibrium of order must be continuously replenished through goodness to withstand the deteriorating pressures of disorder. God instilled awe and fear in Job by reminding him of the divine power that tied a rope around the destructive jaws of Leviathan and tamed unruly Behemoth with a nose ring. Creation is a fragile gift; the tendencies to undermine its goodness are always there. The inheritance bequeathed in the book of Genesis is for human beings to partake of creation and be its stewards by protecting God's life-giving order and contributing our capacities for generative goodness.

Money quintessentially relies on *order*, requiring legal structures for exchange and predictable conventions for value. Chaos is as anathema to money as it is to holy creation, in that it destroys wealth, optimism and trust. When treated as a genuine investment, money becomes a vehicle for communion, for *vesting* the self *in* the aims and risks of a larger group or organization. Even when the motive is competitive, diligent investment seeks some outcome that earns advantage by creating a more beneficial order for customers, employees and communities, as well as shareholders. From this more holistic perspective, we are what we invest in, and we become more through the earnings we deserve for having extended the blessing of order to others. Grace lets us see good, and helps us do good, which means vesting our personal talents and gifts in the ordering pattern of divine life. Money serves as grace when it continues this ordering of new possibilities, enhancing the esteem of persons, strengthening the networks of trust that are foundational to order, and enabling the creative risks to fulfill transcendent needs such as freedom. The global economy very much needs the grace of global order to release the fuller creative potential of both people and money, which is why development bodies such as the World Bank have been so aggressive in fighting corruption in the fight against poverty. Good governance is in demand everywhere, and, whether by principle or regulation, the expectation is to undo the disorder from scandal or corruption and restore the ordering potential from trust and integrity.

Like people, money can be literally *un*gracious, even evil. Overt abuse of money, like the greed of some executives, obviously destroys order as well as wealth, unleashing chaos for companies and communities, shredding security and dignity for workers. Money can also be mean, however, simply by feigning neutrality. This is the much more common source of chaos and disorder, when mutuality is disregarded, or interdependence violated, to serve lopsided priorities for return or wealth. Currency speculation is an example of supposedly neutral money profiting from destabilization, yet often also precipitating it. Money creating chaos for profit is a distortion of potentiality that causes real grief and suffering, trampling material hopes for livelihood, dishonouring the needs of the soul. Companies are forever trying to make money more efficient, reducing costs or cutting waste. Trillions of corporate dollars are now floating in the ether-space of derivatives, hedging risks and trying to stay ahead of any uncertainties that may compromise results. While valuable, these cuts and hedges represent more of a dance with disorder – more an attempt to minimize dips – than a commitment to maximize opportunities, or enable more enhancing and expansive alternatives. Recalling again the parable of the talents, Jesus indicts the servant who buries his wealth out of fear of losing it. Order that is static is disintegrating. The aim of gifts and graces, including talents and money, is to seed harvests of possibility that feed and nourish the dynamic whole of creation.

Uplifting Confidence from Freedom

Creation and life are granted as gifts to every human person, a grace of possibilities that require the additional grace of freedom to be fulfilling. History shows that controlled markets are as repressive to capital as controlling dictatorships are to people. Impositions and protections consistently backfire in economics, creating impediments for capital that almost inevitably impede growth or development and, in the long run, undermine security and opportunity. Money has the power to do many things, and one of the ways it partakes of grace is helping extend and enrich the human experience of freedom. "Expanding the freedoms that we have reason to value not only makes our lives richer and more unfettered," writes Amartya Sen, "but also allows us to be fuller social persons, exercising our own volitions and interacting with – and influencing – the world in which we live."[10] We usually assume poverty reduction to be the aim of development, which it is, but the obstacles to growth in Sen's diagnostic are the fear, illiteracy and degradation of dignity suffered by the poor. Emancipating what enslaves people is interconnected to the emancipation of value. Money and hope are therefore interdependent, again in a dance of grace, to grow mutually sustaining reservoirs of profit and freedom.

As important as it is to honour the practical claims of the poor, we must not assume that human freedom depends solely on quantities of cash. Wealth may bring more choices, but the evidence from numerous polls is that this does not necessarily equate to happiness or fulfillment. Many managers I have worked with sit near the top of the economic pyramid, yet suffer anxiety or soul neglect that qualifies them as among "the poor in spirit" that Jesus grieved for in the Beatitudes. In many cases, money becomes an alternative order unto itself, which squeezes out any qualities of transcendence and enslaves people in vicious cycles of insatiability, including busyness. The cultural economist Juliet Schor writes about the chronic "time impoverishment" in Western society.[11] Since most managers believe there is no remedy or respite, the busyness is actually an imposition and the exhaustion unavoidable. These are the biblical symptoms of slavery, the inevitable imprisonment from investing the needs and hopes of the soul in an order other than the liberating one of God. Too busy to be civil, too busy to be patient or attentive to one another, too busy to recollect oneself in prayer, and too busy to consider the ethical consequences of decisions, we rush to produce without relishing or releasing the underlying magnificence.

Growing Advantage by Obedience

Liberty's paradox that applies as much to markets as to people is its reliance on *obedience* and interdependence with *responsibility*. Money must follow rules or face the chaos that undermines its value. Companies that want free markets but do not obey the rules of grace destroy value and ultimately themselves. This is the lesson from the catastrophic disobedience that happened at Barrings Bank, Enron and WorldCom. The privileges of freedom are secure and sustainable only when supported by commensurate degrees of obligation. It is not just failure or capital loss that is at risk when responsibility is evaded or obedience flouted. Money without such accountability becomes anti-grace, creating growth in the sinister opposite to human becoming that Sen quantifies as "labor bondage," loss of health and even life, and the literal "enslavement" of children and women.[12] Whether because of social regulation or from moral commitment, obligations serve as the grace enabling and sustaining freedom. This demands that we need not only to follow laws, but to recognize their enabling spirit. Simone Weil hinted at this with her evocative characterization of responsibility as "initiative." Doing the minimum to comply with some standard is not enough. Disclosure, for example, is an inadequate substitute for truth; it is more of a mean minimum to satisfy regulators than an enriching exchange furthering dialogue and understanding. Obligations have a much more expansive value. Held as moral duty, and extended as caring service, obligations create the nexus for trust, order and risk taking.

All management involves some act of obedience. When this gets forgotten or forsaken, the structures for obedience get reinforced through governance reforms or new measures for accountability. Grace adds another dimension to this. As a gift enabling participation in divine life, grace requires respect for the unleashed possibilities, including observance for the generosity and reciprocal responsibility that are essential for any relationship of love. Israel recognized this as covenant, a blessing towards holiness invoking cherished fidelity to the laws revealed to Moses. Christians model obedience on Jesus, who responded to the Lord "with all his heart, soul and strength." Haughey calls this "obedient hearing," following not only a system but the impulses of an awakened heart responding creatively to the ever-unfolding question: What does love call for?[13] This is the "double and" claim that obligates money. If we do not discipline money to serve love as well as returns, then it all too easily becomes love's subject or focus. If we do not enrich money with the added value of care, then it too easily assumes primacy as the thing we care about most. For both hearts and money, magnificence is an act of love. And for both, the outcome of denying or thwarting love is meanness.

Lord God, save me from me.

Lord of light, penetrate the darkness of my fears.

Lord of might, sustain me as I exhaust myself.

Lord of mercy, forgive in advance my prodigal son ways.

Amen

Equilibrium from "Equality"

Money is a measure of *equality* because it corresponds to a precise, reciprocal value. Every dollar equals every other dollar, just as for Weil every human being was worthy of obligations just for being human. Grace is the energy of correspondence, what gives value its worth and equality its meaning. In theology, grace is considered super-abundant, in that no situation within God's creation can exhaust it. Because of atrophy and the imperfections that result from not having fully become what we in creation are capable of being, equality requires super-abundance. If all of us put only the degree of responsibility into freedom that we assume is owed to us, the social wellspring would be inadequate. Soldiers have died for liberty. So have martyrs such as Stephen Biko in South Africa and Maximilian Kolbe in Auschwitz. Others have suffered unspeakable deprivations in prisons, or have been bloodied on the front lines of marches, such as those for civil rights. We all have an equal right to freedom, but this enabling is only because of this unquantifiable, super-abundant investment in sacrifice. In transactions, this grace of super-abundance is profits. We buy a chocolate bar knowing that the money we are exchanging for the product is not strictly equal, that some is going to cover the grace of effort, ingenuity and risk that went into its making. Profits are what enable potential, which is exactly what grace does. Equality, like money, needs profits, needs excess, to regenerate freedom. However, those gains of vital excess also hold excesses of grace, which require a parallel excess of obligation. This is the principle of "fair trade," paying the higher price for commodities and goods that reflect their true value in environmental sustainability and human dignity. From those who have much, Jesus said, much will be expected.

Distinguishing Worth from Worthiness Through Hierarchy

The value of life, culture or freedom is not easily conveyed literally, so we often rely on *symbols* to agitate the larger meaning. Symbols tell stories, and we relate to them to fashion significance or hope for our own experiences. This is particularly true in the realm of the soul as the limitations of language foil clear communication of mystical reality. Any symbol stands in the nexus of "double and," representing the concrete thing as well as the metaphoric. Money is a *symbol* for value, a piece of paper or electronic blip that represents a real worth but in an abstract way. That money circulates as a promissory note reminds us that its value relies on a network of integrity – what Weil called *hierarchies* – for redemption. A host of other symbols must interact holistically for money to be money, including central banks, governments, trading floors and the whole backroom infrastructure for processing, securitizing, adjusting and documenting value. Grace is what helps us grasp the transcendent significance that symbols convey. Without grace, the cross is an instrument of death. Through grace, the cross symbolizes the mystery of despair transmuted into inexhaustible hope. If we do not share in the grace for understanding symbols, we can neither fathom spiritual experiences nor transact or exchange value. When we say that markets cannot function without trust, we are admitting that they are dependent on grace-like attributes of integrity: the goodwill, good intentions and good relationships that are the fruit of obligations met and responsibilities delivered. A critical role of governance (too often forgotten) is to frame the symbols for what is right and proper, as well as for what is possible. As they hold fiduciary responsibility, boards must manifest fiduciary imagination, providing the principles, words, stories and example that guide the organization's transactions and reputation. Money is not neutral. How it is earned matters as much as what is being made, since every success or profit is also a sign for the operating values that earned it. Money investing in or obeying systems of trust serves at some level as grace. Conversely, money violating this sacred trust deserves what Weil called the soul's need for *"punishment."*

Responsibility with Cosmic Consequences

Weil argued that all the soul's needs converge on the need for order. *Punishment* is necessary because of the reverse, because disobedience violates every other need. Money stolen or shrouded in false accounting disobeys the rules for order, destroying security (shattering the confidence of markets), compromising equality (damaging investors and employees), abusing liberty (eliciting tougher, costlier new laws) and curtailing risk (causing capital to flee). Honour, truth and all the other needs of the soul are also violated. Such serious consequences warrant serious accountability; however, punishment is not some calculation for revenge but yet another grace, motivating obedience and – more importantly for Weil – healing the breakdown in sacred trust. Money earned immorally and with impunity towards punishment unleashes "destructive destruction" on the whole of society, including its commercial system. Punishment restores integrity by honouring the priority of justice, and providing a means for the restitution or rebalancing necessary for forgiveness and reconciliation.

It is relatively easy to distinguish between good and bad, and to agree on the correctives or penalties for those intentionally using money in wrong, destabilizing or illegal ways. The recognition of grace imposes more nuances. In his book *The Cost of Discipleship*, Dietrich Bonhoeffer introduced a distinction between "cheap and costly grace." Cheap were "the consolations of religion," recognizing the gifts of divine Presence yet surfing on the blessings of this "inexhaustible treasure" without taking them into the heart. Cheap, too, is the grace of forgiveness without repentance, the public relations–sanctioned acceptance of punishment by companies such as Merrill Lynch, Citibank and Marsh McLennan that never acknowledges accountability or regret for intentional wrongdoing. Costly grace instead is "the gift which must be asked for, the door at which [we must] knock. Such grace is *costly* because it calls us to follow, and it is *grace* because it calls us to follow *Jesus Christ*."[14] This is "treasure hidden in the field," and "the pearl of great price" that require not only our appreciation but also the sacrifice, risk and action of our investing to obtain them (Matthew 13:45).

Money, too, can be either cheap or costly. Cheap money is used without conscience, invested for return with no conditions for responsibility other than legality. Earnings are cheap when managers go "for the low hanging fruit," cutting costs rather than increasing innovation, outsourcing on autopilot rather than "lifting up" resources to add value and grow possibilities. Cheap profits come from doing the easy thing, such as packing gas-guzzling pickup trucks with luxuries and marketing them as SUVs. Costly money, on the other hand, stretches for worthiness, looking beyond what is acceptable to what is also right and life-affirming. Earnings cost more to earn, especially in imagination and risk, yet this extra effort – as with Toyota's work in hybrid fuels – actually hones the management and operational skills that sustain order and inspire innovation. Costly money takes value very seriously because of its latent holiness, so much so that accountability is not an after-the-fact safety check, but an ethos of care for consequences that permeates everyday planning, decisions and relationships. Cheap money sustains the lazy thinking that perverts meanness into a virtue. Costly money assumes the heavier yoke of magnificence.

I am present in Your Presence, O God

Seeking wholeness, seeking Your Holiness

Not sure about assuming Your priesthood

But restless to heal and reveal belonging

To bring purpose to teams and add value beyond value

I am present in Your Presence, O Fount of Renewal

Seeking understanding, seeking Your Wisdom

Not clear about prophecy

But certain that we have more in us to aim for

And that stretching will in and of itself become self-fulfilling

I am present in Your Presence, O Accessible One

Not willing to presume Your Kingship

But aware that management and strategy are also skills for hope

Method and process applied to tapping the trembling in our hearts

I am present in Your Presence, O God

Grant me to be more so

Amen

Holy Risks Serving Blessed Creation

One of the most profound intersections between the soul and the market is the necessity of risk. For both, stasis is never neutral and always a degradation. For both, growth and expansion are natural, while stagnation is self-destructive. For both, regeneration is realized through risk that leaves behind what is comfortable to bet on something even greater that is possible. Some theologians explain the moment in which Jesus accepted death even as he felt abandoned by God as the "kenotic risk" – a total offering of self without any certainty that the sacrifice would earn any impact or reward. Indeed, the "scandal of the cross" is that everything was risked and lost by human valuations of success, the temporal risk that achieved cosmic returns. Teachers such as St. Bonaventure explained the movement of the soul as a "journey to God" precisely because it involves repeated shedding of what we achieve to become exposed to what we need more deeply. As with business investments, there are hazards in such exposure, but these are usually less detrimental than those that come from standing still.

Always there is *risk*: that forgiveness will be taken for granted; that healing will be dismissed or received without gratitude – as happened with nine of the ten lepers Jesus cured. Always there is risk that the freely accessible elevating steps will not be climbed, or that freedom will be rejected for the easy comforts of the status quo, as when the Israelites wandering in the desert protested to Moses about the costs of their emancipation, preferring instead the "onions and meat" fed to them as slaves. Love is an offering of self to another, so there is always the risk that it will be turned away or become calcified. But if risk is necessary for love, its aim and supportive roots are *security*. Our human love grounds us, despite the vicissitudes of jobs or economic cycles. Our involvement in divine love provides the bedrock of meaning in both the everyday and those peak experiences of crisis or ecstasy. Forgiving deepens the security of love, as does healing. Elevating keeps the urgency and power of love in sync with the soul's growth, as does growing capacities for giving and exercising freedom. In effect, these risks are how we grow love's security.

Money, too, needs both *risk* and *security* in creative, catalytic tension to realize potential and thrive in stable order. Investors require the minimal security of transparency and accountability before risking their money. They trust that the predictability of the future will be sufficient for earning and rewards to be realized. Money becomes graceful, unleashing opportunities and rewards, when it takes risks within the ordering stability, and when it also risks to renew the integrity that empowers that security. Part of the outrage over CEO compensation has to do with the "distortion of disproportion," with little personal risk earning profligate personal reward. This does "double damage," taking unearned wealth and harming the much wider infrastructure for confidence. Without the grace of risk, security atrophies. Without the grace of security, risk collapses on itself.

Setting Free the Truth

Weil wrote that the most important need of the soul is for truth. Jesus was especially vitriolic towards "false prophets," for nothing destroys integrity as much as outright deception, and nothing corrupts the grace of faith as much as misplaced hopes. Markets, too, hate "false profits." Truth gives value its solidity, validity and relevance. It is the basis for security from which money can be catapulted to take risk. It is the assurance that measures and consequences are fair. Like symbols, truth is at once apparent and ambiguous. To get to the truth often requires discernment of many signals, stories or facts. The truth about globalization, for example, includes aspects of the arguments that both critics and advocates use to advance their position. That both may be right does not exhaust the truth. Companies, too, vector different performance measures to give investors a sense of their true worth and integrity. In this case, the truth relies on the classic "double and" of finance: the current accounts statement *and* the balance sheet *and* the bottom line. Beyond its value, money conveys other truths. Investigators tackling fraud or impropriety "follow the money." Even big bank vaults and centuries of secrecy cannot mute the truth of money, as the Swiss banks found when they had to accede to worldwide pressure and account for assets of Holocaust victims and survivors. The process may be agonizingly slow, but in the course of grace, truth is always on the money.

Truth is the ultimate need of the soul, and the ultimate grace of money. It is also our test for fidelity and personal integrity. This prompts some disclosure and reflection. First, I must own that my optimism about grace and money is the cheap one of never having been without. I learned in Nicaragua from managers involved in addressing endemic poverty that our developed world organizational perspectives tend to be facile, expecting money and systems to behave with universal consistency. In fact, basic principles of liberty, risk and security must be founded with deliberate care, effort and sacrifice. Without such attention to the hard work of grace, we end up with the cowboy capitalism of Russia, the crony money of Indonesia, or the dishonourable money earned from false advice such as at J.P. Morgan-Chase and other supposedly top-notch financial institutions. The truth of money as grace demands that we also recognize the intentional abnegation of grace as sin.

Second, we must be honest that the grace of truth is a value that depends on the integrity of presence, lived and encountered. In terms of the "threefold office," we need priestly comfort and context to deal with money's harsh risks and outrageous hopes. We need prophetic courage to attack transgressions, or to see joyful possibilities from integration. And we need kingly wisdom to recognize the value of hope and administer money with the preciousness it deserves as grace.

The Need for Conversion

One more truth must be broached to prepare us for the work to come: one that relates to Weil's ideas, and to our scope as managers. By orientation, business people tend to focus on utility: the competence of human resources, the functionality of new technology, the incremental value derived from the deployment of capital. Confronting a new equation in which money is grace places many of us on the horns of a dilemma. Do we ignore this and hold on to our standard valuation? Or do we as managers begin to use grace also as an asset for utility and impact? The Jesuit theologian Bernard Lonergan argued that our human method of developing consciousness involved a progression from exploring facts, to formulating knowledge, to realizing understanding, to taking responsibility.[15] That last stage is the moment of conversion when we act on what we know, when we change decisions and behaviours for being awakened to a new reality.

The process of conversion is not automatic, in that not all understanding engenders transformation. Previous generations did not have the environmental facts or understanding about greenhouse gas emissions and global warming. We do, but for the most part this has not stopped us from buying gas guzzlers, has not converted all of us who know and understand the fragility of the earth to more sensible alternatives. Conversion is always a choice, always an act of freedom to commit oneself to another way. Lonergan's notion of understanding was affective, meaning that knowledge has been processed by mind, heart and soul, taken into our very being as humans. Conversion is the choice of an integrated presence towards becoming. It is an act of hope. And it cannot be imposed.

Either way, there are consequences. My friend Mary Joseph is a priest, ordained in mid-life after a career as a lawyer. In her ministry to business executives, she observed a pattern that she called "heads down" and "heads up." Most people that come to her for pastoral counselling are very successful, and very happy with their work for as long as they have their "heads down" on a particular project, issue or responsibility. The ache in their souls becomes active and their dissatisfaction overwhelming when they have their "heads up" and are immersed in the bigger picture. We can hear in the "heads down" the deceptive joy of pragmatism, the sense of real utility and measurable accomplishment. We can hear the despair in "heads up" mode, the realization that effectiveness has been pursued at the cost of hope and integrity. Money by itself is another "heads down" variable, satisfying for being complex, hard to master and clearly measurable. Money as grace is a "heads up" potential, requiring all the functional competencies of management with the very big "and" of hope to animate the pragmatic ideals from the needs of the soul. This is the equation for conversion: for money and grace to dance, we need to make the music.

5

BEAUTY

Freedom in the Balance

There are no "one-minute manager" shortcuts for undoing meanness or realizing magnificence. For business people to stand in the claims of love, for business decisions to serve also the needs of the soul, we must learn and practise the needed expansion of our own hearts and will. The catalyst for achieving magnificence is to become magnificent: doing holy work by becoming holy. In his New Testament letter to Timothy, St. Paul described this as "training in righteousness, so that everyone who belongs to God may be proficient, equipped for every good work" (2 Timothy 3:15-16). The first four chapters drew the scope of human potential as seen from the soul, and defined the aims as well as obstacles for imagining business as soul work. The chapters following this one will dig more deeply into the remodelling of managerial roles to project and protect the needs of the soul, to both leaven integrity and release the graceful possibilities from our business activities. The focus of this chapter is a pause for "training," for experiencing personally the calling and implications of "belonging to God," and for reflecting on the interior "proficiency" that will equip us for this sacred enterprise. Since this is important work, we must prepare for it with the care and competence it warrants. To borrow the imagery from one of Jesus' parables, good intentions will not sprout and take root unless the soil of the soul is made ready to receive and sustain that seed of goodness.

O my God, can this be done?

Do I pray? Or do I run?

O my Heart, can words be found

To clarify confusion all around?

O my Light, can these eyes perceive

Dichotomies' wisdom we're meant to receive?

O my Aim, can the courage be mine

To imagine work and cross the line?

O my Joy, can this be true

Making a living following You?

O my Word, can there be a way

To do the deeds in the prayers I say?

O my Hope, can there ever be

Possibilities without risk from me?

O my Comfort, can I dare withhold

What the cross reveals, what I behold?

O my Glory, can this project be praise

Even if we fail to find other ways?

O my God, can this be done?

Do I pray? Or do I run?

The Transforming Challenge

Managers are all knowledge workers, and most take seriously the need for continuous learning. Prayer and spiritual life require a similar commitment, but the nature of this learning is radically different. Instead of expertise, the aim is encounter. Instead of mastery, the outcome is subsumed and subservient to the Presence we honour as Master. The twentieth-century Jewish mystic and philosopher Martin Buber explained that "The elementary notion in this mystery is a union – more or less corporeally imagined – with God. Ecstasy is originally an emerging into God, *enthusiasmos*, being filled with the god."[1] Centuries of spiritual experience across numerous traditions and religions confirm that prayer does not elevate individual consciousness except by dissolving it. The inexpressible gift of this truly "peak experience" is of wholeness within unity. As if by osmosis, this immersion in magnificence renders us magnificent. "My soul magnifies the Lord," said Mary the mother of Jesus after being taken over by the Holy Spirit, "and my spirit rejoices in God my Saviour" (Luke 1:46-48). We are made for this: to be receivers of God for having the capacities to be in relationship with God. By this relationship we become extensions and extenders of divine stuff. There is no status or badge of honour from this, since the glory belongs to God. Indeed, most mystics stipulate humility as the primary and essential virtue for such ecstatic communion with the Divine. What there is, however, is utter joy and fulfillment from participating in the life and love of God.

When we speak of the needs of the soul, this is the most burning need. When we take steps to assuage spiritual longing, this is the most hallowed destination to which we hope to draw near. God's call may feel like a whisper, but the implications are always all-encompassing. For Simeon, the eleventh-century Greek mystic, this transposition (or trans-possession) infuses our body as well as our consciousness, our actions as well as our perceptions. "We are the limbs of Christ," he wrote, and "Christ is our limb. And my hand, the hand of the poorest creature, is Christ; and my foot is Christ; and I, the poorest creature, am the hand and foot of Christ. I move my hand, and so does Christ, for he, in entirety, is my hand."[2] By implication – and hope – the calling to be a Christian manager is to be Christ managing: to plan with childlike deference and dependence to God as Parent; to order and organize with responsibility for creation's sacred interdependence; and to offer the best of ourselves in expertise as service to community and holy communion. The original disciples went from fishing to becoming "fishers of men" and women for God. Our job, likewise, is to apply profession and skills to God's larger purpose – not ceasing to be managers, but instead doing these indispensable tasks with the delight and responsibility that "magnifies the Lord."

As with the first disciples, this is not an instantaneous transformation. Like any reverse takeover, this change in job description is rarely completed without resistance or fear. Ultimately, the consecration of a person's work goes hand in hand with the consecration of that person's life. We pray to see differently, which for Christians means to see as Christ sees. We stand in the confusion and seductions of temptation, which means to stand firm and hoping as Christ stands. The Incarnation granted and lived in Christ is precious, not as the exception to human history, but as its template. Hope needs a conduit – now, in this moment, in this task, in this meeting, in this decision. Sacred human dignity needs an advocate – now, in my reality, in my job, in my professional judgments, in my encounters with others. Healing needs compassion in action – now, in our most pressing project, in our most urgent objective, in this quarter, in this fiscal year.

As noted earlier, sociologists and theologians have shown that almost a majority of us claim beliefs in God that we hold apart from everyday decisions and actions. I have lived this split, trying to be good, fair and honest, but in a generic way that did not tap the wellspring of Christian faith. What I experienced as a partial or part-time Christian was, of course, partial or part-time integrity. When not all of our core beliefs and intuitions are present, how can we be whole? This is the unspoken disintegration from busyness. The pressures for multitasking overwhelm the conditions for integration. We do not have time to ask the ethical question. We do not have occasion to retreat to the desert to plumb or purify the motives of the heart. We do not take the Sabbath rest to take account of beauty, freedom or love.

Broken Business

While many people acknowledge fatigue or frustration from too much work, we have yet to confront busyness as a form of meanness. Busyness is the cause or justification for much of the discourtesy that has become chronic in our public space, and in our workplaces. Out of busyness, we settle for expediency rather than a richer exploration of opportunities and impacts. Busyness increasingly precludes personal contact, or radically foreshortens human interaction. Just as it intrudes on our social and family life, busyness also stunts interior life. The paradox is that while we adhere to busyness to do the most we can with our talents and ambitions, we in effect cancel out much of the opportunity for magnificence. To put this in Thomas Aquinas's terms, we tend to regard busyness as a virtue for its potential efficiency, when it is largely a vice for actually locking us into the churn of never doing enough, never catching up, never attaining what truly satisfies. The busyness we embrace for aggrandizement or success is all too often the straitjacket that keeps us diminished and unfulfilled.

It seems innocuous, almost an excess of something admirable, but busyness is the cause of many of our ethical problems. Business people will admit that busyness is the bane of their existence. It is much more than that; it is our managerial equivalent of what the philosopher Hannah Arendt called "the banality of evil."[3] From her provocative study of tyranny in the mid-twentieth century, Arendt concluded that systems of suppression rely on small acts of submission or complicity by the silent majority. Fear may play a role in this mass docility, but as often as not it is much more everyday things, such as work or entertainment, that induce moral insomnia. Evil gains momentum not because people assent to it en masse, but rather because they are too distracted or drained by other, seemingly more pressing priorities. Busyness confounds judgment. The heavy liability from this is that we tend to miss the moral moment, juggling balls rather than appreciating those moments of ethical, human or spiritual significance. The squandered asset is that we fail to hone the insight, conviction and imagination to nurture and develop magnificence. There is stimulation from busyness – indeed, a stream of satisfactions – yet, as those of us know who have been consumed by it, busyness ultimately disintegrates, especially the soul. My ugliest moments in business, when I have been most testy, rude or impatient, have occurred in the guise of busyness, presuming myself to be too productive to think about others. The resulting disgrace – the literal distance from grace – has cost me not only the integrity of my working relationships, but also the consolation and creativity of my own heart.

Truth in the Imbalance

Seeking refuge from busyness, many have taken up programs for work–life balance. The goal, sometimes supported by companies, is to protect "quality time" for family or personal interests apart from work. For the soul, however, this may not be enough. Rather than use outside counterweights, we need to renew work by expanding its scope of meaning. Few saints or mystics speak glowingly of equilibrium. Instead, they experience white-hot passion for different priorities, not so much taming excessiveness as giving it over as offering and response to transcendence. Thomas Merton wrote of the perpetual dilemma befuddling monks: whether to follow the example of Martha, who as friend of Jesus attended to the work of service and hospitality, or to follow her sister Mary, who as disciple luxuriated in Jesus' every word and spent herself in devotions such as anointing his feet with perfume. Some monks are so consumed by contemplation that they neglect the action of living and working in the real world. Others are so caught up in the busyness of activity, even aimed at noble causes and good, that they starve the possibilities for reflective prayer.[4] Both are needed, both must be worked at, and both must be savoured.

Most of us in business are overdeveloped in doing, and underdeveloped in just being: just standing still, just hearing the silence. However, the corrective is not necessarily the obvious one of doing less action to allow more contemplation. Turning to meditation to relieve stress, or studying yoga to escape busyness, is like buying a Ferrari to park in the garage. We are acquiring something very precious, but are missing the exhilaration of its power, beauty and ability to transport. The mutual flourishing of contemplation and action inevitably involves "doing differently" rather than "doing less." This is never without tension. We grow wisdom through the artistry and consciousness we bring to life's real and living pressures. We grow holiness by standing in the very heart of intractable options and messy compromises. The call of magnificence is not for facile or therapeutic balance. We may well need to shed frenzy, making time and space for rest, play and prayer. However, it is how we use that balance that ultimately qualifies as magnificence.

An uncanny business example is found in the thirteenth century with St. Bonaventure. In addition to his theology and mysticism, Bonaventure is known as the second founder of the Franciscan order. Before we had such a term, Bonaventure proved to be a master of business administration by reorganizing and restructuring the more than 5,000 followers who were fracturing into acrimonious groups after the death of St. Francis. Bonaventure balanced a host of competing pressures: enmeshing the old with new; reclaiming the original vision of Francis, while introducing systems for organizational coherence and consistency; and combining pragmatism for decision making with prayer for discernment. All of this practical, effective and transcendent balancing was an important outcome, but the animating virtue for balance originated in Bonaventure's profound perception of beauty. In his studies, which were considered the science of his times, and in his prayers, which were drenched in a love for creation, Bonaventure was responding to beauty as what he called the "eternal art."[5]

Our aesthetics have been made relative or turned into commodities. If we think of beauty at all it is in the context of leisure or personal preference. For Bonaventure, beauty served as a manifestation of grace: "All things are beautiful and in some way delightful" for participating in the immeasurably greater beauty of the Divine. From this perspective, we do not need to retreat from the world or its work to encounter this awe. It is all around us, and powerfully transformative, when we have the time and grace to apprehend it. About St. Francis, who loved all creation and even preached to birds, Bonaventure wrote, "In everything beautiful he saw Beauty itself."[6] With our great skills of productivity, we mistakenly assume balance as something to do or to achieve, when it is actually about relishing so as to be transformed. The gift of balance, the gain from eschewing busyness, is recognizing and participating in the beauty intrinsic to matter, life and the soul.

Lord Most High, Watchmaker-Supreme

Your word spoken

Called creation out of chaos

And echoes still in every mountain, leaf and star

We scar this earth but cannot eliminate its awe

We transgress its limits but cannot undo its beauty

We drain and dirty it but cannot escape its loving embrace

Lord of Time and Place

Make green our peace

Make renewal our art

And use this global warming

To melt the hardness of heart

That makes us absent to the earth's agony

And immune to its majesty

Amen

Bonaventure's example is that beauty is *affective* (touching and transforming the person and the soul) and *effective* (impacting, improving and energizing what we do in the everyday). To resolve the differences among Franciscans, Bonaventure did not impose a new strategy or leadership. Instead, he visited the friars, making available his personal presence. He listened to them, and transcribed the stories and memories of Francis that shaped lives and spirituality. The organizational harmony he achieved in so short a time and in so volatile a situation was the result of what Jim Collins would recognize as great humility. He did not impose order from authority but engaged many voices, even angry ones, to allow the rich but hidden wisdom to be revealed. In the end, he did not, as we tend to do, make simplicity the antidote to confusion or busyness.

Rather, he made beauty the inspiration and inducement for simplicity. In prayerful withdrawal, Bonaventure later wrote one of the classics of mystical prayer, *The Journey of the Soul to God*. In this devotional progression, beauty is the catalyst stirring movement and growth, as well as the ultimate, ecstatic aim for human becoming. Beauty is Bonaventure's ordering metaphor as well as his experience, an interaction that provides a glimpse of the relational nature of God as Trinity, and a hint of the perfectibility embodied by Jesus Christ that orients human hearts towards becoming whole as children of God. From this amazing book of the soul's journey, we can deduce a principle, a process and practices that begin to shape beauty as a managerial framework.

The Principle: Prayerful Savouring

For Bonaventure, the work of scholarship or administration flowed from his devotion to prayer. Empirically and spiritually engaged by the beauty of creation, Bonaventure ascended the mystical path by wanting more, by purifying those elements of character that were numb or dismissive of the eternal art, and by surrendering ever more to its pursuit towards wholeness, ecstasy and unity. Our modern conceit is to assume that our pressures are unique, that our challenges are wholly original. Bonaventure in fact faced issues as complex as those for any multinational CEO, and as grave as any clash or contest of civilizations. Beyond being an administrator and university teacher, Bonaventure was called upon as a theologian to resolve long-standing doctrinal differences that had split the church between Roman Catholicism and Eastern Orthodoxy. He died at the council attempting this grand – and still today incomplete – reconciliation, but the metaphor and meaning of Bonaventure's life is that prayer and love are the key resources for integrity. Bonaventure modelled the integration of profession with confession, healing divisions in all-too-petty human organizations, and restoring wholeness in all-too-hostile a society, by making his work part of the exercise of the journey of his soul. This is the vocation at the base of human spirituality, and it cannot be assumed casually. As the theologian Zachary Hayes notes, "Neutrality will not work in this journey. A person must deeply desire union with the divine."[7] Scripture teaches this about wisdom. We do not come to it but receive according to our desire — not desire in the way we may covet a Porsche, but desire lived in what Bonaventure called the "groans of prayer."[8] For Bonaventure, this desire is the bonding material for fusing learning with devotion, investigation with wonder, analysis with joy, insight with love, work with hope. In this context, the prayerful desire for beauty also evokes the integration of needs with ideals.

Can I desire You, O Lord, without the cross?

Can I find peace, O Lord, without being a peacemaker?

Can I experience blessing, O Lord, without passing it on?

Can I hope, O Lord, without confronting despair?

Can I witness, O Lord, without going public?

Can I relish beauty, O Lord, without the dark night of the soul?

Can I desire You, O Lord, without asking these questions?

Amen

The Process: Serious Enjoyment

We develop our capacities for beauty by experience, enjoyment and judgment.[9] Simple words. Profound implications. Experience involves encountering beauty with presence, with sensory and spiritual circuits alive to what grace reveals. All of us have likely had some such sublime experience. I can still feel the chills from when I first saw Marc Chagall's windows at the Art Institute of Chicago, or the glow of holding my newborn nephew in the palm of my hand, or when in mid-life, tutored by my wife, Lucinda, I first felt the swing within an Ella Fitzgerald song. Head, heart and soul in a pulsing food processor of awe, fully alive with one finger touching some mystical hotplate. The grace of prayerful devotion is an awakening so that such experiences are not only life's highlight reel, but perceived in the structure and possibilities of everyday projects, encounters and even problems. More and more marketers are now speaking the language of experience, but this is often facile, such as with Saturn's "no-haggling" price policy. Few go the necessary step to bring beauty-making and beauty-beholding into the encounter and interaction of transaction.

Enjoyment is to *en*ter into the *joy*ful mo*ment*, surrendering to the gift, relishing the sensation and gratification, being pulled into the wholeness or becoming that beauty suggests. This is not about consumption. This is dialogue, an interaction not necessarily of logic or emotion but of unfettered joy that stays with us, that confirms us in the confidence and courage to hope after the experiences lapses. We seem to forget that beauty is also an ethical quality in that it not only satisfies an aesthetic need, but also motivates appreciation. Apple's iPod is a telling example. Most technology has been drab, with complexity bordering on immorality for being dehumanizing and user-unfriendly. In this environment of wires and plastic, we unleashed enormous capacities for communication, only to realize spasms of spam and piracy. In the digital world, art seemed to become a commodity. In the concealing maze of the network, even upstanding citizens used their relative anonymity to download files and steal music. Into this moral quagmire Apple launched the iPod. The beauty of this product is on many levels: it is visually appealing, smart and elegant to use, with great tactile quality, inviting to be seen and savoured. It is an instrument for music – for art. It is so jewel-like that people wear it as an accessory. Its beauty is also in software, which makes it easy to access and organize music files. So rich is the aesthetic experience that the millions who have bought the iPod now happily pay 90 cents to download a song. It is hard to draw the literal line between beauty and propriety, but in this case enjoyment is expansive, generating both a thrill and an obligation. Artists and music executives are now getting their due, which is only fair and right. Consumers do not mind because the value of the beauty and simplicity is inspiring of our whole humanity. The implication is that there is an intrinsic integrity to beauty that is also contagious, satisfying the needs for worth and worthiness, serving both commerce and ethics.

Of course, not all is perfect in Apple-land. The ubiquitous white earphones are another symbol for our increasing disconnection from one another. "Pod-casting" has made it possible for people who are globally wired to remove themselves from presence to the person sitting next to them on the bus. As with anything else, beauty that is strictly personalized or privatized becomes but another factor of consumption. While we need to amplify the public dimensions and savouring of beauty, the iPod confirms that there is indeed a deep human longing for aesthetics that not only raises the inherent value of products but also raises appreciation for what we owe each other. Design is now a high priority in many industries. This is a cyclical awakening, yet many managers still tend to see beauty as either a cost, and therefore optional, or as an aspect of "image," and therefore faddish and frivolous. Bonaventure viewed beauty as central and very serious, deriving his aesthetics from prayer and contemplation of the crucifixion. This was not an adoration of suffering, but an immersion in brokenness and despair through which the power and potential of healing beauty more fully emerges. Beauty is a serious business because it participates in the power and love of God, and because its opposite is damaging, dehumanizing and even deadly. Simultaneously awful and beautiful, the cross is the mystery always at the heart of Christian aesthetics and ethics. Any striving to be managers of magnificence paradoxically involves beholding – and being beholden to – the ugly beauty of God suffering with us.

I mentioned earlier Arturo Paoli's radical inversion of money as grace. It is significant that the conference in which he made his startling address took place only two weeks after 9/11. The air was still heavy with shock and sadness. While the topic was business ethics, most speakers, including Paoli, revised their comments to reflect upon what seemed in those raw early moments an irrevocably changed world. Most speakers also turned up their criticisms of companies, pointing to scandals and runaway executive pay as part of the imbalance within globalization that, while never justifying such terrorism, created conditions of injustice, social turmoil and human anger. It was expected that Paoli, as a liberation theologian, would be even more aggressive in denouncing excesses of corporate power. Instead of the cheap catharsis of hectoring, Paoli went with repentant eyes into the source concept that most people blamed for injustice, redefining money as grace. While most of us were using the grief from 9/11 to confirm existing points of view, Paoli had the radical hope to be transformed by this grief. This was not finding a silver lining. This was becoming fluid silver, an instrument of precious beauty, flowing healing and glistening hope into a moment of disintegration, hurt and despair.

> *Gratitude is grace recognized*
>
> *Thank you*
>
> *Patience is awaiting grace*
>
> *Help me*
>
> *Worship is grace returned*
>
> *For you*
>
> *Supplication is needed grace*
>
> *Grant me*
>
> *Holiness is grace integrating*
>
> *Towards you*
>
> *Fear is missing grace*
>
> *Find me*
>
> *Forgiveness is grace advanced*
>
> *Borrowing you*
>
> *Mercy is given grace*
>
> *Healing me*
>
> *Beauty is grace perceived*
>
> *Hinting you*
>
> *Art is extending grace*
>
> *Inspire me*
>
> *Mystery is grace beyond*

From you

Ecstasy is relished grace

Pulling me

Gratitude is grace recognized

Thank you

Thank you

Amen

The Practice: Responsibility for Balance

With enjoyment we are taken over by beauty. With the third step, judgment, we become co-artists responsible for the degree, depth and quality of the integrity circulating in our world. Bernard Lonergan recognized responsibility as an outcome of understanding. In St. Bonaventure's process, responsibility flows from our being immersed in beauty, through our sensory experience and the abandonment to joy. From having been penetrated and remade by beauty, we become responsible for its preservation and continuous remaking. The artistry involved is of the soul, which has in beauty received a tantalizing sample of the awesome joy of mystical union with the divine. It is an artistry of ethics and morality, judging reality in its relation to wholeness and integrity. Bonaventure spoke of beauty's "proportion," the balance of elements and parts, the holistic composition, that we recognize intuitively as a practical as well as metaphysical aesthetic. Even with abstraction or deconstruction, we are still playing with elements of proportion, distorting or reconfiguring the elements of balance to convey meaning or challenge perceptions. Proportion is a principle of relationships, apparent in the equilibrium of tightly interconnected ecosystems, finely calibrated engineering tolerances suggesting the fit and feel of quality, or high-performance teams. Proportion is also a principle of justice, weighing evidence and violations in correspondence to the impact on the whole.

When proportionality is missing, as with executive salaries, we experience the absence of integrity, including the real disintegration that results from not trusting. When proportionality is abused, as with surreptitiously introduced banking fees, we disconnect with suspicion. Much of what concerns globalization protesters that managers have failed to take seriously is the valid issue of disproportion. What markets regard as corrections are in reality reboots from disproportionate "bubbles" to more truthful proportions between risk and reward. Monopolies are acknowledged as destructive of innovation and as threats to free markets exactly because of the disproportionate concentration of resources and power. In these cases, the remediation involves the clear exercise of judgment, refashioning balance through the millions of acts of independent investors, or re-imposing balance through antitrust interventions. The business writer Geoffrey Colvin argues that even Wal-Mart will inevitably "lose steam" as "societal resistance, competition and cultural exhaustion" exert their inexorable pressure.[10] Other behemoths, such as GM, AT&T, Sears and IBM, once seemed unstoppable, until their very size became a liability for fuelling complacency and arrogance. Markets, competitors and customers have, in the end, exacted a harsh rebalancing. Of these once-dominant companies, only IBM has managed to resurrect its greatness, in large part through an ethos of proportionality, making its resources and power at least in part subservient to the needs and desires of customers.

In its true vocation, the charge of corporate governance is to maintain viability through the prudent exercise of proportion: enough value to earn customer loyalty; enough vision to guide innovation; enough reward to warrant risk; enough profits to secure investors; enough ethical courage to claim integrity. It is through their judgments that directors fulfill their fiduciary responsibility. Rather than focus on the moral and strategic quality of these judgments, we are trying to renew governance simply through systems of transparency or processes for accountability. Not yet have we cracked the harder nut of inciting the fully rounded care for magnificent judgment. Such thicker integrity serves the claims of beauty as well as results, demonstrating the proper proportionality between investment and return, shareholder gain and executive pay, company success and community development, corporate gains and employee participation. Such beauty makes transparency an instrument of discernment and judgment. Such beauty makes accountability a canvas for expressing ethical maturity. With these and the other measures of organizational balance, we get a picture of the whole, which is a picture of integrity, a judgment of artful management that is morally responsible.

Beauty is efficient.

So is prayer.

Om

Balance in Action

Our principle for beauty is that it starts in prayer, as a desire for ecstasy that we prayerfully extend to nature, work and relationships. Our process is that we first experience beauty, enjoying it with the full extravagance of presence. From this we then come to its responsibility, practising the ethical and moral judgments to preserve and promote beauty's integrity. How do we apply this? How do we make beauty a moral basis for management? The short answer is artful balance. The long answer, which will take the rest of this chapter, provides the device for prayer and practice that will be used later in the book to give life to the needs of the soul.

We tend to think of balance as a state, perhaps as an ideal for which our pragmatism is too impatient. In his work and prayer, Bonaventure modelled balance as a mode of being. Using the retrieval and relaunch that I noted as an objective for this project, he went back to the teachings and example of Francis to discern a spiritual foundation for the order, and then re-envisioned the future. This was an artful balancing of tradition with renewal, of spiritual devotion with organization efficiency, of human history lived within a transcendent becoming. Bonaventure led through inclusion, consulting and drawing upon the wisdom of his friars, yet moulding this group to his vision. He also had something special in his bones, the saintly talent that was at once outrageously confident and authentically humble. He and his contemporary the great theologian St. Thomas Aquinas were both commissioned to write the definitive *summa* of Christian teaching. An elaborate presentation to authorities and scholars was orchestrated, but after hearing Thomas's inspired exposition, with its still resonant beauty and clarity, Bonaventure withdrew without presenting his summary so as to not diminish the integrity of what Aquinas had achieved.

Beauty is wise.

So is silence.

Om

Balance is hardly a new issue for managers. In the mid-1990s, several programs for organizational recalibration were launched, including the "Balanced Scorecard" developed by teachers and consultants Robert Kaplan and David Norton.[11] The concept situates financial performance within a cluster of other important measures, including environmental responsibility, human resource development, and aspects of social contract. A very valuable extension of operational horizon, this respect for the totality of pressures and opportunities harkens back to the original intent of the financial balance sheet. From its inception, double-entry accounting was to provide the wider context and implications for the bottom line. In our pragmatism we forget that the balance sheet is an art, with inherent possibilities for beauty, for understanding the interconnection of parts and harmony of the whole. This has made it easy to accept what are often self-fulfilling off-balance-sheet entries. In finance, playing with the balance undermines it. Pro forma is too often dis-forma – disfigured, out-of-proportion, ugly business.

Reclaiming beauty for the balance sheet holds "double and" possibilities, balancing the needs of corporate performance for more accountability with those of the soul for more integrity. To restore the balance sheet – to use this instrument to its utmost potential and benefit to management – requires that we animate and measure both of these dimensions. In addition to financial terms, our opportunity is to weigh and discern, through the prism of "assets and liabilities," the terms of holistic performance that include the needs and ideals of the soul. Beauty is a fulcrum for most of the needs Simone Weil identified, including order (wholeness), liberty (art), equality (accessibility), honour (significance) and truth. The balance sheet's harmony between assets and liabilities is only accurate when it portrays both business metrics and moral ones.

This is a relaunch perspective, recognizing that in a knowledge and information economy, value is generated by human, social, creative and moral capital as well as by financial capital. These deserve serious definition and measurement. This is also a retrieval perspective because the original conception of the balance sheet was of commerce within "the divine proportion" of the divine milieu.

Modern corporate accounting is premised on an interdependent trinity: the balance sheet, which identifies the assets and liabilities that reveal the organization's financial strength; the income statement, which gives the bottom-line results once expenses are subtracted from revenues; and the statement of cash flows, which discloses the source and use of revenue towards the operations' "opportunities and responsibilities."[12] All three are important; however, while income and cash flow point to outcomes, the balance sheet points to inputs. It is this "balancing" of risk factors with opportunity values that reveals true worth and viability. It takes a trained eye and rich imagination to read a balance sheet – which involves literally reading between the lines.

There is some cosmic serendipity to the fact that it was a monk who originally codified double-entry accounting: the fifteenth-century Franciscan and mathematician Fra Luca Pacioli. Almost all the historical sources begin by calling Pacioli a Renaissance man. More accurately, he stood at the nexus of colliding worlds: religion with science, theology with commerce, Islam with Christianity, and the Middle Ages that formed him with the Renaissance that he helped to shape. As with Bonaventure, beauty was central to Pacioli. In fact, his aptitude for mathematics was honed in an art studio where, as a young man, he studied with Piero della Francesca – his hometown compatriot and the artistic genius who helped define the geometric principles for perspective. Pacioli went on to learn the basics of accounting as an apprentice to the Venetian merchants who were the globalization trendsetters of their day. After becoming a monk, Pacioli studied mathematics at universities in Bologna and Padova. As is again happening today, expanding trade created a parallel and significant exchange in knowledge. He was voracious, taking in the precepts of the ancients such as Euclid, as well as the theoretical and practical works of mathematically more advanced Muslim traders.

Pacioli met and served popes and princes, he designed a still-impeccable typography based on mathematical harmony, and he frequently consulted on both architecture and merchant practice while teaching at universities in Perugia, Zara, Rome and Bologna. The fusion of art and accounting was characteristic of Pacioli's work, so much so that in his later years he collaborated on numerous projects with Leonardo da Vinci. Some scholars think it likely that Pacioli's insights about proportion inspired Leonardo's famous drawing of the "universal man" with outstretched arms inside a perfect circle within a perfect square. What is certain is that Leonardo provided drawings for the various spheres and geometric shapes that Luca designed – constructs of such clarity and imagination that many anticipate by four and a half centuries the geodesic inventions of Buckminster Fuller.

While practitioners and textbooks continue to call him the "Father of Accounting," Pacioli never claimed to have created anything. Although vague, the historical evidence suggests that double entry was already in use by some of those cutting-edge merchants of Venice. As happens with ideas, the Venetians may well have imported this accounting expertise from Byzantium, which for centuries before was trading goods and concepts with Islamic cities. As was the publishing practice of the time, Pacioli started by compiling and disseminating best practices. However, more than an anthology, his *Summa* organized the various pieces into a coherent system. This was accomplished with such originality and clarity that his core structures for accounting are those still in use today. Pacioli was a teacher and a priest. His *Summa* provided a textbook for students, as well as for the merchant class that was just developing the professional skills for measuring risk. While not a theology as we understand it, this accounting treatise was designed by Pacioli as a commercial participation in the beauty and fullness of what he called "divine proportion." As R. Emmett Taylor noted in the definitive biography on Pacioli, he was "the first experimentalist to put theory into action."[13]

It is true that the Renaissance unleashed a great sense of secular freedom, but for the most part the great leaps in understanding from science and reason were still perceived in the context of religious ideals that then predominated. Galileo's observations of planetary movement shook the world view of society and deeply threatened the church, but his faith remained constant. Knowledge was not seen through a binary lens as some denial of God, but instead as a peeling back of the ignorance that obscured humanity's vision of divine things. For Pacioli and his intellectual peers, God permeated creation, and all knowledge was doubly valuable for what it enabled for human beings, and what it revealed about the divine. In his *Summa*, Pacioli repeatedly enjoins readers to recognize that what is important is not the practice of accounting or the success of commerce, but the intent of everyday activities, which is always to serve the call of the soul towards salvation (literally, healing). Albert Einstein claimed to see the mind of God in the potential of his theorems to define the physics of creation. For a monk of the Renaissance, the relation to God was only more profound, especially since mathematics – in theory and applied to merchant activity – repeated the actual theological process of creation by wringing order out of chaos.

Even though our postmodern sensibilities are radically different from Pacioli's, the ultimate basis of accounting is inextricably moral. Fraud is theft, destroying value as well as trust. Corruption is a lie, cheating shareholders and cheapening integrity. Off-balance-sheet sleights of hand that conceal performance failures violate investors as well as the truth. Whether the perspective is secular or religious, it is impossible not to acknowledge the morality of accounting. This is why we assign auditors and regulators with the "public trust" and why we define the duties of board directors as "fiduciary responsibilities." The task of this book – the intersection of the horizontal goals of business with the vertical demands of the soul – in many ways simply retrieves Pacioli's integrating aesthetic. The question for us becomes how to mix these distinct categories to replenish the spent reserves of trust, recreate confidence, and inspire magnificence as well as excellence. There are three interconnected dimensions to the answer: *content*, or the factors we introduce for evaluation into the balance sheet; *skill set*, or the expertise needed to discern the truth as both present and with presence; and *orientation*, or the aim and attitude for doing the hard work of setting new norms.

As discussed, content for this new balance sheet will be derived from linking the systematic needs of business with those of the soul. As the focus of the next three chapters, this will involve structuring qualitative rather than numeric values, juxtaposing priorities of good management with the corresponding ones for moral good. Imagine a zipper. One set of teeth are composed of business essentials, including:

> Vision •
> Governance •
> Structure •
> Strategy •
> Innovation •
> Investment •
> Competitive advantage •
> Measurement •
> Disclosure •

The other set identifies the corresponding needs of the soul:

> • Order
> • Accountability
> • Hierarchy
> • Fairness
> • Creativity
> • Stability
> • Liberty
> • Obedience
> • Truth

Each side of the zipper has its own integrity: vision has value only if it shapes structure and finds realization in strategy; order is effective and enabling only if it provides liberty and is grounded in the truth. Beyond this coherence on each side, the two sets of teeth zip together into an integrating and potentially very strong whole.

The skill set, explored in this chapter, involves aesthetics as well as analysis. Just as financial understanding is wrestled from co-holding assets and liabilities, spiritual understanding requires the active, prayerful and open-hearted examination between the tasks of profession and the needs of the soul. These are not opposites; nor, however, are they easy complements. This particular challenge calls for insight with integration. Reading a balance sheet is always a creative act, yet St. Ignatius of

Loyola also showed this immersion in the tension between opposites to be a critical competence for wisdom in our relationship and attentiveness towards God. In his classic Spiritual Exercises, Ignatius challenges us to see beyond the black-and-white duality of good and evil, and instead make the more creative and conscious choice between the lesser and greater good. With his conversion in the sixteenth century, St. Ignatius experienced God's call not as a single demand but an ongoing dialogue that he called "discernment." The strategy or process for accessing this deep inner truth involves a creative movement between polarities just like those of a balance sheet, in this case involving the spiritual or psychological factors of "consolation" and "desolation."

Theologian Ronald Modras explains the brilliance and simplicity of this interior discipline: "As we walk through the day, besides the gifts we note the gaffs. Small pleasures bring to mind sore spots; pleasant surprises conjoin with annoying frustrations. These too call for prayer. Feelings, whether positive or negative, are an index to what is going on in our lives and force us to look not so much at our actions and failures as the motives and reasons behind them."[14] Once again the happy overlap: what we need as souls to discern God's will involves the same imagination and judgment as does deducing the organizational truth between company assets and liabilities. We must decide to see on these sacred terms and to evaluate with moral care. The wisdom is arrived at the same way: with respectful reflection and the alert imagination to recognize causes as well as effects and implications as well as results.

This desire to see differently leads to the third dimension of orientation. We often mistake ethics to be a knowing what to do. Rules and laws may demarcate some aspects of right and wrong, but the ethical process involves a living discernment of variables to achieve the best, most humane outcome possible. The core competence is creativity, not compliance. Orientation sets the aim for that creativity, using principles and conscience to do what is most reasonable and responsible. Back to Zachary Hayes: we are not neutral when we infer the value in a balance sheet; rather, we are agents and advocates of the values we hold and the ideals we aspire to. Pro forma exceptions to the balance sheet can be either legitimate or deceptive, either helping reveal true worth or helping conceal it. Authenticity depends on the orientation we bring to the exercise of discernment and discovery.

Amazing God

Within and beyond

Yin and Yang

Divine Mother and Father

Tsim'tsum.

Word and silence

Presence and absence

How I long for Your embrace

Amazing God

Transcendent and Immanent

Source and Aim

Darkness and Light

To be grasped and to be lost

Crucifixion and Resurrection

Mystery and meaning

How I rejoice in Your face

Amazing God

Fullness and emptiness

Dance and stillness

Justice and mercy

Gift and obligation

Consolation and desolation

Apart and a part

How I float in Your grace

Amen

Broken Bottom Lines

The bottom line, when honestly accounted, documents results. The balance sheet, when viewed holistically, reveals the larger truth of possibilities (both positive and negative) and potentialities (both commercial and moral). The balance sheet is by tradition financial, but by process, intent and potential it is intrinsically dialogic, involving movement into a new, dynamic, often inexpressible middle that also transcends differences.

The bottom line atomizes; the balance sheet integrates.

The bottom line reduces; the balance sheet expands.

The bottom line provides the partial truth of data; the balance sheet constructs a deeper truth from the interplay of opposing realities.

The bottom line is time-specific, only a partial snapshot; the balance sheet relates memory to future.

The bottom line sees management as a technical procedure that must focus on performance while complying to the minimal morality prescribed by law; the balance sheet sees management as a moral calling that can contribute to the kingdom of God through attentive practice of faith-filled profession.

The bottom line regards ethics as a cost or curtailment – a parallel but secondary procedure to the priority of strategy; the balance sheet regards ethics as a contribution to both creation and management – the glue holding together in other-enhancing mutuality all the nodes that sustain relationships, including commercial ones.

Again, it is not only business that suffers compression from too tight an embrace of outcome or results. Bottom-line theology reduces salvation to a singular calculation of law or expiation; balance-sheet spirituality invites immersion in a reality of never fully disentangled nuances involving freedom, love and self-emptying in a cosmic dance with evil, power and suffering.

Bottom-line morality assumes a definitive checklist of rules and norms to assign culpability; balance-sheet morality instead unravels complicity, acknowledging the shared equality of sinfulness to co-bear forgiveness and co-create a less imperfect reality.

Bottom-line morality is impatient to fix blame, ascribing evil to caricature; balance-sheet morality is dialogically calibrated for reciprocal responsibility and reconciliation.

In morality as in business, the bottom line determines results; a balance sheet recognizes the interaction between limits and ideals, intent and consequences, hopes and incompletion to receive, when receptive, a discernment.

The habits of a bottom-line practitioner are analytic and strategic, a focused mind seeking certitude; the virtues needed and taught by balance sheet are experiential, a simmering heart aware and assured by the reality of risk.

A bottom line is an act of reporting; a balance sheet is an absence or withdrawal for reflection.

Business fixated on the bottom line has done untold damage when it reduces persons and resources to means, when it manages ethics as an expense. Theology fixated on its bottom line has caused parallel damage when it reduces faith to formulas, when dissonance or difference is denied or silenced. The balance sheet blows open the doors not only for intra-renewal, but also inter-renewal – for the inter-penetration by which wealth creation is situated in God's creation and morality frames and informs management. This is Arturo Paoli's insight when he recasts money as grace and insists that economic transactions can be part of sacramental possibilities for life-giving exchange. When, as a Roman Catholic, I participate in the Eucharistic prayer, I believe that bread and wine become sacramental flesh and blood. When Christians proclaim Jesus as Lord, they are echoing St. Paul's Christology of descent into humiliation transmuted by the Spirit into ascent and glorification. When Christians live within the stories and symbols of Holy Week, they walk in faith through death on the cross to a life of transcendence in the Resurrection. Although these mysteries are infinitely more than what we mean or understand by balance sheet, they participate in and signify the transformation that occurs when we move the human heart to be present to the awesomeness and awfulness of paradox.

Beauty, if we again practise "receivement," can be where prayer and managerial practice meet and intertwine. Through beauty, we are attuned to balance, both as a spiritual virtue for the journey of the soul, and as a business competence that earns trust. As the proto-ideal, beauty includes and brings together the needs of the soul. As an approachable, enriching, enjoyable experience, beauty evokes our human artistry and creativity. With the balance sheet, we have an instrument latent with potential for intermingling the management and moral factors that participate in the grace of beauty. What is required for this movement into balance is a willingness to dialogue, to shed some of the lean and mean rigidities that have bled into our souls, and to experience, enjoy and exercise judgment using new performance criteria that dare to hope. When our hearts are open, we can thus begin to examine the content of this new balance sheet and, later, the skills for unleashing its beauty.

Lord of Sparks

Fusion refuting confusion

What a gift this work of management

To make meaning out of facts

To find opportunity in need

To invent what can be

Lord of Sight

Focus out of hocus

What a responsibility this managing can be

To draw from creation without despoiling it

To add value while adding hope

To use human resources for human becoming

Lord of Links

Connecting the dots

What a cross this job entails

To bless the poor while growing wealth

To heal the displaced while carving share
To serve the Spirit while making returns
Lord of Beauty
Sublime without sub
What a mystery this work invites
To apply strategy to wholeness
To exercise expertise to hope
To extend control by relinquishing it to grace

Part III

Integrity from Doing It

6

PERSPECTIVE

Where Horizons Meet

Beauty inspires hope, and provides a reason for seeing differently. Business can be beautiful, which is part of the reason it so engages our lives and imagination. However, this potential cannot be realized apart from the moral aims of society and the soul needs of human beings. The challenge imagining a fusion of categories between theology and business is at heart systematic, not simply interconnecting wisdom with expertise but achieving a synthesis that is transformational. All too often we manage objectives or solve problems at stress points without respecting the systemic factors, including human attitudes and relationships that shape the final result. This is a shortcut we often take in spirituality as well, seeking mastery without a master, comforted by a general faith without growing through the discomfort of a specific, immediate and life-altering transcendent relationship. To finally manage the alchemy of total quality, or to deliver the respect required for authentically managing customer relationships, some companies have learned to think through and attend to a whole complex of interacting people and processes. Making prayer and spiritual consciousness work within work involves a similar reconsideration and re-enmeshment of parts. The meshing is between systems, which brings us to the heart of the book: zipping the zipper.

Previous chapters laid the foundation. Presence is anthropology, a point of view about our nature as humans and about our destiny as souls in relationship. Hope, which is called eschatology in theology, is a point of view about our human potential, meaning and becoming. From grace, which holds and sparks holiness, we developed a point of view that recognizes the giftedness and therefore sacred interconnection of all creation and human activity. With beauty, which is sacramental in its power to signify the Divine, we began the opening to being taken over by the point of view of faith so as to participate through ecstasy, artistry and devotion in sacred creation. The challenge for the next three chapters is quite different, moving from reframing to redoing, from understanding anew to working and managing from this newness. Theologically, this could be described as the work of salvation: bringing together the parts into a liberating, healing and sanctifying whole. An obviously loaded word, salvation agitates and inspires what the theologian Walter Brueggemann calls the "prophetic imagination."[1] Salvation at root means "restoring to health," which is exactly our challenge: restoring to health the broken disciplines of management that compromise professional integrity; restoring to health the overstressed, often dehumanizing workplace; restoring to health the prudent governance of boards and responsible leadership of executives; restoring to health the real promise of technology and globalization; and restoring to health the practice of faith within the urgent, turbulent and yet powerfully creative reality of modern business.

Systematic Approach to Magnificence

In human terms we understand health as a complex of interrelated variables, involving genes, nutrition, exercise and diet, as well as emotional, psychological and spiritual well-being. Organizational achievement similarly requires a systematic alignment between vision, resources and strategy, and synergy between skills, processes and values. Theology, too, is premised on a network of interconnected beliefs, values and behaviours. To conceive of God as Creator tumbles other dominoes: situating human reality in a web of relationships, including with the discernible source; imbuing past, present and future with more than transitory significance; elevating all creation to be a sacred gift; and linking as precious and indispensable every human life to the unfolding story of creation. To believe as a Christian produces another set of inextricable implications: placing Jesus at the centre of human history, as well as at the heart of our relationship to God; relating the mystery of the cross and resurrection to our daily freedom; and inviting a personal response to the possibilities and implications of this life-altering personal relationship. This is not shorthand for orthodoxy, only the recognition that any belief has consequences, that conversion is real only if it converts perspective, expectations and action as well as personal prayer. The example of the saints is that holiness is very much like high-performance business leadership. We need to be systematic, comprehensive and highly disciplined. We also need to stay sharply focused on the animating vision, taking care with hard work and passionate attention to detail to deliver the mission.

The inclination when addressing systems is to disaggregate parts and processes, eventually connecting symptoms to cause so as to reform goals and redesign practices. We now know from re-engineering that this approach often only exacerbates disconnection by polishing small increments of expertise without growing the relational competencies for belonging and unified action. With postmodern consciousness, we better appreciate that systems understanding is never neutral, never free from the contextual dynamics of our personal assumptions, motivations, perceptions and cultural conditioning. That this seems obvious does not make it easier to escape a point of view that is much closer to a telephoto lens than a wide-angle one. It takes a great deal of distance to recover a more genuine systems perspective, and such distance-making almost inevitably also involves contemplation and self-discovery. To envision what is necessary, we must sometimes pull back from the plausible. To innovate from hope, we must sometimes make space for the impossible.

> *Magnificent Lord*
>
> *Your arms on the cross invite my embrace*
>
> *Hold me to hold You*
>
> *Your words of life illumine my heart*
>
> *Fill me to express You*
>
> *Your call to follow agitates my being*
>
> *Mould me to be You*

When impatience breeds despair

Be my hope

When complexity obscures purpose

Be my clarity

When problems defy solution

Be my inspiration

O Lord Jesus

Bless my work as offering

Receive my work as labour in Your fields

And as You are wont to do

Transform this work into that which glorifies God

Amen

Management history shows that one of the greatest challenges for success is cohesion. It takes a lot of work to do vision and strategy, and a lot more to implement with consistency and passion. In Jim Collins's analysis, mediocre companies usually have the same information and prospects as great companies, but either they fail to grasp the insight for transformation or they carry out the implementation badly. The art of greatness involves the stubborn pursuit of ideas and ideals at every stage of the management process, across the breadth and depth of the organization. Most people give up on change because it is hard: the difficulty that undoes many smart and necessary renewal projects is having to contend with the details for achieving cohesiveness. To envision these systematic factors, I have clustered them into the basic categories for management and leadership.

- We start with analysis and planning.
- We continue with resource development.
- We make bets and control implementation.
- We follow up with measurement and learning.

In broad terms, these managerial categories correspond to the stages of soul development.

- First comes "seeing anew," the beholding of the possible that will be unpacked in this chapter as "Perspective."
- Second comes the resulting reorientation of priorities and values, which Chapter 7 defines as "Proportion."
- Third comes the development of transforming skills and processes that, as in Chapter 8, is "Practice."

What often undermines organizational cohesion is that these three stages involve disparate needs and engage different skills. Great strategists are not necessarily strong managers; entrepreneurs who master innovation rarely have the personality or acumen to institutionalize processes and control. The same variability is also true of discipleship. There are times or circumstances in the life of the soul that require peering over the horizon, applying "the prophetic imagination" to set new direction and priorities. Other times call not for designing but for doing, attending to human, relational and productivity details in the proper proportion to realize their transcendent significance. This is the work of "priestly consecration," not as clerical ritual but as the calling forth of the holy in everyday situations and decisions. Other times, the need is to get to what both works and endures, performing the "kingly duties" of oversight, authority and administration to create structures of equity as well as prosperity. Much more detail about these roles will follow, but what is important now is the pattern and correspondence: Perspective, especially to perceive magnificence and agitate for its realization is served in business and for the soul by prophetic imagination; just and sustainable Proportion, especially as participation in divine magnificence, is realized in business and for the soul through the priestly invocation of holiness; and the attention to pragmatic detail of Practice, especially creating wealth that matters and magnifies magnificence in business and for the soul, is achieved by "kingly integration."

Faith has implications and responsibilities. In his apostolic letter on the laity, Pope John Paul II wrote of being made anew by discipleship, receiving "grace and dignity" to "participate in the threefold mission of Christ as Priest, Prophet and King."[2] These are "double and" roles: to see and to interconnect and to act; to envision and to make possible and to make real; to be moved by God's magnificence and to share its holiness and to bring forth its beauty and truth. Some of us may have managerial gifts that are especially prophetic or priestly or kingly. The truth is that for integrity in life and work, we will need in various ways to exercise all three.

Needs of the Soul — Roles and Responsibilities

PROPHETIC	PRIESTLY	KINGLY
• Agitate	• Consecrate	• Integrate
• Criticize	• Empathize	• Symbolize
• Inspire	• Enable	• Empower
• Dislocate	• Educate	• Adjudicate
• Humanize	• Divinize	• Systematize
• Reorient	• Reveal	• Restructure
• Point	• Anoint	• Appoint
• Incite	• Reflect	• Wisen
• Debate	• Discourse	• Dialogue
• Proclaim	• Pray	• Pronounce

Simone Weil did not categorize the needs of the soul, but what is clear from her writings is that she valued and studied conceptual patterns. As a philosopher, such motifs were the currency of her trade, revealing what she called "underlying interconnections." And as a mystic, these models of thought allowed Weil to experience what she saw as the "geometry" of beauty and meaning. Systems are inherently based on patterns: we order and organize activities to conform to some expectation of consistency. Managers are tasked to think systematically and implement systems. For Weil, the "ordering pattern" of systems, whether in society, church or the economy, served to expose "interlocking necessities." We create strategies and structures to facilitate what we want to do. We constantly refine processes to achieve greater efficiency. Weil made *need* the fundamental feature of any system: not the autonomy of parts or individuals but their interdependence, not rights or efficiency but obligations and accountabilities. The task now is to re-pattern the pattern, taking business roles and revealing the corresponding need of the soul, organizing management as prophetic, priestly and kingly work.

With Prophetic Imagination

Scanning the horizon of technology, opportunity and need to fashion an inspiring and compelling *Vision*. •

• Scanning the horizon with awe for what is possible and grief for what is broken to insist on moral *Order*.

Creating rules and monitors for boards and management that fulfill existing laws while anticipating future stresses on integrity and new norms of *Governance*. •

• Exercising moral respect for consequences by demanding not only honest disclosure but also the restraint and repentance that signify *Responsibility*.

Organizing systems and processes to grow competence and deploy resources in an effective and responsible *Structure*. •

• Orienting professional practice to achieve honour by advancing human dignity and situating work in its proper moral *Hierarchy*.

With Priestly Consecration

Practising fair principles of reward and merit to motivate staff and realize authentic *Advantage*. •

• Making healing and healthy communities by including those disadvantaged or marginalized in the experience of *Equality*.

Adding value and growing relevance for long-term sustainability through ongoing *Innovation*. •

• Uplifting dignity by inviting and supporting participation in beauty and its creative *Risk*.

Using management skills for planning, implementation and measurement to satisfy the market's need for *Sustainability*. •

• Revealing the sacred significance of tasks, projects and outcomes to experience the hope that grounds human *Security*.

	With Kingly Integration
Deploying and renewing the control tools and values for ensuring *Accountability*. •	• Operating within the rights and privileges that moral law enables through *Obedience*.
Making bets within the free market through smart and differentiating *Strategy*. •	• Adding moral value and wisdom to programs and projects by recognizing their role in securing and advancing human *Liberty*.
Delivering value and results with rigorous, far-reaching and responsible *Transparency*. •	• Unifying operations and realizing personal integrity by living up to the demands for *Truth*.

The rest of this chapter, which delves into perspective, also serves as the prototype for the two that follow. After definitions, we undertake a diagnostic to bring the major impediments to integration and renewal to the surface. The exercise part of this work involves a dialogue, juxtaposing and inter-informing theology with business to derive insights, options and opportunities from a methodic and prayerful commitment to balance. Respecting the bias to action of managers, chapters 7 and 8 will outline deliverables and questions of implementation.

Definition

Perspective in Three Dimensions ("Double And")

The first movement in transformation, and the primary role of any balance sheet, is to realize the perspective not yet revealed by facts. To gain perspective, we must see more than we see, interpreting the relationship between points, figuring out the potential qualities of interconnection, deducing which questions can or cannot be answered, and assessing the risk from any opportunity, threat or action. In business, perspective serves as the raw material for strategy, for matching resources to the task, motivating staff towards goals, justifying change or plans. For spirituality, perspective also serves to situate and connect, this time providing context from beliefs, experiences and hopes, attributing meaning to obstacles, possibilities and relationships. As Avishai Margalit suggests, morality defines our obligations to humanity at large, with much of this deriving from our perspective about human nature, becoming and belonging.[3] We hope because something in our perspective warrants it; we pray because our perspective includes some dynamic of transcendence or divinity.

Without perspective, companies flounder, which is why vision statements are now everywhere – posted in elevators and distributed in wallet cards. However, while almost all companies now have such statements, few are prophetic, with most sounding trite or tired or familiar, and therefore the opposite of visionary. Without perspective, souls, too, flounder, facing the exhaustion of isolation from incoherence. St. Teresa of Avila likened the soul to a bird that cannot flutter and stay aloft indefinitely. Perspective provides the destination to fly to while also recognizing the branches for possible rest along the way. Perspective is to strategy what belief is to spirituality: the hope sustaining faith; the aim compelling improvement. In either the commercial or spiritual realm, to be without perspective leads to waste: flapping our wings endlessly and aimlessly, forever reacting, and eventually becoming exhausted from mastering tactics without making progress towards the real goal and reward.

Perspective is a type of dialogue, a transforming immersion similar to an encounter with beauty or art. We are not neutral bystanders: instead, we bring memories and expectations along with truth and hope to the formulation of understanding. Panoramas or insights that afford perspective are frequently stunning or amazing in some way, inspiring surprise, delight and even wonder. Two people standing on the same spot will not necessarily see the same view, not because the contours of landscape or facts of analysis vary, but because sensibility and experience colour vision and interpretation. This means that we create perspective, working as artists with our unique talents to shape the meaning of what we apprehend. For painters and physicists, perspective is where two lines converge on our horizon but continue endlessly beyond, with the finite pointing to the infinite, the world of "and" linked to that of "double and."

While we all have some perspective, we also miss or lose it all too often. To be honest, few managers see new patterns and paint from original perspectives. Most follow. Companies rushed to remake themselves into the image and likeness of dot.com companies, suffering loss and disappointment because they adopted the broken paradigm of the herd. Others look to Warren Buffet for managerial inspiration and GE for organizational guidance. Companies mostly merge because conventional wisdom values economies of scale. However, big is not automatically better. Nor is big more prescient. GM bought Saab and parts of Fiat; Ford bought Volvo and Jaguar; Mercedes merged with Chrysler and invested in Mitsubishi. While these behemoths struggle to make money and stumble to keep market share, their smaller and more nimble competitors – Toyota, Honda and BMW – are growing their base of satisfied customers and taking the technological lead in hybrid, electric and hydrogen vehicles. Conventional wisdom, by definition, is not visionary wisdom. Yet in industry after industry, magnificence is lacking because conventional assumptions lead to conventional strategies that produce conventional mediocrity.

Souls, too, are prone to substituting tired conventional wisdom for perspective. Sometimes, as with the Israelites released from slavery in Egypt, we grow tired of the risks from wandering in the desert, and, frightened of the perspective-making work demanded by freedom. In most cases, as Douglas Porpora reminds us, perspective gets diffused by complacency.[4] We are smart enough to see what is wrong. We have imagination to see what is possible. We have the empathy to recognize what is called for. Despite these skills, we all too often turn away from the exposed truth or keep our heads down, ignoring the human claims, consequences or obligations. Perspective in this case is hollowed by hollow emotions, stunted by outrage that does not seem to last much beyond the next commercial break, and trivialized by easy sentimentality that equally denies the hard commitments of remembering and hope.

Presence awakens longing

Longing seeks relationship

Relationship inspires devotion

Devotion enables understanding
Understanding exhausts words
Words bookend silence
Silence exalts awe
Awe invites veneration
Veneration bends knees
Knees elevate perspective
Perspective precedes communion
Communion frees presence
Presence awakens longing…

Prophetic Attributes

When the status quo becomes static, assumptions become rigid, and what is wrong, evil or destructive becomes invisible for being banal. Consider the environmental risks posed by driving unnecessarily big cars, SUVs and pickup trucks. Oil companies, automotive manufacturers and consumers are in co-dependent denial, which few politicians or regulators have the courage to confront. As Hannah Arendt observed, the damage here does not involve some massive, evil scheme, but instead is sustained by small acts of daily insouciance on the part of average people who are trying to get on with life as easily as possible.[5] Despite the understanding that current practices cannot be sustained, precious decades of intellectual development and investment in alternative fuels and technologies have been lost. The prophetic voice unmasks the harsh truth that our million acts of individual choice enslave us in a system that chokes the natural environment as well as human lungs. The smart task, which is also honest, is for dramatically greater fuel efficiency. The responsible task, which is also strategic, is for breakthrough innovation. These are prophetic agitations that are extreme only for being candid and necessary.

God of Codes,
You have programmed creation, and our hearts to see it
Grant us insight to understand what causes our system crashes

Grant us artistry in designing new applications
And grant us the courage to upgrade
Amen

The prophetic role is for authentic vision setting and strategic planning, adding to the perspective of opportunity and advantage the "double and" of what *ought* to be. Again, this is not extraneous to executive planning, but prudent, as it often clarifies the real issues that corporate governance must address, and the real innovations that operations must achieve. The Jewish and Christian scriptures are inherently prophetic in motif and narrative, and all of Islam is a following of the Prophet. To think and behave prophetically is therefore also the central feature of faith, for encountering God, living in hope and growing holiness. There are times when prophecy prods business from within. There are times when prophets demand correctives. And there are times when prophetic integrity demands standing outside the management structure to speak unheard truths or instigate radical change. As theologian Walter Brueggemann shows from his study of scripture, prophetic figures are usually at odds with the powers that be, exposing systems of privilege that inevitably threatens the brokers of that power.[6] This is always precarious work, which is why even today we stigmatize people who speak the truth in companies as whistle-blowers.

Brueggemann identifies four attributes of the "prophetic imagination" that have direct application to strategy.

- First is "long memory," the respectful remembering that brings forth context, values and relevance from the defining stories or patterns from history.
- Second is "sense of pain," the deep grief for grievances that fuels outrage at injury or injustice, and compels condemnation of systems or individuals that exploit unfair advantage.
- Third is "practice of hope," the conviction for what is good, right and magnificent inspired by wonder, and driven by love of the holy ideal.
- Fourth is "effectiveness at discourse," using communication and persuasion to challenge complacency and pull people into transformation that they need but do not always recognize.

Each of the attributes is worthy of considerable reflection, with implications for professional as well as spiritual development. As managers, we tend to understand the pressure for short-term results as a compression of what is at stake in the future. It is that, but it also often imposes a compression of memory: we forget what history has already taught about what matters most. Business books make their sales helping companies rediscover the mastery of quality, service, learning, governance and innovation. The real question is this: How did we forget the pivotal importance of these management skills? How did what is essential, including ethics, become expendable or merely appended? An important lesson from Brueggemann's work is that prophetic imagination is inspired and sustained from the heart. It is by allowing our hearts to experience the wonder of God's creation and continuing Presence that hope is stirred. It is from empathy with suffering that the claims of truth and justice become clear. Managers call what is needed for success "core competencies." By etymology, this means competencies from the heart – from the *coeur*. As with St. Ignatius's Spiritual Exercises, the prophetic heart moves between polarities: experiencing the consolation of what is possible along with the desolation from what is distorted or broken. We stand in awe pondering beauty and recognizing the gifts of genius and ingenuity. We stand in grief witnessing what is unfair, inhuman or enslaving. Awe and grief are the assets and liabilities of the prophetic balance sheet. Strategic planners do SWOT analysis, identifying strengths and weaknesses, and, through creative analysis, projecting opportunities and threats. Prophetic planners do SWAG analysis, identifying strengths and weaknesses through the heart's prism for awe and grief.

A lot of strategic planning today is in fact budgeting. We still perform some blue-sky imagining but with little real consequence, because the goal of most plans is simply to reach some pre-set target. Rather than imagination, plans have become templates for implementation. Spirituality has become equally thin and forgetful, disconnected from the memories of the community, and disengaged from either outrage or hope. For both our companies and our souls we want straight-line trajectories, linear "how-to's" that will ensure success and satiation. The prophetic breaks the rigidity of these straight lines, forcing the deviation into paradox that thickens and enriches our encounter of human life and spiritual transcendence. Hearts alert to "awe" and awakened to "grief" not only critique what is dysfunctional, but also push for what is restorative and healing. Neither pole is definitive of human reality, so it is by holding both, and entering into the implications between what inspires awe and what brings grief, that prophetic perspective takes shape and gains force. This back-and-forth pattern between liabilities and assets is as much prayer as analysis, fashioning vision from empathy and deriving wisdom from the visceral encounter with both disintegration and communion. There will be alternative poles to explore later as part of the balance sheet exercise for priestly proportion and kingly integration. Not for intellectual Ping-Pong, this exercise of engaging polarities – in this case of awe and grief – is for a prayerful opening to truth, the silent contemplation within contrasting parentheses by which what we need and what we dare fuse into action.

PROPHETIC PERSPECTIVE

Awe	Grief
Opening the heart to perceive in childish wonder the beauty of life and the mystery of Divine Presence •	
	• Opening the heart to feel the trauma of poverty, brokenness or inhumanity
Feeling in the heart the urgency and breadth of God's love made present in our gifts, talents and prayers •	
	• Solidarity with those mourning, thirsting for justice, risking comfort and detachment as peacemakers
Responding to the shock of God's call and the scandal of God's suffering presence among us in Christ •	
	• Responding to the whispers from those most vulnerable, including children, the poor, the lonely and the marginalized
Inspired by ideals, honoring that which ennobles human beings and enables their magnificence •	
	• Outraged by the hard-heartedness or complacency that turns a blind eye to violations of basic rights, freedoms and hopes

Standing in continuity with humanity's greatest achievements so as to call forth its greatest possibilities •

• Recalling the most tragic inhumanities of our shared history so as to expose latent capacities for death and destruction

Overflowing from the prayerful encounter with God, transformed and compelled by ecstasy to pursue what is infinite, lasting and good •

• Angered by the arrogance that denies God's law or by the busyness that fails to recognize the beauty and obligations of our fragile interdependence

Burning with God's light, the purifying fire in the soul that lights up dark corners of our collective heart and flashes the beacon to guide the way forward •

• Serving as "salt of the earth," stinging open social wounds, adding the tang of conscience to social discourse

Soul Needs for Perspective

The three needs of the soul especially attuned to prophetic perspective are *Order*, which is also the job for corporate vision, *Responsibility*, which also relates to governance and accountability, and *Hierarchy*, which also attends to structures for implementation and control.

Extraordinary Vision for Extraordinary Challenges

Simone Weil marks order as the first need of the soul. Why? The book of Genesis begins with the story of creation in which God called forth "order out of chaos." More than the defining imprint of creation, order is the characteristic by which we know and recognize the handiwork of the Creator. As children of God, we are by inheritance and ambition children of order. Creation is a work in progress that has surprises, risks and mysteries, but it seems that some pattern for ordering is always being revealed, whether it be DNA, natural ecosystems or the latest theorems and discoveries from science. The pattern for human order is set by relationship, living and growing as social beings dependent on one another, drawing purpose and meaning from dependence on God. Our souls desire different blessings: we want peace or freedom from doubt, we hope for understanding or wisdom, we petition for comfort or help in distress. All of these prayers and longings of the soul are answered by some restoration of order. The very commitment to explore spirituality or practise religion is an exercise in ordering, seeking to heal what is broken or incomplete through participation in an alternative, higher and holier structure. Disorder not only disturbs the soul, it also buries it. What animates the soul and agitates its development is the fullness of order, which is holiness. "My soul is restless," wrote St. Augustine in his *Confessions*, "until it rests in Thee."[7]

Order is inherent in the job description of managers. There can be no strategy, quality, efficiency, productivity or control without it. However, while these implements for structure and activity are important, the most critical ordering of companies is set by vision. As noted, few companies are visionary, so few can be said to have true vision. Most follow, offering specific increments of value or innovation that may make the road travelled smoother. But few companies chart the map. As a result, corporate visions have become innocuous rather than inspiring, like the motivation posters that preach a pithy insight below a seascape sunset. If there is wisdom in vision-making, many companies have let it slip through their fingers by thinking the task complete by projecting trends or creatively teasing the data. This surmising can be creative and valuable, but it remains locked in existing patterns rather than giving birth to something original.

A new paradigm is a new way of envisioning order. In religion or art, vision is something received, not constructed. There are disciplines for preparation, including both study and withdrawal – what in the scriptures is often portrayed as time in the desert. It is from standing outside the current reality that we have the best chance of being overtaken by a new one. This is the charge to be visionary. When we are taken over, as mystics, artists or leaders, the vision that is realized belongs to others as well as ourselves. It moves them to also be overcome, to be inspired and connected to totally new possibilities. For this to be genuine, something about the vision must make good as well as make sense. This was God's criterion for the labour of creation. After each effort to make order, God "saw that it was good." Without this promise of goodness, visions are only lofty objectives. Without enhancing the common good or the personal good, there is no "vying" in vision.

Disorder destroys value. Markets that are not level playing fields are anathema to investors. Companies that are disorderly are inherently inefficient and wasteful. Accounts or reports that are messy impugn professionalism and warrant suspicion. Bureaucracy is often the antidote for absent vision. When we cannot inspire workers or assure customers, we create structures for documenting the follow-up to the follow-up. The more rigid the bureaucracy, the more it is clear that vision is absent or irrelevant. Order framed by an inspiring vision instead promotes what theologians call "subsidiarity." Since the vision unleashes goodness, people participate to the best of their talents and abilities in delivering and upholding the emancipating order. There is less need for control and supervision because individuals feel a personal stake and responsibility for the possibilities being jointly created. Structures and roles have their place, not to regiment but to empower, and not to protect bureaucratic reputations but to enable outcomes and innovations of goodness.

Order is a high-level capacity because it involves judgment, linking parts and activities into a cohesive whole, evaluating what is happening against an imprint for functioning harmony and balance. Any spiritual discipline is an investment in order as a structure of prayer, ritual or reflection. Religion simulates divine order in human time and space, with prayers, beliefs and laws that evoke personal goodness within the common good. Human order is never complete, never perfect on its own, which is why the relationship to God must be continuously lived and renewed by the individual and community. Sacraments signify this privileged relationship of goodness, and grace is the active hand of God's love gently continuing the creative work of elevating order. The risk from too-privatized spirituality is that the sense and expectation for order becomes relative rather than cosmic, something to consume rather than contribute. However we may come to it, redemption is ultimately about order restored with the holy at the very centre of human history. However we may regard it, sin is what corrupts order, displacing the divine and distorting our interdependence. For mystics, the journey of the soul is personal but never ad hoc, a free commitment and individual experience, yet always within an ordering structure of preparation and relationship.

Companies that struggle with innovation or renewal are missing the fire from a new and relevant ordering principle. This is what Jesus called "storing new wine in old wineskins" (Matthew 9:17). The important task of change cannot be cosmetic. Nor can it be "continuous" without some orienting aim satisfying purpose and engendering trust. Economists speak of "creative destruction" as the natural cycle of competition, yet the wealth created by companies hinges instead on "creative creation" – stabilizing new order to mine the investments in innovation and create steady returns for risk. This "creative creation" produces order not simply by advancing technology or benefits, but by literally extending generosity. The Internet exploded into global usage by offering almost as a gift largely free access to information and free e-mail. Conversely, the biggest threat to the Internet is from spyware, spam and identity fraud, which represent the exploitation and irresponsibility that are the opposite of generosity. Warren Bennis, who teaches business leadership, argues that people within companies that are making a contribution to society are "much more likely to bring vigor and enthusiasm to their tasks."[8] Higher purpose is the fuel for passion; the greater good is the motivation for inspiration. Many corporations showed this latent capacity for goodness in their response to the tsunami crisis in Southeast Asia. FedEx and TNT, for example, put their fleets and logistics to work delivering essential relief supplies almost overnight.[9] This magnificence in exceptional circumstances is always with us, and always longing for expression. Prophetic managers attack the daily numbness that stifles this impulse for magnificence, and crack open this capacity for beauty and goodness in visionary plans and goals.

I have seen many CEO road shows and town-hall meetings to sell the corporate vision. Such orchestrations are a good sign that the vision is incomplete or missing the necessary quotient of goodness. Real vision does not need persuasion, but only experience. The paradigm breakthrough Jesus offered was linking love to forgiveness. Rather than retribution or enmity, forgiveness creates a whole new order that any of us can immediately understand, since we are all transgressors and victims. Jesus taught by healing, and he initiated healing often by extending the blessing of forgiveness to the person petitioning for help. Forgiveness reorders our relationship with God and with one another. It is vital to remember that in the time of Jesus, illness or impairment were viewed as the consequence for sinfulness. People suffering infirmity therefore faced the double wound of stigmatization and social exclusion. When by his touch Jesus healed the lepers, the relief was for the person, but there was also reordering for the community, which needed to challenge its prejudices and make space for the now whole individual. The goodness was experienced, not marketed. The reordering was compelling for its beauty and justice, not positioned.

Prophetic vision generates human wholeness. It inspires awe and provides guidance; it secures the flow of goodness as well as results. Prophetic priorities are not abstract. Quite the opposite – convictions and outrage are rooted in the pain and dislocations that people face every day. Prophetic vision deals with concrete details of goodness that also release value: respecting people's time by making access not only easy but elegant and enjoyable, extending service by making technology secondary to the experience, adding value by subtracting busyness. Prophetic planners ask different questions:

- How do our strengths embellish or renew order?
  - What strengthens freedom and dignity?
  - What enables creativity and wisdom?
  - What lifts exclusions and facilitates belonging?
- How do our weaknesses contribute to disorder?
  - What adds disrespectful complexity or busyness?
  - What short-term fires consume long-term capacities?
  - What breeds unfairness, despair or exclusion?
- What can we do that is awesome in its potential for goodness and beauty?
  - What is the aim of inspiration and motivation?
  - What is the moral purpose for innovation?
  - What is the WOW that raises pride and integrity?
- What grief are we accountable for or must we attend to?
  - What responsibility has been abused or exploited?
  - What are "collateral" risks and "unintended" consequences?
  - What requires repentance and forgiveness?

ORDERING BALANCE SHEET

Thriving Order for Souls	Thriving Order for Managers
God's creating gift, making form, substance and harmony out of chaos to enable and sustain life •	• Creating value within creation's sacred project, advancing freedom, dignity and belonging to keep destructive chaos at bay
Principles for meaning, connecting the person to the eternal •	• Principles for contributing goodness and fairness to the "level playing field"
Orienting imprint for social capital based on what "ought to be" •	• Organizing imprint for trust from operational and moral excellence
Reference points from memory and hope to guide present action towards greater freedom and becoming •	• Reference points from competence and ethics for guiding responsible implementation
Predictability to thrive within a nexus of trusting relationships •	• Predictability to manage risk and develop reputational credibility
Continuously renewed structures for exercising and expecting justice •	• Systematic care, internal and external, which demonstrates integrity
Place and role within history and community as equal children of God •	• Place and role within organizational structures designed for creativity and hope as well as productivity
Ineffable experiences of beauty that invite appreciation and awe •	• Elegance in design for systems and products that enhances quality and grows wisdom

Parousia, with the many gathered up as one: the unified humanity with elevated consciousness Teilhard de Chardin envisioned as "Omega Point" •

• Contribution to globalization as a moral infrastructure for humanity, nature, technology, knowledge and commerce to activate ennobling potential

Promise of salvation as the healing and sanctifying union with transcendence •

• Accountability to bequeath organizations that meet the tough criteria of sustainability

Governance from Love of the Law

For any system or structure, order pivots on the law. The legal rights of the corporation are essentially those of a person, so the dependence on law is for both protection and freedom to operate. There are always pendulum swings. For a time, companies became the fiefdom of managers, and operated removed from responsibility to shareholders. Today the emphasis has largely swung to the other extreme, with executive performance so tied to immediate shareholder returns that other legitimate obligations have suffered. Directors swing as well in their understanding of governance. New laws and regulations are imposing tougher standards for audits, director independence and performance. These are meant to define accountabilities more precisely and assure markets, investors and the public that proper prudence and judgment are exercised with consistency and integrity. While there is no doubt that progress has been made on a global front, it is also clear that the pendulum has neither budged too far nor settled. Already there is substantial "undertow" from CEOs who find new transparency laws too onerous. Already the emphasis in governance renewal is for achieving compliance. History teaches that government structures are never perfect, and that laws are forever catching up to circumstances. The prophetic task in business, as it has been in scripture, is to incite overreach beyond the minimum requirements of regulation, to spark the loving embrace of the spirit of the law as the basis of our collective freedom, dignity and order.

The prophet Ezekiel ate the Holy Scriptures, ingesting the word of God so as to metabolize the law. Jesus taught that the law is not to be usurped but inscribed on the heart. There is a practical reason for this. Dry, minimal adherence to rules always robs them of their capacity to generate order and elevate dignity. Rigid rules empty of care lead to systemic unfairness, with dangers and damage for people and societies as well as organizations. There is also a theological reason for bringing the law into our bloodstream and pumping it through our hearts. By the law we know God. By the law we receive its freedom and graces. By the law we participate in God's holy order, benefiting from its blessings and contributing to its liberating harmony.

We cannot be magnificent when we are parsimonious with the law. Prophetic directors do not govern with disdain for results, but instead recognize success as an outcome of interdependence within a living, fragile order. The prophetic respects professionalism, only expecting that the noble norms of any vocation be upheld. The harsh challenge of prophetic criticism is for those who compromise their principles. The same with profits: the number is valued in terms that I earlier referred to as "worth and worthiness." Praise goes to wealth that serves order and spreads human dignity, satisfying the high expectations of the market while satisfying the higher norms of moral integrity. Prophetic directors do what they are charged to do, only more so. They are slightly more aggressive in questions of discovery to expose moral dilemmas within strategic quandaries. They perform double due diligence to fathom implications for both principle and objective. They debate and decide with conscience as well as competence. They assume responsibility not simply as the place where the buck stops, but as an expression of their care for order and fairness.

Corporate governance is a subset of personal governance, and not the other way around. In other words, we need to develop the moral capacity of individuals to upgrade the moral imagination of boards and their organizations. Developing the personal prophetic voice is part and parcel of any Christian discipleship.

- To perform with prophetic intent and intensity, we too must withdraw to the "wilderness" for prayer and the humbling experience

of our utter dependence on God and nature. Rather than executive retreats to golf courses, we must risk retreating to ghettos, garbage dumps and global "hope spots" where entrepreneurs are experimenting with new modes of stewardship and new projects of social justice.
- To enliven the prophetic imagination and see what ought to be, we too must come back into our communities and jobs with repentance.
- To question the status quo with moral authority, we too must inscribe God's law and love on our hearts through meditation and frequent prayer.
- To break through the comfortable assumptions of our managerial class, we too must stand in desolation with the widows, orphans, homeless, imprisoned and despised, with the women unfairly stuck below the corporate glass ceilings or with workers disposed of through outsourcing.
- To see the truth, we must risk exposing ourselves to the surprising claims and perspectives of others, engaging corporate protestors or critics with the same amazement that Jesus found in the great healing faith of the Roman centurion.

Human perspective is a moral as well as creative capacity, implying accountability for what we perceive, as well as for the consequences of choices that enhance or disrupt order. For governance to be wise, for responsibility to be commensurate with knowledge, we must take the prophetic action that Bernard Lonergan called "conversion." Responsibility inheres in our human transcendence as the obligation corresponding to our freedom and morality, rather than as finger pointing or scapegoating. What we see and do matters. When we are wrong, when by omission or commission we destabilize order or ignore the hierarchy of principles and values that frame human moral interconnection, accountability serves as the means for healing and recovery, for personal recommitment to the whole, for restitution, reconciliation, forgiveness and redemption.

RESPONSIBILITY BALANCE SHEET

The Charge for the Soul	The Charge for Managers
Consequence for judgments and actions: freedom and wholeness are at stake in every decision and action •	• Accountability for the public trust: what we decide and implement matters profoundly to the natural environment and social reality
The price for being free, and for being in the image and likeness of the transcendent creator •	• The licence to operate in which justice serves to keep the system functioning stably and dependably
Not a regressive burden but a process for purifying to liberate the potentiality for holiness •	• Not for simply finger pointing but an ownership of consequences that accepts responsibility with honour and care as part of a mutually sustaining relationship with society
Commissioning for justice, to serve the repairing and reciprocities that help with healing and reconciliation •	• Commissioning for integrity, to build the assurance to market and stakeholders that justice will be served
Entry into grief and penance, recognizing our human complicity in systems or attitudes that dehumanize or destroy •	• Entry into visceral presence in the world, owning and responding to the human, social, natural and moral impacts of strategy
The foundation for hope: to serve justice enmeshes us in its benefits and fulfillment •	• The foundation for renewal: to make a contribution bigger than the benefits to the enterprise

The terms of discipleship: to embrace the law with an open, receptive heart, to not only adhere to structures but also love them as gift and grace •

• The terms for discipleship at work: to meet the requirements of the law cheerfully and expansively, and to "walk the extra mile" to serve what is needed beyond what is required

To recognize that we cannot grow towards God alone, but need the intervention of the Holy One who heals, forgives and completes •

• To recognize the holy norms of integrity, trusting grace as well as competence to help judge what is right

Hierarchism as Honour

Simone Weil identified the needs of the soul while in exile during the Second World War. Her experience of upheaval and death makes it understandable that she recognized order as essential and foundational. Her experience of displacement and oppression makes it understandable that she gave priority to obligations, regarding the rights for freedom not as secondary but as second for being dependent on the complete exercise of responsibility. Weil also witnessed the power and corruption of symbols, which makes it understandable that she would acknowledge the indispensability of what she called "hierarchism."[11] The principle for this involves three truths: that not all values are of equal worth; that not all people are of the same moral sensibility or maturity; and that not all responsibilities are of equal weight. The development of the soul involves an upward progression, an ascent from broken or partial perspective to one that is whole and holy. This ascent from disintegration to integration recognizes the primacy of God and the priority of God's law. The first commandment stipulates this hierarchy by prohibiting the idolatry of placing other objectives, desires or false images before God. As Weil noted, symbols and structures are imperative for order, since these allow for priorities to be set and for obligations to be discharged. The authenticity of symbols hinges on invoking veneration for what matters morally. The legitimacy of structures hinges on effective implementation that honours "the nobility, heroism, probity, generosity and genius spent in exercise of profession."[12]

Management is premised on hierarchy: defining goals and roles; delegating tasks and responsibilities; creating systems for expertise and control. Brands serve as symbols of honour and trust, conveying principles and qualities to customers and stakeholders. However, while structures and symbols are intrinsic to business, there is evidence that hierarchies have become too rigid and less than honourable. As noted, Peter Drucker has long argued that most companies still deploy a management hierarchy from the industrial age. One dysfunction of this broken paradigm is executive compensation that is so out of whack with merit and performance that it qualifies as obscene.[13] Another potential cancer in our obsolete hierarchism is the terrible growth in the number of working poor. The credibility of structures becomes suspect when working hard does not get you ahead, and working irresponsibly does not get you caught. Most of us work somewhere in the middle of hierarchies, benefiting from how they extend our reach and possibilities, yet also constrained by them for the stress and disposability they impose. That we are nearly always restructuring confirms that there are serious problems with existing hierarchies. That we rarely see changes through to the end also validates that we do not yet have the key for ordering the roles and obligations that the unfolding future demands.

Prophetic managers take symbols and structures seriously for how they shape the purpose and experience of the lives lived within the organization. These managers do not paper over the black holes of accountability with facile ethics codes, but instead insist on the truth. In the area of strategy, Jim Collins calls this intellectual discipline "confronting the hard facts."[14] With regard to prophecy, this confrontation is of the even "harder facts" revealed by the heart and expected by the soul. Rather than re-engineer processes, prophetic truth-tellers recalibrate priorities, focusing on the smooth, efficient flow of moral productivity. Alert to the human stakes from lost opportunity, prophetic managers are outraged by what wastes human commitment, creativity and integrity. They stand on soapboxes decrying the value being destroyed by disrespectful meanness. They shine a beam of light on the dark corners of decisions or operations not yet made transparent.

They quantify the costs and damage to dignity and innovation from unrelenting busyness. When others see stress, the prophetic bias is to see enslavement. When most others assume that "business as usual" is good enough, the prophetic urgency is to do much, much better.

As Walter Brueggemann reminds us, the prophetic role is for creation as well as critique, for pointing out possibilities as well as problems. This means imbuing symbols with meaning and ideals: not just brand equity, which measures worth, but also brand integrity, which measures worthiness. Prophetic organizations value knowledge for its wonder as well as utility, creating continuous learning that allows us to be continuously childlike in the terms described by Jesus: open, dependent, trustful, playful and in need of security and belonging. Prophetic organizations also value dialogue, not as focus groups for dissecting perceptions, but as conversations to affect conversion – change, growth, relishing diversity, and learning from dissent.

HIERARCHISM BALANCE SHEET

What Honours the Soul	What Honours Managers
Establishing the priority of God in covenantal deference to the First Commandment •	• Establishing moral priorities that situate shareholder value in its proper relationship to sustainability
Ascending towards an ideal, purifying those habits that distort integrity or stifle relationship •	• Ascending towards professional excellence, undoing systems or processes that stunt moral judgment
A relationship of dependence towards the Divine: assuming the open hearts of children •	• A relationship of interdependence: maturing self-interest to have regard and responsibility for the common
Recognition of the stages for spiritual growth, that beginners require what Bonaventure called "the willingness to be led" •	• Recognition that moral discernment is not a constant but requires disciplined practice to become as robust as strategic imagination

Using scripture and tradition for sustenance during the "dark night" that is an inescapable step in the soul's ascent •

• Having diverse, non-business voices inform governance and ethics to engage the breadth of human wisdom in critical discernments

Opening to the reforming and reframing possibilities of grace as God's gift of presence and love •

• Opening to the unknown, allowing facts to simmer in the silence of possibilities and unintended outcomes

Moving up from sensory experience and temporal understanding, seeking truth and beauty, and at the pinnacle goodness and communion •

• Moving up the scale of accountability, offering truth rather than transparency, and the multiple-bottom-line results that serve interdependence

Striving for St. Bonaventure's *synderesis*: the summit-awakening that melds wisdom with watchfulness to attend passionately to the moral moment•

• Striving for clarity and consciousness about roles, with accountability and access commensurate with privilege and power

Prophetic Rubber Meeting the Operational Road

Perspective fashioned with soul needs provides an effective diagnostic for where we have been in business. The new economy was an attempt to project a new order from new technology. Globalization is another matrix for wrestling order from new nodes and interconnections of trade. Neither of these has been realized to their imagined potential because other essential needs were neglected. When vision is indeed thick with ordering relevance, a hierarchy of honour and an embedded sense of accountability, companies excel and souls soar. This is what happened at Johnson & Johnson (J&J) during the Tylenol tampering crisis. For generations, managers and employees had shared a perspective that ordered their work around priorities of care for patients or customers using their products. This was defined in a Credo, which has been much studied by business schools trying to codify crisis management. For J&J, the response that won such admiration was not based on the code, but from the order, priorities and consequences it envisioned, including the responsibility throughout the company. As then-Chairman James Burke has explained, the decision to pull product from store shelves was not a top-down hierarchical one, but spontaneously made by hundreds of employees according to a hierarchy of values. In the face of a crisis, these employees took upon themselves the obligation to reorder the chaos. An integrated perspective was the foundation for a response of integrity.

Forgive me, Father, for:

— Confusing monologue with monotheism

Thinking that because there is only one of You

I can pray as if there is only one of me

— Mistaking the certitude for what I want to say

For the clarity from the silence I avoid to hear

Forgive me, Mother, for I keep winning

— Confusing success for satiation

Thinking that as long as I am a good person

I am entitled to all the goods I can buy and have

— Mistaking choice for freedom

Making truth and obedience options of pragmatism

For the soul, as well as for companies, shrunken or incomplete perspective leaves us exhausted from ceaseless tactics and disoriented from continuous firefighting. Something more fundamental also comes apart when we lack perspective (which, by definition, is a view of what is holding everything together). Inevitably, the mistrust for what is unclear or deceptive leads to growing, hardening isolation. Silos are assumed to be symptoms of territoriality, but they more accurately reflect the absence of ordering perspective that connects relationships and motivates integration. Indeed, the reason we opt for silos is often to preserve order within a reality of growing confusion, threat or disorder. Operational silos in companies have hardened in part because top-down decisions to merge or re-engineer rarely took into account the underlying disruption in culture, operations and patterns of relationship. Initially erected as barriers to keep chaos out, silos – as we know all too well in management – have become the walls imprisoning innovation, information and interaction.

Spirituality, too, is often practised in silos. Seemingly an act of freedom for being completely a matter of individual choice, this spiritual silo-making has instead created an existential imprisonment in which our beliefs have little bearing on who we are, what we do and what we hope to become. These silos are in part capricious: individuality is so rigorously applied that it presumes to redefine presence and divine relationship. Yet part of what makes building silos so compelling for the soul is a rationale similar to that in the corporate world, with walls going up partially to distance us from religious traditions that claim unifying wisdom yet trip over disordering hierarchy, truth-monopolizing dogma, or sexism that is the opposite of liberation. As with companies, spiritual silos defeat efficiency. We are always starting over, always having to reinvent wheels rather than proceeding along clearly marked, well-trodden and therefore smoother pathways. Spiritual silos also impede synergy, both in the sense of our possible contribution to integration and our missing the opportunity to participate in the grace of what others have wrought.

For companies, the habits that come from operating from silos are very costly, undermining the co-operation needed for quality, frustrating access and accountability for customers, and ultimately curtailing the creativity of employees who remain withdrawn and risk-averse. Spiritual silos have the same diminishing impact on the soul, with generic prayer as proxy for sacramental depth, generic transcendence substituting for relationship to awesome Presence, and imagination constrained by self-imposed concrete boundaries. When God calls prophets in the Hebrew scriptures, the project is usually to break the golden calves of idolatry or to call people back to obedience of divine law. In our context, God is smashing silos, using the prophetic voice to take down the silos of slavery, to break the excluding concrete of hatred or injustice, to disintegrate the personal appropriation of the ineffable that makes us into walls impeding grace rather than mirrors magnifying it.

The God of Israel is the supreme silo-buster, so much so that the divine preference was for a tent rather than a temple, for an empty ark denoting perpetual movement and easy, ubiquitous access. The mono-relationship that stemmed from monotheism shattered the divide between cosmic God and temporal humanity. The gift of the Law created the mechanism for living in a unifying, sanctifying and liberating intimacy with the Divine. In his ministry, Jesus, too, challenged and defeated the structural and attitudinal silos that are often constructed of material much harder than cement. To the blind, he gave not only sight, but also the physical wholeness that qualified for reacceptance into the community; to the bleeding woman he gave not only relief from her hemorrhage, but also the ritual purity to resume the fuller personal life within free contact and exchange with others. Especially with his radical teachings about forgiveness, Jesus sought to penetrate the silos of exclusion and shift possibilities towards an order that held in dignity and unity those most broken and impoverished.

> *Mother of waves*
>
> *Agitate my surf*
>
> *Mitigate the undermining undertow*
>
> *Mother of horizon*
>
> *Elevate my view*
>
> *Prop up my height impediment*
>
> *Mother of day/break*
>
> *Break open this day with holiness*
>
> *Distract me from distractions*

Mother of edges

Sharpen the encounter with truth

Discipline discipleship

Mother of awakening

Designate my driver

Close the gap that isolates me

Mother of Jesus

Conform me to the cross

Entangle the possible with the needed

The global economy is becoming a silo economy, with protections for products of mature industries such as steel, subsidies for agriculture, and fiscal policies that impose structural reforms in developing countries – such as water privatization – that few, if any, developed countries have mastered. These high-level, highly rigid silos keep the poor, poor – a point made repeatedly by James Wolfensohn, the former president of the World Bank. Silos of poverty are also the disordered breeding grounds for despair, fuelling antagonisms that few gated (silo) communities are strong enough to repel indefinitely. Consultants, myself included, receive much work helping organizations identify their silos. Most of what we do only scratches the surface: few silos come down; fewer of the ones that do stay down. The reason is that we are a silo culture, with silo values, within a silo system. Even as we shed one layer we find ourselves, as if inside the innermost compartment of a Russian doll, free only so far as the next bigger one.

Prophetic critique is never a PowerPoint picnic. The objective is to encounter in as authentic a way as possible the pain and grief that we usually miss or have become immune to from within our own everyday silo to unleash hope, grace and courage. Prophets have edge because there are tons of concrete around our hearts, hardened by fatigue and reinforced by the steel of practicalities. Prophets have irritating insistence because they see what we do not, and they hope for what we have stopped aspiring towards. Whether for or against it, the reality of globalization includes not only progress but also regress. We suffer from issues fatigue as our hearts skip from crisis silo to crisis silo. We also have belonging silos (not in my backyard); accountability silos (not in my job description); attention-span silos (flavour of the month); ideology silos (crossfire); and program silos (strategic philanthropy), which create conscience silos (as long as I am a good person) and accountability silos (survival of the fittest). We see our problems from silos and proffer silo solutions without recognizing that silo-making and silo-sustaining are systemic problems.

Silos – even well-reasoned ones – eventually become prisons. The enslavement gaining momentum at the fringes of our silo society and economy is a metaphor for the whole system, as well as an indictment of what happens between its cracks. The business of prophets has always been emancipation; the prophetic role within business is now to penetrate the mutually enslaving silos to authentically co-create order, co-define honour and co-share accountability. Paul Ricoeur argues that we cannot use fact-based approaches to close the distance or penetrate the isolation that facts have created.[15] In many ways, it is expertise that has made silos necessary and thrive, so throwing more expertise at the problem does little to awaken hearts, agitate urgency or invite silo-rending outreach. What is needed, Ricoeur says, is a much more provocative "second naiveté"[16] that allows wonder to dissolve the distance caused by facts, and awe to undo the numbing from perspectives of utility. Whether in corporate or spiritual silos, the way to freedom and integration is not through more "heads-down" homework but through a "heads-up" encounter with ineffability.

Paradoxically, the perspective shift that results from an encounter with God presumes or demands a perspective about the nature of this relationship: a way of bringing order to what otherwise remains abstract, to have some hierarchy for access to what otherwise remains absolute and apart, and to exercise worship with freedom and accountability to what otherwise remains as discretionary and displaceable as Santa Claus. For Christians, the order, hierarchy and accountability of perspective are seen through Jesus. Whether from "high Christology," which believes Jesus came into human form as divine, or "low Christology," which believes Jesus perfected his humanity to reveal and participate in divinity, the consequences for following Jesus are specific. His humanity, which we share, relates us through him to the Father/Mother/Creator and through Jesus to each other as brothers and sisters. This is a cruciform reordering: the vertical connection bridging temporal with eternal, human with divine, and personal with transcendent; and the horizontal connection bridging past to future, humanity with creation, and individuals with community. There is also a hierarchy for this order, with God as the aim and Jesus at the centre, and a radical equality premised on every human being bearing as a constitutive gift of life the image and likeness of God. Finally, there is accountability, not only for choices and mistakes we make in freedom, but for living in the healing and whole-making pattern of Jesus.

It took several centuries for Christians to understand that the relationships and possibilities unleashed by this cruciform reordering involved, and could only be possible, through the agency, wisdom and sustenance of the Holy Spirit – the third element of Trinity and the first, original understanding of spirituality. Reading the prayerful language of the English mystic Julian of Norwich, we come to realize that one perceptible characteristic of God in this mystery of Trinity is as a being of surplus. God is indivisibly one and more than that. God is more than Trinity, more than knowable, more than Father or Mother or Spirit or silence. Abundance in abandonment is part of the nature mirrored in Trinity, and part of the quality that results in creation and rubs off in its unfolding. From the subatomic to the intergalactic, creation reveals profound efficiency within the imperceptible redundancies and randomness that we call chaos theory, but which we now know is not chaotic at all. Souls for holding the eternal memory and longing of our source and aim crave for this surplus, and thrive in its abundance. We need order for more than stability, to also belong, fashioning identity within the trajectory of creation, and exercising the latent potency of our creative gifts. We need hierarchy for more than security, to also have a program for becoming, for ascending through love, forgiveness, invention and reinvention to wholeness and holiness. We need accountability for more than reciprocity in obligation, or for punishment and expiation, to also grow towards God by sharing in the responsibility for the integrity of the whole, for the dignity and potentiality of one another. The needs of the soul are for God, and in the pattern of God these needs are for more than the minimal, for the extravagance of Trinity and the excessiveness of creation and human life.

What has this to do with silos? Very simply, the emollient for softening the hard walls of separation is generosity. The acid for dissolving the cold concrete of keeping experts isolated and departments apart is hope. Meanness is never the solution, since it only spreads fear and hardens segregation. Only magnificence unifies. Only participation in beauty and truth sustains the shared sacrifice for common cause. Order based on relationship with God is the prophetic call. Accountability shaped in mutual care is the prophetic demand. And hierarchy designed to realize hope is the prophetic legacy.

More than I think You are

More than I name You contain

More than become You overcome

More than create You generate

More than are You are more

More than relate You love

More than apart You impart

And by Your gift I too am more

More than be I belong

More than dependent I am free

More than empowered I can liberate

More than work I can create

More than redeemed I can forgive

More than en-gifted I can heal

More than apart I can receive

In the image of more than

I am only me when I am more.

7

PROPORTION

Fair Asymmetries

Since they are responsible for strategy, most managers have some appreciation for prophetic contribution. Already the term *prophet* is conferred on executives who have been proven right on a bet. It is much harder for managers to fathom what it means to be priestly. Prophetic agitation at least gets things moving, but how can we afford to be priestly in business? The answer, which puts this capacity at the heart of operations, is that priestly managers see and reveal holiness in what is happening every day. No matter how smart, strategy always depends on the details of implementation. In priestly fashion, business people with open and careful hearts serve one another in the trenches of implementation, honouring courage, consoling injury, remembering divine purpose and potentiality in the mundane situations of getting it done. Change is disruptive, often damaging, and the priestly orientation to community keeps people together using a framework of meaning during the tumult of transition. As Rabbi Dow Marmur explains, "one of the most important functions of religious community is *sharing of failure*, especially moral failure."[1] It is because we underappreciate these vital contributions to purpose and belonging that so many companies struggle when transforming vision to action: it is because we rush into continuous change without attending to human consequences and holy priorities that we have so much unproductive churn, disillusionment and change fatigue.

The spiritual premise for priestly management is that our relationship with God is in the here and now, not on some far-off horizon of perfection. God's calling is effusive. God's grace is pervasive. Any divide between mundane and holy is an artifice with destructive and desecrating consequences. Any faith is a hope and commitment to dissolve that divide. Insisting on integration, the priestly act exposes the sacred that inheres in the daily grind and glory, and even in the detritus. Quaker theology is premised on "that of God" in every human individual. It is this sliver of divine stuff that we all share that automatically anoints us priests. This same sliver demands that we stand in witness and service to one another. To be clear, this priesthood is not a clerical designation. It is instead a gift from God to live by the rules of love and forgiveness in the everyday stress and mistakes of life. No doubt this is a daunting job description. The consolation is that we are already consecrated for being "children of God." We are already ministers of hope for being sisters and brothers of Jesus. Our challenge is only to be human from the healing integrity which that relationship enables.

Perspective is the gift of prophetic imagination. What engages and stimulates the priestly heart are issues of "proportion." The time for prayer on the Sabbath was bequeathed as law and gift by God to protect against the enslavement of ceaseless work. In the story of creation in Genesis, God pronounced the six days of labour as "good" and the seventh day of rest as "holy." (Genesis 2:3) This playful and prayerful absenting from work is a prototype for balance, the liberating proportion between productivity and relishing. In the scriptures, God asks not for rituals of sacrifice but for acts of service: protecting the widow, sheltering the homeless, raising the orphan and visiting the sick or those imprisoned (Isaiah 1:17). Each of these priestly acts corrects disproportions of exclusion or indignity. The temple for this work is the human body, with its basic physical needs, and the human heart, with its basic longing for respect, acceptance and creativity. Jesus prescribed other norms that again reveal God's proportions: to love one another as God loves us; to do unto others what we would have done unto us; and to "forgive those who trespass against us" as God has forgiven our transgression. These priestly proportions are not necessarily reciprocal. As with the father welcoming back the prodigal son (Luke 15:11-32), or with the injunction to forgive "seventy times seven times" (Matthew 18:21), Jesus teaches that God's proportions are always profligate in the same excessive yet imperative scale as for magnificence.

The prophetic balance sheet juxtaposes what is with what ought to be. The priestly balance sheet corresponds the temporal with the eternal, consecrating what seems ordinary by bringing forth what is numinous and transcendent. Proportion is foundational to morality, beauty and the corporate balance sheet: connecting distinct parts into a working whole, assessing cause with effect, discerning viability from the dynamic symmetry of operating factors. Most religious ethics systems are disciplines for proportion, striving for the relational obligations of the golden mean or the detached presence of a middle way between materiality and spirituality. In its ethics and outcomes, proportionality is also a synonym for integrity. Conversely, our most troubling problems in business, society and even spirituality, including the following, are from the unsustainable imbalances from disproportion:

- too much executive compensation, not enough accountability;
- too great a short-term focus, not enough care for the long term;
- too many greenhouse gases, not enough restraint or innovation;
- too exclusive a focus on share price, not enough focus on governance;
- too many men on boards, not enough women, minorities or non-executives;
- too many stretch-targets, not enough imagination;
- too much drive for efficiency, not enough valuing of relationships;
- too much managerial firefighting, not enough managerial insight;
- too much data, not enough discernment;
- too much competition, not enough co-operation on shared consequences;
- too many auto-attendants, not enough service people;
- too big a to-do list, not enough Sabbath;
- too much personal stress, not enough inner peace;
- too much consumption, not enough satisfaction;
- too much "bowling alone," not enough community involvement;
- too much preoccupation with image, not enough memory, meaning and hope.

Why is the work of addressing disproportion priestly work? First, practically addressing what is out of proportion involves a different skill set than does critique. It takes patience and persistence to develop the soul skills for renewal. It takes stone-by-stone building of community to create structures for liberating order and prayerful creativity. During apartheid, many companies agitating for social change in South Africa adopted the Global Sullivan Principles. Created by Leon Sullivan, an ordained African-American minister, this code leveraged corporate investments and practices to correct institutional discrimination, opening doors of opportunity and dignity beyond the norms of local or international law.[2] This was very much the priestly task of making new possibilities for society and organizations by insisting that God's presence in the here and now made unfair policies null and void.

Second, the process for rebalancing is tricky because our inclination, especially as managers, is to do something about it. In pursuit of simplicity, many of us become exhausted trying to imitate Martha Stewart. Undoing destructive imbalance is less about doing less, and more about becoming more. A higher achievement of purpose, magnificence is the antidote for disproportion, as the "double and" that fills in the emptiness that results from unceasing busyness. This is the working outcome of the soul reaching for God, and the role of nurturing transcendence and consecrating work is again priestly. This ministry, which we all share, is to bless work, offer it as praise and prayer, witness God's gifts in profession and practice, create communities of purpose, and make space for grace to give life to our hopes in decisions and actions.

One of the puzzles of our corporate reality is that so many companies that have the public trust became its most extreme abusers. The exemplars of disproportionate excess worked in industries such as electricity (Enron) and telecommunications (WorldCom and Global Crossing) that were held to a higher standard because they are utilities. Also conspicuously culpable have been what used to be called the pillars of the financial establishment, including banks (Citibank and CIBC), insurance companies (Marsh & McLellan and AIG), and brokerage firms (Merrill Lynch and Solomon Smith Barney). Perhaps most damaging of all have been the failures of industries (accounting) and services (mutual funds) that were assumed to be the custodians of transparency and fairness. Analysts have dissected each situation, with regulators imposing fines and penalties along with stricter rules for disclosure. Despite this serious attention, we have not yet recognized the systemic nature of this imbalance, nor dealt with the paradox that the biggest deceivers were those most trusted. The obvious implication is that deregulation has been interpreted by quite a few managers as "no regulation." The priestly manager venerates the moral grace of rules and respects the fragile interdependence of laws. God made God's presence available to Israel through the Ten Commandments, and by Israel's experience we remember that adherence to Mosaic Law delivered freedom while its violations led to defeat, chaos and exile. Markets have many virtues, but moderation and temperance are rarely among them. Rather than promote the usual debate that is ideologically split between "regulators" and "deregulators," the priestly invocation is to find a middle way that exercises obligations commensurate to opportunities, setting limits that are both responsible and catalytic.

Regulations and rules are important, but still only part of the answer. Sense of proportion is often lost because managers are stretched taut between the lofty goals of vision and steep demands of performance. We have plans to scope out "what" to do. We have practices and processes for "how" to get it done. Yet we give only casual consideration to "why." Proportion connects the objective and outcome to its animating purpose. We are all, to a degree, motivated by rewards. Priestly proportion adds the inspiration from magnificence and the conscience from responsibility. Unless we tap what is essential, the cure for imbalance becomes its own curse. This happened with "0% financing," introduced by North American auto companies as a tactic to clear inventory. Since it did not address real issues of quality, design and fuel economy, the promotional device became a hard-to-break addiction that still plagues sales and profits. Today, Ford consistently makes its money as a banker for car loans and loses money making cars. Some will argue that this is only poor marketing or bad product design. My view is that the addiction to rebates should alert managers to a more significant erosion of ethics.

Having to bribe customers to buy a product indicates that trust has been lost for any traditional precept of value. This represents a "soft corruption" that many more companies are afflicted with, yet misunderstand. Unlike fraud, which is an explicit breach of trust, soft corruption involves the thousand cuts of indignity that are the thin border between what is legal and what is right. The wounding is not instantaneous; it accumulates by bumps and bruises into injuries that, in the end, cross the ethical line. Stress is one of the most common indicators of soft corruption, with human needs for play and renewal made hostage to pressures for productivity. We all rally to do more in times of crisis or threat, but when the imbalance becomes a norm, then employees are paying the price in health and purpose for the leadership's failure in scoping an ordering vision. Other symptoms of soft corruption include fatigue, with employees subsidizing competitiveness through longer work, and complexity, with customers being robbed of precious time to deal with services or products that companies failed to engineer for respectful simplicity. These seem like bad management practices but are instead examples of bad ethics and morals: bullying workers; extorting productivity; short-changing value or dignity to customers.

Reframed regulation may, for a time, restrain the usual nuts-and-bolts types of corruption. For the "soft" variety, which is more banal, the necessary corrective is to attend to the thousand cuts with a thousand courtesies or consolations, and to signify by everyday decisions and actions that fairness, freedom and beauty do indeed matter most. Soft corruption ruptures trust and hope. Paradoxically, it is a breakdown that we often contribute to by going with the flow or not expecting better. The priestly role is to lift the group's eyes to behold an alternative horizon of possibilities, and to create the spiritual resources for flexing more moral imagination in the processes and contact points of productivity. Rather than deal with its first union, Wal-Mart closed down the store where workers bravely voted for certification. This is a company that is very smart and resourceful in providing value to consumers, but it is also a carrier for the virus of disproportion that breeds soft corruption. If unions are not corporately acceptable to Wal-Mart, what other solutions are there to a business plan that is now seriously imbalanced? Markets like the bottom line, so no pressure will be forthcoming from there. Regulators are reluctant to intervene against what is now the largest employer in North America. Consumers are reluctant to sacrifice value, even if, as workers in other industries, they are paying the productivity price for operating in a Wal-Mart economy. The stars seem aligned for despair, which is why priestly imagination becomes invaluable. Markets may make their corrections or competitors force reform. In the in-between, priestly managers invoke God's word, standing for truth and making real the implications of fairness from God's law. In small ways, within small decisions, the priestly instinct is for expansion to let in grace, to foster goodness, and to remake ordinary acts into special ones as offerings to hope and justice. People need belonging when they have been victimized. They need community when options seem oppressive. And they need consolation and inspiration from the word of God.

The questions posed by this soft corruption are of personal as well as professional significance. It is not just that companies are demanding. It is also that for reasons of either ambition or fear, we managers are more docile. Jim Collins writes that "good is the enemy of great."[3] He means that acceptable mediocrity undermines achievements of excellence. I would restate this from the perspective of lost magnificence. Companies have largely ceased being great for missing the importance of goodness. The absence of corporate meaning motivates the desire for spirituality at work, but this can be vacuous, perpetuating despair and meanness, if it becomes only an exercise in personal seeking or comfort. This spirituality becomes priestly and affective when we managers take seriously the possibility of consecrating our work to the glory of God, offering precious quality in praise and inspired innovation in gratitude, returning magnificence for the gifts and graces invested in our human nature and professional privilege.

Out of gas, I can't stop guzzling

Refuel me with what matters

Out of time, I can't stop working

Downsize my addictive ambitions

Out of touch, I can't stop e-mailing

Connect me to serve your Server

Out of extinguishers, I can't stop firefighting

Open up the hydrants of hope

Out of meaning, I can't stop churning

Re-engineer my inefficient prayer

Out of communion, I can't stop privatizing

Stretch my targets beyond me

Out of control, I can't stop rationalizing

Forgive me my dysfunctional norm

The Priestly Role

The Christian prototype for priesthood is, of course, Jesus. Called "Rabboni" by his contemporaries, Jesus taught in the synagogue, interpreted scriptures and presided over everyday events of encounter, such as shared meals, which became the basis for sacraments. In addition to a conventional ministry – a shepherd leading his sheep – Jesus also embodied an offering, living in response to God's love by giving himself as a gift to those whom he encountered, and most especially those in greatest need. From this emptying of self in gratitude towards union, Jesus lived and made manifest a seamless, intense and all-encompassing intersection between divine and human realms. Symbol as well as priest, Jesus healed the sick, fed the hungry, gave comfort to the widows, and brought dignity to the most excluded – both to children, who were the most vulnerable, and to tax collectors, who as power figures collaborating with the occupying Romans, were the most reviled.

Busy, forever travelling and in great demand, Jesus nevertheless withdrew often to pray, reflecting and attending to the interior dimensions of his spirituality. With prayerfulness – with fullness from prayer – Jesus intervened in life's distortions, performing whole-making miracles, and by his acts and words incarnating a rebuke to social and religious systems that disproportionately benefited a few at the expense of suffering by many. This "in-breaking" of divine justice and mercy was not simply a metaphysical concept, but was made practical by Jesus in tiny acts of heartfelt generosity: "Come to me, all you that labour and are burdened, and I will give you rest" (Matthew 11:28).

Markets and other public institutions are often hostile to religion and suspicious of overt spirituality. There are historical reasons for separation of church and state, but some of the antipathy can subvert human rights rather than protect them. The issue is rigidity. Even the most enlightened human structures eventually calcify. In his theology of power, Walter Wink observes that those with disproportionate privilege in any society always seek to protect and advance their interests. Hard-heartedness becomes a characteristic of the status quo, dehumanizing those victimized by the structure. This is why innocuous business words such as *outsourcing* and *right-sizing* are so dangerous. Reinhold Niebuhr, a mid-twentieth-century theologian, pointed out that the root of evil is "rigidity." The harsher the lines of exclusion, the more fixed the boundaries of separation, the more damage to individuals, and the more restrictive the freedoms of the community. The most rigid systems, such as communism and national socialism, ended up killing the most people. Not to say that markets or companies are like that; rather, no human system of economy or politics is ever exempt from making fast and firm the disproportions that benefit those running the show. Since rigidity is latent, so is evil.

An Example for the Ages

It is because the risks are serious and the stakes high that I have taken the unorthodox step of modelling organizational priesthood on Etty Hillesum – the young Jewish lawyer killed in Auschwitz. Let me begin unequivocally by saying that I am not trying to appropriate Hillesum or in any way diminish her Jewishness. We can love and admire her, but we must not use her heroic faith to lessen even by one iota the awfulness of the Holocaust. Nor can we forget that this travesty was perpetrated across a Christian continent, aided and abetted by Christian managers running transport, chemical, information and finance companies. Hillesum would never have used categories of priesthood to describe herself, but we can learn from her example what it means to serve with a pastoral heart within systems of annihilating rigidity. She practised what has been called "a mysticism of honesty."[4] Even before her arrest,

Hillesum understood the scale of the tragedy then unfolding. All too human in her despair and doubts, she refused to let cruelty and terror destroy her personal convictions for meaning. This did not mean creating intellectual sandcastles for holiness. Instead, Hillesum performed small, tedious and seemingly unimportant acts with great love. Herself a starving prisoner, she cared for others with simple courtesy, passed messages within the camp and to the outside world, helped mothers with young children, and dressed the wounds of the injured. She did not delude herself about the murderous forces around her, yet with lucidity and prayerful intention she blessed the moments in the camp, as well as those imprisoned with her.

There are four patterns to what we may call Hillesum's assumed rather than ordained priesthood.

First, she began with prayer, longing for it and insisting on praying even within the harried chaos of a world being systematically destroyed. The pressures from disproportion do not readily accommodate strategic critique; the quandaries from disproportion rarely unravel in logical sequence. Prayer brings us into the encounter with divine mystery, which may be our only antidote for or response to the mystery and intractability of evil. In her diary Hillesum wrote, "Sometimes the most important thing in a whole day is the rest we take between two deep breaths, or the turning inwards in prayer for five short minutes."[5] That space between two breaths is where infinity leaks into the ordinary, where the cloud of unknowing helps fill in the emptiness of what we know, where presence leaps into hope despite the despair on either side of our inhalation/exhalation.

The second pattern involves sensibilities and actions of consecration, finding beauty and echoes of infinity in the midst of the ordinary, finding sacramental significance in even the most humble acts of human practicality. Hillesum did not deny but rather held onto the irreconcilable contradictions of her situation, using these as fuel for creating meaning and sustaining actions of service. She wrote, "Every day I am in Poland, on the battle fields, or we could say in the slaughter fields. Sometimes I have a vision of a battlefield running green with venom. I am with the hungry, the tortured, the dying every day, but I am also near the jasmine and the piece of heaven outside my window. In life there is space for everything. For a faith in God and for a miserable death."⁶ Consecration does not mute but transmute, releasing the integrity of either suffering or joy by integrating these into the holy entirety of God's being for and within creation.

To insist on hope in the face of numbing indignity requires a third priestly virtue: courage. An integrating perspective fusing the holy with the everyday cannot be claimed without risk. Hillesum saw this as the test that was also the aim: the impossibility that became impossible to deny. She wrote, "This thought has pursued me for weeks: We have to dare to say that we believe. Dare to pronounce the name of God."⁷

The fourth characteristic of Hillesum for this universal ministry relates to compassion. While consecration restores balance by recalling the priority of the divine, compassion deflates disproportion by giving priority to others over self. "I would like to be the thinking heart of my barracks," Hillesum wrote in her diary several months before her extermination. "I would like to be the thinking heart for the whole concentration camp."⁸ A "thinking heart" seems like an impossible aim for a death camp. The wisdom at work in Hillesum's perception was not that it helped her make sense of the evil around her. Nothing could do that. Rather, to paraphrase a rabbinic saying, it was a view that allowed her to remain human within terrible inhumanity, kept her whole and becoming within a rational and ordered factory producing disintegration and death.

We cannot relate to Hillesum's experience, but we can be uplifted by the dimensions of her spirituality to imagine a real spirituality at work.

- Making space for prayer is necessary, and is possible even in impossible situations.

  – We may need to steal moments at the beginning of every day to dedicate our efforts to God.

  – We may need to offer silent prayers before every meeting, blessing those gathered with the call to peace that Jesus gave to his disciples.

  – We may need an "examen" at the end of the business day to audit what we did as managers that hurt or healed, that liberated or thwarted potential.

- We may need to pray for forgiveness or grace.
- Recognizing magnificence, and being overcome by its beauty, is available to us in even the busiest or most ugly circumstances.
  - We must relish the wizardry of our technology or science with childlike wonder for its hopeful possibilities.
  - We must see our tools and skills as blessings that bestow great opportunities for human advancement.
  - We must be restless to create value that is also beautiful and enduring.
  - We must look to history and the dreams of the heart for the ambition and inspiration to make a difference.
  - We must "receive" the gifts of wisdom and holiness that are inherited because we are made in God's image, and shared because we are in fellowship with Jesus Christ.
- Daring to speak God's name rescues hope even in the most cruel and hopeless environments.
  - There are times when truth must be trumpeted.
  - There are times when God's name must be spoken, not as a challenge to diversity but as a right.
  - There are times when speaking as a Christian creates anxiety, testing both our authenticity and perseverance.
  - There are times when pronouncing God's name is the greatest risk.
  - There are times when God's name on our lips is our only protection and solace.
  - There are times when God's name seems to change nothing, except that it is so holy that it always transforms something, particularly our hearts.
- Having a "thinking heart" changes everything.

When the Heart is the Vector

A "thinking heart" is more than a grammatical distinction. While mind probes reality for context, heart seeks relation. While mind learns and calculates, heart loves and plays. While mind critiques and judges, heart mourns and rejoices. In synthesis, we could say that the mind has the capacity for mastering parts and the heart for perceiving the whole.

Obviously, we need both, but when the mind dominates, it makes emotions factors and enablers of intelligence. When thinking instead serves the heart, we use facts without being automatically constrained by their limitation or pragmatism. The heart's predisposition for relation serves to weave us into the web of life, connecting us through intimacy and love, but also through identity to community and history, and through hope to the future. Thinking serves the heart, providing utility and understanding as basics for smart living, but also for aiming critical scrutiny at breaks or threats to the wholeness.

Other voices have critiqued managers' overdependence on IQ, with some now advocating "emotional intelligence" as the corrective.[9] There is important learning in this material that suggests aspects of richer human presence. What does not work for me is that the emphasis is reversed. Perhaps this was clever strategy for gaining credibility among a fact-based target group, but the inflection qualifies and gives precedence to "intelligence." This is too calculative, positioning the productivity of the heart (emotions) as an asset of the intellect (intelligence). A "thinking heart" puts data and knowledge to the service of that organ or capacity that connects and completes us. IQ is smart. EQ (emotional quotient) is smart about emotions. THQ (thinking heart quotient) is wisdom. Since as managers we are usually disproportionate in valuing brainpower, we must double or triple the priority of the heart to achieve equilibrium of perspective. Jesus modelled this reverse wisdom, giving precedence to healing, responding first with his heart to those blind, mangled, bleeding or excluded. Teaching followed: the understanding of the head in tow behind the compassion of the heart.

We cannot go from vision to action effectively, nor can we aspire to magnificence without hearts that think in God's time and in human terms.

PRIESTLY BALANCE SHEET FOR PROPORTION

Consecration: Work as Eucharistic Prayer	Compassion: Work from a "Thinking Heart"
Living spiritually in the relational life of the Trinity, invoking the "sign of the cross" •	• Living socially and within professional duties from the prerogatives of the "thinking heart"
Purifying intent through sincere recollection of past mistakes, "confessing" for forgiveness and for self-knowledge •	• Extending "mercy" to ourselves as well as others, filtering projects and priorities through criteria of human impacts
Venerating scripture as the Word of God, desiring its wisdom and inscribing its laws on the heart •	• Testing projects and assumptions with the moral rules that unleash dignity and justice
"Offering" the gifts of intellect and expertise to God, remaking desks and desktops into altars for praise •	• Witnessing the dignity of others, honouring contributions and creativity so as to mirror the Divine within them
"Consecrating" work, calling upon God's Spirit and willing human hearts to make holiness real and present •	• Demanding governance and strategies that treat human beings as a worthy end rather than only as a productive means
Praying the Lord's Prayer to make present the divine relationship and reciprocities that undo disproportion and extend "peace" •	• Daring to "hallow" God's name, to seek "God's will," and to settle for the right proportions of "daily bread"

Inviting others to "communion,"
including those with diverse beliefs
or expectations •

• Sharing fellowship in meetings, research and "contact points" through dialogue and celebration

"Blessing" the ongoing work, carrying grace forth into the world to make peace •

• Challenging facts of expertise from the unifying intelligence of the heart

Soul Needs for Proportion

Proportion is relational (involving an assessment of balance between parts), dynamic (requiring continuous adjustment to recalibrate for change) and foundational (serving as the basis for belonging and co-operation). The three needs of the soul that in this model best correspond to proportion-making are *fairness*, which is the claim for dignity from being one and all children of God; *risk*, which relates to the insuppressible creativity inherited because we are created in the Creator's image and likeness; and *security*, which reflects our inescapable dependence on God and interdependence within creation. Fairness is the experiential test for proportion. Risk is the skill for undoing disproportion or for creating the renewal that restores the health of broken systems, structures and persons. Security is the aim and outcome of proportion, the state for realizing both participation and belonging. Again, the three are important standing alone, but also in interconnection. Fairness – what in business we call "the level playing field" – is a basic prerequisite for risk and a defining characteristic for security. We know from research into innovation and creating minds that risk flourishes within the stability of friendship and support, and we know from markets that risk abounds when there is an opportunity for fair rewards. Like most things spiritual and social, security is not so much an asset as a continuous tension between renovation and conservation. Too much entrenched stability, as we have seen in communism, markets and church structures, destroys fairness and stifles risk. Too little stability, as we have seen with heavy-handed deregulation, creates disproportions, such as the Russian oil oligarchies.

Excesses Required for Fairness

The need for fairness is for more than rights; it is to have rights seen and responded to in practice. Fairness is the claim we make from our inalienable equality, and it is at the heart of all ethics, including the dignifying reciprocity encoded in the golden rule. Fairness is also one of the knives we use to cut right from wrong. Like other Jewish prophets before him, Jesus taught fairness measured by the situation of the most vulnerable, least appreciated, especially the poor, and those broken by suffering and condemned or imprisoned. We have become immune to its significance because of its easy familiarity, but the prayer Jesus taught – the Lord's Prayer – overflows with the radical hope and revolutionary expectations of practical fairness. "Our Father" identifies us as children, equal, free and utterly dependent. The priority from this familiarity with divine source is to stand within and serve the sacred will that is the foundation and meaning of creation. God's kingdom, which we both await and contribute to, involves heavenly proportions manifest on earth. This means speaking God's hallowed name, expecting fair portions of daily bread, and extending the forgiveness that has been extended to us in the life, mercy, joy and acceptance that are the root of our being (Matthew 6:9-14).

Importantly, the fairness exemplified in this prayer is animated by two asymmetries: from God we receive completely unmerited gifts of life, sustenance, familial relationship with the sacred and the healing mercy of forgiveness; and from each other we receive the respect of co-being children of God, which includes the restorative gift of human forgiveness. In this kingdom, fairness is not simply some utilitarian quid pro quo. Rather, it is a gift premised on giving and not necessarily receiving, a right extended in generosity and not necessarily reciprocity. Equanimity is enjoyed in the generosity, is available to all in the superfluity, and is fair to all in the indiscriminate extravagance of grace. We become disintegrated as souls (separated and fissured) and we experience lapses in integrity in business (with separated and fissured accountability) when we exempt ourselves from the asymmetrical giftedness of fairness.

In management, the key relational factor is merit, which is an important consideration for honour but not a complete substitute for what is fair. Companies, like individuals, are not self-sufficient or self-sustaining. Indeed, the licence to operate is a privilege composed of innumerable historical, societal and even moral investments in facilities and supports for fairness. Any economic activity that isolates itself from this framework of fairness eventually destabilizes the very environment and society upon which it depends for production, consumption and profits. Many of today's reforms in governance are aimed at re-equalizing outcomes so as to honour and reinforce the essential terms of moral fairness. Transparency is a tactic for fair access to information. Board independence and diversity are acknowledgments that boards have unfairly underrepresented entire segments of society. Corporate social responsibility, although often positioned as philanthropy, is a strategic investment in social, cultural or environmental assets that are often forgotten yet nevertheless essential to the equilibrium of the whole system.

From disproportion it is not possible to enact fairness simply by returning to some equalizing balance. In equity markets, analysts provide special briefings and customized research for large investors. Making these available to small investors as a result of being penalized for previous omissions will not in and of itself win integrity and assure fairness. The same is true in the mutual funds industry: eliminating after-trading exemptions that advantaged big clients and penalized individuals will not satisfy the criteria of equity. In both instances, efforts to restore credibility require not the averaging of access, but the shift in mean so as to serve the needs for fairness as defined by the least powerful and most neglected. As with any other capital, trust needs investment. And as with any other currency, social capital needs a payout, some overflow or profits, to escape entropy.

In global terms, there is growing attention to fair trade, a policy by which commodities, such as coffee, or manufactured goods assembled in extremely low-cost labour conditions, are priced at some premium to enable a minimal living wage. Developing countries are also striving, as they have done for more than a decade, to win the access to global markets that they were promised in return for their structural reforms. In most cases, tariffs in agriculture and other low-cost manufacturing goods have foiled this access, serving only to drive prices and wages lower. In this case, fair trade as a nominal tactic for aid hardly qualifies as equalizing or *equi-liberating*. Fairness, in its historical and moral sense, requires creating opportunities on a whole other order of magnitude, accommodating a long-term imbalance of trade favouring poor countries to compensate for the long-term imbalance in opportunity that has gone excessively the other way. By implication, fairness demands systemic re-fairness – extensive two-way change that deconstructs conditions, expectations and disproportions for us while trying to reconstruct balance through the "double and" of dignity and opportunity for others.

Simone Weil's priority for obligations is particularly relevant for fairness because structural disproportions cannot be rebalanced without some more-than-mutual contributions to the social capital. This has not been our pattern, but such aggressive generosity will be a critical competence as we begin to deal honestly with the fast-approaching constraints of sustainable development. In truth, sustainability actually requires "de-development," at least for the few of us who consume and pollute so disproportionately. More than new technology, we will need new priorities supported by new attitudes and substantiated by new actions. Such genuine sustainability, which is in effect "enduring proportion," will force all of us to take drastic risks, reimagining what we mean by security, redefining happiness and opportunity, creating new solutions for career, production and consumption as well as meaning. Fortunately, the soul is enlivened by risk. The twentieth-century philosopher Emmanuel Levinas believed that human beings finally develop identity and self-understanding in the encounter with the identities and freedom of others. In his typology we find authentic home in the risks of leaving home, discovering truth by risking familiar certitudes, realizing belonging by paradoxically risking the solitude of becoming the stranger.[10]

With a thinking heart we encounter unfairness not only through empathy, but also with analysis. For business people, this means we must learn to let ourselves feel, to encounter the moral moment in its sadness or hope, and then do the factual work to respond to that visceral truth. In remaking General Electric for the new millennium, CEO Jeffery Immelt has adopted "virtue" as one of the organization's critical leadership objectives. Neither the most ethical nor environmental of companies, GE, in the person of Immelt, has chosen corporate social responsibility as the linchpin for company renewal and for rehabilitating GE's reputation for integrity. There are practical motives for this dramatic change. Interviewed by *Fortune*, Immelt said, "Businesses today aren't admired. Size is not respected. There's a bigger gulf today between haves and have-nots than ever before. It's up to us to use our platform to be a good citizen. Because not only is it a nice thing to do, it's a business imperative."[11] The exercise that awakened this strategic insight is telling. Senior managers were charged to visit the countries and communities in which GE operates. They also met with other companies for advice on best practices. The breakthrough came from personal encounter and conversation, feeling as well as studying the situation.

Immelt and GE are not alone. Many other companies are assuming goals for social responsibility, which are in essence extracurricular exercises to undo unfairness and restore balance. Domenic D'Alessandro, the CEO of Manulife, goes even farther, stating that a key attribute of corporate integrity will be its "generosity."[12] It will take time to see whether these aspirations take root, but this corporate ambition for magnificence must be taken seriously for two other reasons. First, it is needed, which means that there is commercial opportunity in attending to environmental clean-up and social development. Second, it is a critical motivator for employees who desire jobs and stock options, but also, as Immelt points out, "want to work for a company that makes a difference, that's doing great things in the world."[13] Broadcasting moral purpose raises both serious expectations and serious questions. Aiming high for virtue will require managers to learn to dig deep into the reservoir of the soul: growing compassion as a validated probe of strategy; using hope as a yardstick of performance; blessing and confirming those risking the generosity to generate fairness; and creating communities for satisfying the needs of the soul at work and within business. It will also require utterly different questions to be raised in governance, research, planning and measuring. For a thinking heart to take root in corporate culture, thinking hearts will have to be planted: bringing poets, activists and theologians onto boards; interviewing those who usually do not matter to company goals; taking plans into the field to be validated by the human beings directly impacted; auditing compassion and its ROI.

FAIRNESS BALANCE SHEET

Fairness for the Soul	Fairness for Managers
The middle way between heaven and earth •	• The middle way between productivity and responsibility
Holding in the heart both the grief of the world and its hopes •	• Holding in the heart strengths and weaknesses, including for holiness
Participating within and contributing to a dignifying social harmony •	• Participating in and contributing to true economic sustainability
Corresponding the freedom and opportunity in the everyday with the inheritance for being one and all equal children of God •	• Corresponding risk, reward and merit not as an enclosed calibration but within our social, natural and moral interdependence
An ideal already savoured in Christ but not yet fully, finally realized in time •	• A smell test with unfairness serving as an early indicator for dysfunctions not yet exposed
Requiring "Jubilee:" a once-a-generation intervention to undo systemic disadvantages and liberate equal opportunity for all •	• Requiring "Program Jubilee:" an intervention in every project or program to expose unfairness and instill values for renewing integrity
Forgiveness and mercy experienced as divine gifts become modes of being with one another •	• Repentance goes beyond public relations to authentically create contrition and social responsibility

Reciprocity as the lopsided gift of Covenant with God, requiring our lopsided priority to serve those with the most need and least power •	• Reciprocity beyond terms of contract to contribute the magnificence that renews social capital and makes more elastic the skills for tolerance, forgiveness and risk-taking
Equilibrium to fuel "equi-liberation:" not the principle of freedom but its universal practice •	• Equilibrium as wealth creation with magnificence: extending worth by extending worthiness

Bets, Beliefs and the Rewards of Risk

By definition, all faith is a risk in that it defies fact-based empirical certitude. The mystical path of prayer marks this intrinsic risk as the passage through doubt of the "dark night of the soul." Bearing the cross of Christian discipleship, blessing the poor and suffering, walking the extra mile and turning the other cheek are not formulaic building blocks for holiness. Rather, these are the risks in whose freefall we experience both the abyss of surrender and the transformational power of God's love and grace. As exemplified by God's covenant with Israel, we do not come to God with an equal negotiating hand. We must risk our brokenness and isolation to the encounter and be uplifted by God's healing wholeness. While a contract stipulates reciprocity and mutual protections, a covenant promises a disproportionate imbalance with the powerful party ensuring the rights of the dependent. God gets much less from us as God's nation of peoples, church and believers than we do from having God in relationship. As our dignity and capacities for growth are derived from this enabling unfairness, we are charged to live a similarly lopsided beneficence in ethics and morals. In Levinas's framework, the very basis of our personal home is the welcome we extend to outsiders and strangers.[14] Covenant is God's taking a risk on us, the explicit invitation for friendship intruding decisively in the unfolding history of creation. Faith, which can only mean faith lived in practice, is, in turn and in response, the risk we take in God.

The soul is at home in God's creation and bears the imprint of God as Creator, so within spirituality, as in life itself, there is an essential drive for creativity. Whether it is in countless small ways of striving for improvement or in grand outpouring in art, the tendency towards magnificence is innate. Risk, as it is for business, is the currency for this creative growth. In his parable of the talents, Jesus tells of three servants who were entrusted with gifts (Matthew 25:15-25). Two took these and risked them as investments, but earned returns that doubled the value. Out of fear, the third simply buried the small treasure and later returned it diminished for being stained and dirty. We, too, have personal talents and the creative capacity to live richly our human life as an art. As souls we have particular gifts. We are rich also in the treasure of spiritual tradition, memory and wisdom. As professionals, we have additional talents of expertise, vision and imagination. Within our domain as business people we have a wealth of resources in information, in capacity and for investments. All of these blessings have the potential to earn compounding interest, provided we risk this treasure in pursuit of goodness and truth. This is what is so exciting about Amartya Sen's challenge to reimagine the measures of economic productivity. By gauging development in its true human dimensions of freedom, we elevate the scope of our economic talents and activity to serve growth in dignity, hope and opportunity as well as trade. We can always opt to do the minimum, as did the servant who buried his talents. Or we can bet our money and skills as grace towards a "double and" return.

Our caricature for creativity is of eccentricity, with the lone genius having a "Eureka!" moment. In his research on creating minds, Howard Gardner shows that it is neither so simple nor so romantic. There may indeed be disparity in talent or restlessness, but artists such as Picasso, Stravinsky and T.S. Eliot, and social innovators such as Gandhi, Freud and Einstein, were also surprisingly dependent on others for their creative productivity. Creating minds share three characteristics. First, they work very, very hard to master their craft and break through its conventions. Second, they do not stand still even in the glow of success that has been difficult to achieve. Third, they function within a caring cadre of friends, colleagues and benefactors. This community is essential to incubate ideas. It is also a resource for withstanding the winds of public or critical rejection. By its support and convictions, the group also sustains the integrity of the artist during the vulnerabilities and failures of risk-taking.[15] One talent can revolutionize our models for beauty or justice, but this one talent is usually rooted in a sustaining community of friends and believers. In theology, this coming together to share, bless one another and raise offerings of gifts is the basis of Eucharist. Private prayer is essential for mastery, but to use Gardner's topography, we can really only take the risks of remaking ourselves, and only take the risks for magnificence, when we draw nutrients from the rich ground of communion.

- Jesus risked breaking the law to heal the man with the withered hand on the Sabbath. We, too, must risk surpassing the laws for corporate governance or regulatory compliance to serve what is right.
- Jesus risked calling simple fishermen to be disciples. We, too, must risk acts of discipleship within our work or profession.
- Jesus risked the ingratitude of the ten whom he cured of leprosy. We, too, must risk doing what is needed, knowing that it may go completely unappreciated.
- Jesus risked acting in faith across the deep divide of cultural differences. We, too, must risk speaking truthfully to others, respecting diversity enough to relish it as a right and extend it as a responsibility.
- Jesus risked the enmity of the religious authorities by ministering to the sinful and impure. We, too, must risk unorthodoxy by pointing out what is holy and possible to those enmeshed in the competitive-aggressive reality of commerce.
- Jesus risked forgiveness. We, too, must risk forgiving, including of our own lapses and failures, the hyper-acquisitiveness of society, the moral forgetfulness of business, the arrogance of leaders and the reduction of human values to economic value.
- Jesus risked kenosis – the complete self-emptying of self to serve others and receive God. We, too, must risk self-emptying, shedding those priorities or distractions that fail to satisfy the soul's need for God.

BALANCE SHEET FOR RISK

What the Soul Needs to Risk	What Managers Need to Risk
Seeking: Risking the journey of the soul to find ecstasy from what Martin Buber calls "entering into God"[16] •	*Scanning*: Reviewing the horizons of opportunity and risk to set goals for performance with presence
Trusting: Risking that faith matters in the everyday by making space for the efficacy of grace •	*Investing*: Deploying capital in all its forms to risk outcomes that lift freedom as well as profits
Hoping: Risking to see signs of God's wonder latent in daily reality •	*Planning*: Imagining "double and" benefits that risk going beyond the simple offers that fuel addiction
Mourning: Risking the availability of the heart to grieve for what is wrong in "solidarity" with the suffering •	*Accounting*: Measuring moral consequences that risk repentance as well as renewal
Belonging: Risking Eucharistic inclusiveness to welcome the stranger and thereby find our own home •	*Connecting*: Rooting operations in the community to risk interdependence
Remembering: Risking to stand in the lessons of tradition to frame current reality and "invite" wisdom •	*Disclosing*: Auditing with transparency and honesty deliverables of both worth and worthiness
Honouring: Risking the creativity of the talents received from God to offer our magnificence as praise •	*Rewarding*: Aligning compensation and promotion to those who risk the double productivity of quality and beauty

Giving: Risking our talents and skills to read and serve the "signs of the times" •

• *Giving back*: Going beyond corporate social responsibility to risk integrating responsibility for society's needs

Proportions of Security

One of the follies of a reduced anthropology is that we also accept a reduced notion of what constitutes human happiness. Many of today's most intractable problems result from having reduced happiness to a simplistic hedonism of things and experiences. Whether as individuals or as managers, rarely do we have ambitions or take risks for liberation, beauty or wisdom, settling instead for getting more of the success, status or possessions that we imagine as security. This premise of human fulfillment as a lifestyle in effect reverses the corrective imbalance of covenant. Instead of disproportionate fealty from our dependence on God and creation, we operate with disproportionate entitlement towards what we want for ourselves. The now-accepted profligacy from this reversed covenant threatens environmental sustainability and global security. Not only that, the normalizing of obsession also destroys personal security. Some of our children and many adults suffer from bulimia. More and more of our children and adults suffer from obesity. Either extreme represents the insatiability in which we are becoming consumed rather than satisfied by our consumption. Rather than release the beauty of the soul, we opt for ever more radical cosmetic surgery. This is literally a self-annihilating incarnation, a melting away or disfigurement of presence. Individuals suffer a social ailment: a thin view of freedom that insists only on choice, and thin expectation of happiness determined only by gratification.

This upward creep in accumulation and downward spiral in satisfaction are in many ways a bigger threat than terrorism. In the name of self, we enact creative self-destruction. In the pursuit of this one-dimensional happiness, we become immune to the great disparities created in the global economy. Lately, even the structures of power, such as the Davos Economic Forum, have turned their attention to fighting global poverty. Perhaps more by default than by conversion, these groups are recognizing that the security so coveted by investors and managers utterly depends on a much wider experience of fairness, hope and participation. Such altruism from self-interest may not be enough. Markets, by their nature, cause instability through the ceaseless pursuit of innovation, advantage and efficiency. This churning renewal, when unmoderated, becomes self-destructive. Robert Heilbroner points out that none of the major economists who have contributed to the current paradigm believed that free markets would survive. Their view was that either for reasons of greed (Adam Smith and Joseph Shumpeter), limitation (John Kenneth Galbraith) or prosperity (John Maynard Keynes), disproportion would prevail to the point of destructive disorder.[17] This specialist insight in fact echoes Mosaic Law, which recognizes that society's structures turn rigid and personal hearts turn hard when we assign absolute value to any object or system other than God.

Ominous warnings from economists and prophets have not prevented managers from sliding into the faulty assumptions that seem to be accelerating disproportion and destruction. In a provocative article on 21st-century management, professors Sumantra Ghoshal, Christopher A. Bartlett and Peter Moran argue that executives have increasingly confused the true nature of their vocation. Their point is that while companies operate in the market, they are not mini-markets unto themselves. Quite the opposite: companies succeed by forging pockets of stability and security that create predictable value within the market's forces of disruption. As a result of mistaking responsiveness to markets for being taken over by them, managers have made the share price the disproportionate determinant of success. These authors argue that companies have therefore "become victims of the market straightjacket, unable to create the conditions required to enhance 'the level or speed of performance' because of their total focus on fully utilizing their resources and relationships to whatever advantage the market dictated to be best."[18]

Companies are like boats floating on the rough seas of markets. You have to always be aware of the water, but the expertise for boat-building and boat-captaining are in fact aimed at holding the water out, finding new ways to cut through it and go faster, improving systems and techniques for weathering its storms. To base company direction and performance primarily on market criteria overburdens displacement and bails water directly into the boat. The more this water gets in, the heavier and less manoeuverable the boat becomes until – like Westinghouse, in the example cited by the authors – it finally sinks. Markets do not have vision, nor are they guided by principles of fairness or long-term sustainability. The business of business is to create anti-markets, striving for the predictability and security that allows risks to be translated into a complex of sustaining value, including fair return for shareholders, fair benefit for society, and fair opportunity for employees. "When its people act alone, and only in their own interest," the professors caution, "the company loses its very essence as an institution of modern society – the essence of what distinguishes it from a market and endows it with the ability to create value in ways the market cannot."[19]

Security is a need of the soul for providing the dignity of place that comes only from predictability. This is why we need communities for prayer, memory and hope. Security is also a basic need for companies, providing the stability of a level playing field from which to imagine investment opportunities and secure advantage with some probability of a return. This, too, is why we need healthy, vibrant, sustainable communities. For both the soul and companies, security is the foundation for taking risks towards growth and self-realization. Without security we have little freedom, either as individuals or as markets. Security is a synonym for fairness and balance. It is also a test for integrity in that our true personal character is revealed by the justness of our decisions and actions. Although fairness, risk and security all imply some harmony that balances investment and reward, the achievement of each need depends on something more than literal reciprocity. As modelled in the covenant, we achieve a working equilibrium through a disproportionate dependence that invites, and thrives with, self-sacrificing generosity. As Jesus taught, from those who have much, much will be expected.

SECURITY BALANCE SHEET

Covenant for the Soul	**Managers of the Covenant**
Situated within a network of belonging for carrying God's imprint, receiving God's gifts and flowering in God's mercy •	• Situated within a network of fair systems and supporting infrastructures that enable the creative risks for innovation and return
Predictability from the overarching and eternal claims of justice, to expect and inspire right choices •	• Predictability from justice applied as the criterion for adapting to continuous change
As the foundation for hope, standing on the ineffable mystery of divine access and intimacy •	• As the foundation for risk taking, expecting not a guarantee, but the reasonable probability that the right outcome will be realized
Trusting relationships that support the exercise of our personal freedom and creative growth •	• Trusting relationships that accelerate problem solving, enhance creativity and add meaning to results
Unleashing the eternal and the infinite within the everyday: opening to worship, gratitude, remembrance, and petition, and basking in the embrace of God's love •	• Unleashing the long-term within the short-term: creating the learning community and relevant productivity that realizes what Arie de Geus calls "the living company"[20]
The resource for moving through the inevitable experiences of doubt, disintegration and dark nights •	• The confidence to persist with difficult strategies and credibility to recover from inevitable setbacks

God's surprising loyalty to us, given as calling, forgiveness and talents to invest in creation •	• The moral and productive consistency that earns loyalty among workers, customers, investors and stakeholders
Revelling in grace, illumined by the Spirit, awakened to brimming emptiness in contemplation •	• Revelling in the problems and messiness of everyday work as the opportunities to heal and make whole what is broken and of risk to all

Knowing When to Stop

In a recent lecture at Newman Centre in Toronto, Rabbi Dow Marmur observed that as a culture of consumers and believers, "we have lost the capacity to know when to stop." Limits are at the heart of morality, defining our dependence and marking our ethics. Not knowing when to stop describes the "tragedy of the commons." It is the missing restraint that depletes fisheries, clear-cuts forests and rejects even the modicum limits on greenhouse gases prescribed by Kyoto. Not knowing when to stop is the cause of our fatigue and stress. It is the endless ambition that feeds the bottomless emptiness of our many addictions. Not knowing when to stop leads to corporate fraud and corruption. It is the blank cheque that executives use to overpay themselves. Not knowing when to stop is the ailment that corporate governance renewal is trying to address. It is why those of us who have so much increasingly think that everyone should be personally responsible for their own health and security. Not knowing when to stop gives 24/7 priority to the economy. It is why we have surrendered virtually without complaint the Sabbath rest that liberates and renews wholeness and holiness.

Perhaps our toughest question as a society and as individuals is this: What would it take to stop? The very few systems for dealing effectively with addiction have two basic requirements: first, an honest acknowledgment of the truth – what in the therapeutic vernacular is called "owning" – and, second, the not-very-scientific or quantifiable reliance on a "higher power." To unleash this wisdom in companies, we need priestly managers. Admitting to a problem is obviously a precondition for solving it. This is very hard to do, because it involves speaking the truth. As Kraft and McDonald's have come to realize, there are consequences for fast, fatty foods that implicate the manufacturer and marketer in the illness or addiction of the consumer.

To effectively own these larger responsibilities within companies requires not only the prophetic whistle-blowing to call attention to the liability, but also priestly ministry of the word, "preaching" to focus innovations and processes on effective remediation. So, too, the reliance on the "higher power" requires signs and symbols to make Divine Presence palpable and urgent. This again is a priestly function. Jim Collins stresses humility as a critical virtue of great company leadership.[21] The priestly manager genuflects to the relationship that the soul most needs. If God is not the first priority, if love of God is not the ordering principle for the heart, our innate excessiveness gets misplaced into disproportions that qualify as both idolatry and addiction. Thus, the simple way to know when to stop is to know what matters most: seeing God in all things; recognizing magnificence in all possibilities.

8

PRACTICE

Details of Devotion

Receive this work as offering

Guide this effort as prayer

Awaken these questions with consequence

Shape these decisions with care

Receive our talents for the greater good

Open our hearts to hear other voices

Draw us to the grace within expertise

Keep us constant seeking wiser choices

Amen

Organizations and souls often flounder during implementation. Whether we are promising to improve customer service or deepen the personal spiritual practice of contemplation, we seem to be forever starting over on that same frustrating treadmill that we get on every year to meet our New Year's resolutions. Doing the details that deliver excellence, as with doing the details that enliven and realize devotion, requires an exercise of power. This is why we need kingly expertise: to bring to bear the full majesty, authority and nobility of human potential, to translate our innate dignity due to our being in the image and likeness of God into lives of honour and grandeur. Many models have been advocated for business leadership, invoking everyone from Gandhi and Winnie-the-Pooh to coach Don Shula and Attila the Hun. Kingship operates on another level entirely. While leaders stand on top of an organization, kingship stands at a nexus of boundaries that serve identity and purpose as well as administration. Through symbolism, the kingly role links the present with the past, summoning memory to help shape the future, and connecting individual achievements to the common good. The good of the realm means defending what is most precious while also investing in what is most worth sustaining. As an embodiment of the values and aspirations of the community, the kingly leader also sets boundaries for what is proper and of priority, conferring the balance between the rights of the individual and the obligations to a larger realm that sustain order. The kingly ruler adjudicates, as the highest power for marking the boundary not only for what is lawful, but also for what is right. Such potency needs to be faced and defined – a privilege within obligation – resulting from standing on the metaphysical boundary between heaven and earth.

To be children of God is to be princesses and princes: not feel-good equals but co-anointed co-inheritors of inestimable power and potential. Despots are not kings, which is why God initially resisted Israel's petition for a monarch. As the chosen people of God, the ancient Israelites already had a defining allegiance to a majestic, merciful ruler. Their enslavement in Egypt had already provided firsthand experience of the injustice of and abuse by those wearing crowns for their own human pleasure and profit. Even with the dignity and equality enshrined in the law, the people of Israel longed for the status and identity that come from having their own king among nations. God relented, showing again a love and respect for human freedom. In very short order, though, the Israelites' kings reverted to the tyrannies of power and ambition. Saul stopped listening to the wisdom of prophets and succumbed to hubris. David slipped into idolatry for the love of a woman. Solomon, whose reputation for being wise turns out to be millennia-old spin, squandered the nation's treasure and imposed servitude on his free people to build grand royal structures. Israel's anointed rulers did model worthy aspects of kingship: the warrior fierce and resolute in moral causes; the poet who conjures symbols and frames meaning; and the builder who creates the infrastructure for work and worship. But the prototype was incomplete and finally only fully defined by Jesus Christ.

With the inscription "King of the Jews" nailed to his cross, Jesus exemplifies power emptied out to liberate others from suffering and enslavement, fashioning that most radical realm that makes space for even the least powerful. Power is necessary and yet corrupts; it is an inescapable birthright and yet deludes even responsible kings unless it is made holy in the self-consuming service of others. The perspective that comes from prophetic imagination alternates between grief over human suffering and awe towards the possibilities of our divine calling. Proportionality and justice involve a similar juxtaposition between priestly compassion for those in need, and the hopeful view that consecrates everyday things to reveal the sacred. Getting on with it – implementing kingly change and administration – involves another shifting, this time between the practical short-term needs of the realm and the long-term investments in unity, confidence and beauty. Like David, kingly leaders dance before the Tabernacle, celebrating human achievement in the streets of community and in the presence of the Divine. Like Christ, kingly servants outstretch their arms to bring all peoples into the embrace of dignity, hope and love. To summarize: the prophetic incites what can be, what must be. The priestly agitates the interior capacities to change. The kingly uses drive, determination and power to excite the realization of what honours the realm and dignifies the individual.

Power is grace. We still call those who abuse their power "disgraced" for being distanced from grace, for dishonouring and distorting it. A deceptive reversal in our society (and within our companies) is that we worship power as the highest fulfillment of our personal individuality, while increasingly adopting a morality based on powerlessness. In business we have the authority from our expertise and station, but remain passive about what depreciates humanity, even our own. Good people who do not blow whistles accept impropriety as proof that they have no choice. As theologian Walter Wink observes, such powerlessness has the discomfiting outcome of letting everyone off the hook, and the disgracing result of actually hooking us all.[1] The task for the kingly within every one of us is to own and not deny our power as God-made and God-sharing. More than therapeutic self-esteem, kingship elevates human dignity to both its potency and obligations, to live and work in the glory of our innate nobility. The soul is already magnificent, so powerful that Jesus said an iota of faith could make mountains of difference. This inherent splendour, if denied or abused, can equally make mountains of evil. The needs of the soul reflect our blue blood, and those that align to kingship help us stand humbly in the glory.

As we all have this royal power, we all have stark choices about where to invest our fealty and allegiance. In his Spiritual Exercises, St. Ignatius explained this as the choice of which "standard" to follow: that of the light of Jesus Christ, or the opposite one of annihilating darkness. With so much at stake, the first kingly need is always to make power accountable, corresponding to the soul's need for *obedience*. The second need of this potency must be to make power enabling, corresponding to the soul's need for *liberty*. The third must be to make power integral and integrating, corresponding to the soul's need for *truth*. Obedience places power within its obligations, honouring ancient moral laws and working out their meaning and relevance in the unique challenges and unknowns of our own situation. Liberty simultaneously exercises and shares power, deriving dignity from God's gift of free choice, and realizing its zenith only when those deemed by politics or economics as powerless are helped to be free. Truth enflames power as its authority and aim, forming the bonds and motivations for bringing words to life as deeds. Those in kingly roles obey to be the models of moral fealty and to discipline power with its true divine purpose. As agents for glory, kingly rulers empower and enable individuals towards free choices for their personal destiny and holiness. In its respect for the word, kingliness diffuses relativity and the cult of individuality, counters the disintegration from spin, and interrupts the exclusions from absolutism.

What does this kingship mean in business? As followers of Christ, we continue the incarnation, embodying the royalty won for us by his death and resurrection. The actual chore of discipleship is kingdom building, making our work and practices on earth a holy prequel for eternal life with God.

- Kingly managers not only set governance, they also embody it, modelling in highly visible ways their obedience to ethical norms and obligations beyond the rules.
- Kingly managers construct living structures for ethical discernment, going beyond facile programs for compliance to embed and reward moral decision making throughout the organization.
- Kingly managers symbolize accountability, owning consequences, disclosing privileges, and sharing in the sacrifices caused by cost-cutting or poor performance.
- Kingly managers not only delegate authority, they also liberate staff to apply talents and make decisions to the best of their abilities.
- Kingly managers free up the time for the organization to think, creating efficiencies that have the flexibility for experimentation, dreaming and Sabbath.
- Kingly managers observe not only unintended consequences, but also unintended enslavements, correcting imbalances and protecting the equity of even the lowest-level employees.
- Kingly managers design products and services that go beyond convenience and actually free the time or enliven the creativity of customers. Here too they keep a watch on unintended enslavements, such as addictive product usage or dependencies on image and acceptance.
- Kingly managers have the authority and conviction to speak the truth. Not spin. Not legalese. The truth that sets people free is the truth spoken by royalty (even when it is our truth setting free our liberty!).

Practice Makes Perfect

Practice involves the hard work and creative persistence to finally make those possibilities real. For as long as companies have sought to improve performance or excellence, managers have undertaken methodic approaches to practice. We benchmark "best practices." And we re-engineer "processes," which are practices set in sequence. Since ordering and controlling practices are at the heart of the manager's job description, we should expect a startling impression of enhancement from all the programs of continuous improvement. Of course, we have not. Such inconsistency between aim and outcome is more than an organizational dilemma. It is more profoundly a human one. The executive mantra for "walking the talk" is simply business buzz-speak for the more ancient proverb to "practice what we preach." Operationally and morally, what we know to do and what we end up doing all too often misalign, resulting in sin instead of synergy. As managers, we have come to accept that the antidote to "continuous change" is "continuous improvement." This trying to be incrementally better forgets altogether that we are already magnificent. Unlike kings, we settle for less, substituting efficiency or productivity for what could be of historic worth and grandeur. A low bar is also characteristic of much of our spirituality. We shop around for wisdom just as we assemble best practices, only to find that without steadfastness and commitment, even the great truths of the great religions become the nothing more than the flavour of the month.

It takes practice to perfect kingship. Never easy to achieve, practice has become more elusive because we have shortchanged the aim while also diminishing the object. We no longer really believe that perfection is possible, which means we no longer subscribe to the perfectibility of the human being. This is why magnificence, which is our natural state, feels so alien and idealistic. Kingliness reminds us that magnificence is inherited and innate. To be less so is to be less than who we are already. Rather than studying more case examples of what other companies have done, we need to practise our own perfecting acts, aspiring to be the Mozarts of management. Rather than spirituality per se, we need spiritual practice as the serious vocation of the soul, unbounded to allow us to contribute with big imagination and hopeful plans to humanity's moral and economic perfection. That is why this is the work of kings: only the intermediaries between heaven and earth can presume such ambitions; only kingly power can commission such eternal art-making; only kingly bloodlines would accept so noble an inheritance and burden.

That I glimpse Your glory

Inspires fear and hope

That I flounder in Your mystery

Arouses apprehension and awe

That I grasp so little

Conjures hungry doubt and thirsty faith

That Your choosing me precedes my choosing You

Anoints my confidence

That Your mercy overflows Your judgment

Assures my trepidation

That Your call echoes in my heart

Awakens my talents

Infinite God

If everything is possible in Your flow

Then everything is possible when I clasp You

Please keep me close, then

Even when I do not know

How to be so

Amen. With love.

Our business version of leadership is devoid of royal glory. The magnificence bar is so low that in a special issue dedicated to "the mind of the leader," the *Harvard Business Review* (*HBR*) did not publish a single article about ethics or morality.[2] Other than generic references to "outstanding human qualities" and infrequent axioms about "keeping ethical values front and center," the issue was embarrassingly thin on the very topic of integrity that so challenges governance, undermines investor and employee confidence, and directly affects performance. Even the "five components of emotional intelligence at work" that *HBR* calls "the *sine qua non* of leadership" fail to define or unfold any of the dimensions of moral sensibility, which presumably should have some role in crucial moments or decisions. Our most august business publication, exploring the most essential practices of managerial leadership, misses the mark by focusing on competence without acknowledging the consciousness.

In his book *The Trinity and the Kingdom*, Jürgen Moltmann disparages the reduction of Christian discipleship to ritual or ethical practices. More even than the response to a motivation or aim, practice needs to be the very means by which we live within truth and hope. This is practice not for competence but for caring, not for checks and balances against impropriety but for the expansive possibilities from communion. Like Ignatius, Moltmann envisions practice as the substantive interplay between contemplative reflection and responsible action. The radical variable for mastery of any practice turns out to be time: time to absorb, integrate, mutate, rest and, as with the Sabbath, exercise freedom, creativity, receivement and relationship. Integrity resides in the wholeness that comes from the interior deepening that inspires and takes responsibility for exterior doing.

Expertise or virtue is only a by-product of practice. The true value, as Moltmann reminds us, is the experience of God. We practise worship for the experience of awe, gratitude for the experience of gift, prayer for the experience of conversation, offering for the experience of sharing love, adoration for the experience of inadequacy before mystery, petitions for the experience of intimate access, and silence for the experience of utter unspeakability. As with covenant, there is an unimaginable asymmetry in this encounter. We can never be little more than a little less stupid about God, yet despite this disparity, this one-sided relationship unleashes a type of reciprocal dependence. God is all-powerful, and the power bequeathed to us is the freedom to practise the meaning and claims of this lopsided meeting. Going to action from this experience means that we practise with "God behind" us and "the world in front." With choice, commitment and risk we practice "in the domain of open potentialities," personally shaping the future by "which of these potentialities" we "realize" or "reject."[3] On this scale, practice becomes kingly work, anointed by God, and noble as the glory-making "movement from potentiality to reality." That we chose and realize this movement through our own effort is what it means to perfect through practice.

Practice makes perfect because practice encounters Perfection

Practice makes perfect because it unleashes what we have been bequeathed

Practice makes perfect because this is what Duke Ellington proves

Practice makes perfect because the soul's imprint already is

Practice makes perfect because this is the way of wisdom

Practice makes perfect because we stand on the perfecting practice of others

Practice makes perfect because it invests the talents entrusted to us

Practice makes perfect because perfect mercy forgives in advance

Practice makes perfect because perfectibility is already ours in Christ

Practice makes perfect because this already potential is not yet there

Amen

Again the question: How does this relate to our work as managers? Of course we need to improve processes and efficiency. Of course we need to practise disciplines for innovation and excellence. The charge from the soul is to hold these projects and hopes as means, not ends, as serving human freedom, not exhausting it, as realizing possibilities for relationship, not simply expertise. Expressions of strategy need to go beyond demarcating what we must do to succeed to also resonate with who we can become as integrated and integral human beings. Programs of process renewal need to go beyond improving efficiency and outcomes to also improve the conditions for integrative reflective action that strengthens relationships and belonging. Human resource supports need to go beyond training or self-improvement to enable self-understanding and genuinely empower self-becoming. As much as we drive to learn new things and master new skills, we need to go beyond expertise to also develop the expertise for togetherness. This is not to suggest that the undertaking and disciplines of practicality are not important, but to realize again that these are not enough. Just as prophetic perspective and priestly proportion are incomplete as a bottom line and fuller, richer and more truth-revealing as a balance sheet, so too is practice.

THE PRACTICE BALANCE SHEET

What To Do (Thin)	Who To Be (Thick)
Aiming for improvement •	• Aiming for human perfectibility
Focusing on growing competence •	• Focusing on realizing relationship
Breaking down increments of process •	• Strengthening nodes of network
Calibrating dynamics of expertise •	• Engendering creativity
Striving to minimize defects •	• Striving to minimize dehumanization
Working towards efficiency and productivity •	• Working towards integrity and sustainability
Growing proficiency •	• Realizing potential
Exercising continuous learning •	• Alternating contemplation with action
Mastering the complexities of change •	• Living the consistency of conversion
Reaching targets •	• Contributing magnificence

Business aims for advantage and is motivated by self-interest. The soul aims for unity and is motivated by love. As irreconcilable as these forces seem, they are paradoxically interdependent. We suffer terrible consequences when, by our practice, we keep them apart, or assume them to be forever in conflict. A painting never ceases to belong to the artist, yet its value as art and meaning as beauty rests in the experience and humanity of those who view it. Kings commission art for this very reason, to highlight the practical excellence of artisans and to create the social bridge by which the glory of the realm is refracted and made relevant to every person. Self does not dissolve, but instead experiences the transcendence from belonging. So, too, self-interest does not end, but instead realizes its sustainability from within the hard truths of limitation and the glorious potential of interdependence.

Kingly Inheritance

Borrowing Plato's distinction, leaders leverage expertise while kingliness personifies wisdom. We need both. Of course, the distinction between leadership and kingship is less about the person holding that role than about our relationship to him or her. We follow leaders because of delegation; we follow the kingly because of duty. With delegation, power is parcelled out in tightly constrained increments to enable those with responsibility to discharge their accountability. With duty, power flows as honour, dignifying every task with the pride of place that fulfills the terms of trust. Leaders engage and reward expertise, with the consequence of usually undervaluing or making disposable our personal humanity. The kingly use of expertise makes the magnificent visible as a concrete expression of our human power and glory. Plato's philosopher king exercises wisdom in four broad roles: finding truth and creating its twin, beauty; distinguishing what is enduring from what is transitory to reveal meaning; practising justice, making the broken whole; and synthesizing, making a realm out of parts by unifying personal needs and expertise with common purpose and ideals. From the perspective of myth explored by Carl Jung, kingliness is also the archetype of great power, the human offspring of divine coupling. Like the religious memory of being created in God's image and likeness, Jung's archetype simultaneously projects kingship as an external, eternal otherness, as well as an internal, infinite fulfillment of self. The royal symbol for wholeness stirs and strengthens the interior integration of the person.

These trajectories are evident in Jesus, who practises kingship to the perfection of transforming it. After a prolonged time of prayer in the wilderness, Jesus comes forth to serve in ways that would eventually be perceived as messianic. Early in Luke's gospel we are given a four-part job description for this reign: bringing good news to the poor, letting

captives go free, giving sight to the blind, and liberating the oppressed (Luke 4:16-19).
- Good news is truth revealed.
- Freeing of captives breaks down systems or addictions of enslavement.
- Sight involves the capacity to apprehend truth.
- Liberation for the oppressed fulfills the all-enfolding criteria of justice.

These principles were already definitional to kingship. Luke, in fact, is intentionally echoing the more ancient law of Jubilee by which kings intervened to cancel debts, free slaves and recalibrate with justice the social relations within society. By professing to fulfill this prophetic text, Jesus claims the prerogatives of kingship, embodying a royalty that did not depend on the temporal understanding of noble lineage. He is the prototype, however, not for perfecting the existing model, but for radically restoring the practice of kingship to its origin and essence as a constitutive aspect of our human creation.

Kingship by and through Jesus is *kenotic* – the Greek term explained earlier as pointing to "self-emptying." One of the hymns the earliest Christians prayed to make meaning of their experience of Christ's death and resurrection is embedded in St. Paul's letter to the Philippians. The poetic structure is in "V" form: the descent into suffering and ignominy with Jesus confronting as victim the violence of evil; the nadir moment of annihilation emptied of power with self-emptying love; and the ascent mysteriously mutated through the Spirit of God into crowning dignity, power and glory. More than a corrective for the ego pleasures of privilege, the self-emptying love of *kenosis* exposes the ultimate powerlessness of brutal hatred and domination. We know violence is wrong: Jesus' loving kingship renders it and its masters impotent. We bend our knee in awe and veneration, yet also in examination of conscience, for the ascent to glory qualifies the king in the role of judge. Purified and illumined, the king's authority is over right and wrong, setting criteria for good and the consequences for evil.

The reality of moral accounting, particularly having to assume responsibility for sin, turns out to have a salubrious effect on economic performance. Poring over hard data from 59 countries, two Harvard scholars have begun to bring to light the quantitative proof for contributions to economic development from religion. This is a 21st-century update of Max Weber's original thesis about the role of Protestantism in advancing capitalism. The perspective from Robert J. Barro and Rachel M. McCleary "is that religion affects economic outcomes mainly by fostering beliefs that influence individual traits such as honesty, work ethic, thrift and openness to strangers."[4] Too much dogmatic religion has the opposite effect of actually stunting the economy, but it seems that belief "in an afterlife – especially hell" stimulates growth. Hell is as much a mystery as heaven, and for all the associations with Dante's *Inferno* in pop culture, theological understanding is pretty thin. If hell is such that – as Jesus said to Judas – "it would be better not to have been born," then we can assume at the very least that it is a state devoid of hope for being conscious yet deprived of the presence of God. In Catholic theology, there is no certainty that any being is in hell, or that anyone can be judged as forever damned because the mystery of God's mercy is as unfathomable as God's judgment. Whatever the theological expectation, the insight from Barro and McCleary is that morality from our religious consciousness – what in this context are the needs of the soul – matters. The needs of the soul provide an essential underpinning for economic development and sustainability over time, especially when we operate with a consciousness for others and with conscience for the consequences of our actions.[5]

Majesty in the Details of Practice

From art, business and saints we know in general terms the practices for mastery. It is already hard to do a good job, to achieve outcomes that are above average. With passion added to effort, we move up the scale of achievement towards excellence. One precept of practice is that adherence to demanding discipline is the springboard for freedom: the tighter and more rigorous the parameters of practice, the more liberated we are for experimentation and improvisation. Today's excellence usually stands on the wisdom and craft skills of generations before us. Part of the gift of practice is that it situates us in the larger continuity of creation – to the past through memory and imitation; to the present through benchmarking and learning from best practices; and to the future as the inspiration and aspiration for what we can bequeath.

As with any creativity, the effort for magnificence involves sacrifice and yet is also a gift, something very taxing that is also easy for being completely natural.

Our Puzzle

Who art in our hearts

Many be Your names

Your kingdom come in our boardrooms

Your will be done in our workplaces

In our companies

As in the global economy

Give us this day our daily cashflow

Forgive us our transposing priorities

As we forgive those who piss us off

And lead us not into the next Enron

But deliver us from the rigidity of bottom lines

For Yours is the wisdom, the flower and the story

Now and after the closing bell

Amen

Embodying Obedience

Religious experience is predicated on obedience: to yogic practice in the Upanishads; to the Eightfold path in Buddhism; to the Mosaic Law in the Hebrew scriptures; to the claims of the cross in Christianity; to submission in Islam. Obedience was the one condition that God placed on Adam and Eve, and the implication of violating this command was estrangement. Practising obedience is practising relationship. Mystics teach that love and obedience are interchangeable: we can only be genuine in loving by attending to the priority of the one we love. Freedom, too, rests on this willingness to obey the claims of others, to subject personal desire to the ideals that only by our willing adherence create the reciprocal conditions for liberty. For Israel in its sojourn out of slavery, this relationship with freedom and divine love came to fruition in the embrace of the covenant of the Ten Commandments. These were the ordering rules for living in creation, for living in the image and likeness of God, for living in recognition of this image and likeness in others. As a rabbi ministering and teaching, Jesus did not want to abolish this framework of obedience, but to fulfill it by renewing adherence through the expansive and transcendent priority of love (Matthew 5:17). We obey the commandments of giving precedence to God and making holy the Sabbath because we experience and return divine love. We obey the commandments to respect life, property and truth, not because we have to, or because of reciprocity, but because love compels this honouring. St. Teresa of Avila wrote, "The important thing is not to think much, but to love much; do, then, whatever arouses you to love."[6]

Although business thrives in free markets, the reality again hinges on obedience. On a macro level, this submission is to the invisible hand. For companies and managers, the parameters for what is permissible and what is not are designed in a dynamic involving competitive pressures, regulatory structures, public disclosure, social acceptability and fiduciary responsibility. The everyday activity of business – completing projects, fulfilling job descriptions and doing the concrete work of meeting the contract – sets conditions that require obedience to some standard or norm. Our challenge as managers involves two sets of problems. The first is functional compliance. Market pressures, personal foibles and process shortcomings combine to make it all too easy to slip from towing the line to crossing it. The pace of change and exponential spread of information only puts more grease on ground that is already treacherous. Like society, business usually operates within a not quite stable balance between sound practice on one hand and ethical grey areas on the other. Reality is forever entangled but workable, until scandals become so pervasive or infractions so outrageous that the integrity of the system is itself put at risk. Reforms that respond to destabilizing disobedience usually rush to rebuild credibility by imposing stricter compliance. This is necessary, but far too thin an assurance. As its true responsibility, the exercise of governance is to secure the long-term health of the organization by operating to principles that obey the norms that contribute to the health of the system and society. While business operations focus on competition, governance is responsible for living up to the demands of interdependence.

We know from history that obedience at the point of a sword is hardly sustainable. Research shows that the majority of companies that adopt ethics policies in response to crisis are likely to succumb to repeat offence. Just as with addiction, the solution is not in rigid regimens curtailing damaging behaviour, but in undoing the tight grip of underlying motives, needs and brokenness. This level of obedience does not circumscribe propriety as a must-do list but frees it, realizing healing integrity as the outcome of integrating the beliefs, values and actions that define our being and personality. As happens with the soul, this deeper submission is for the sake of relationship, to the presence of others with whom we share creation and to the Presence that is Source and salvation. This is kingly obedience, owed to the sovereign in gratitude and for the good and glory of the realm. This is also the obedience that earns authority by submitting privilege to personally follow and therefore uphold the moral law. When we obey, we make space for others, make room to accommodate needs or differences that seem not to be our own, yet, like the golden rule, secure the enabling empowerment of respectful reciprocity. Always the choice is ours: to obey from compulsions of fear or minimal compliance, or to obey with the expansive care of love.

OBEDIENCE BALANCE SHEET

Obedience for the Soul	Obedience for Managers
Gets beyond the tyranny of desires to purify, peeling away assumptions that prevent "seeing anew" •	• Gets beyond industrial-era operating models and information-era excesses to fashion moral-era management practices for interdependence

Activates personal governance from submission to God's will and law •

• Submits strategies and tactics to the integrity requirements of social capital

To help transcend the isolation from unchecked self-interest •

• To help channel self-interest to generative rather than destructive possibilities

As the pathway for personal spiritual growth and ultimately communion •

• As the pathway for taking International Organization for Standardization (ISO) or Six Sigma disciplines to the necessary heights of ethical excellence

Practising discipleship, following the guidance and norms of a master to escape the rigidity of idolatry or the chaos of subjectivity •

• Practising accountability, following the intent as well as the letter of the law to co-contribute to a fair and moral playing field

What we owe to enable one another's freedom •

• What we owe to earn the charter to operate

The hard, detailed work that releases artistry •

• The hard, detailed work that releases excellence

Willing acceptance of constraint to respect limits •

• Willing acceptance of constraint to respect sustainability

The paradoxical self-subjugation that breaks enslavement and realizes personal freedom •

• The paradoxical self-control that breaks the exhaustion and annihilation that comes from unmitigated self-interest

As proof of fealty towards the divine Source and aim •

• As the practical benchmarks for integrity

Liberty and Justice for All

Few disagree with the importance of freedom, but why does this need of the soul qualify as a factor in practice? The simple answer is that in our postmodern reality, we clearly already hold dear the principle of rights. Our struggle is not with the universality, but with the practicality: the everyday stresses, decisions and habits that deflate the sustaining structure of obligations. The Hebrew prophets premised freedom on responsibility to the Law because enslavement always resulted when humans presumed self-sufficiency. Even when the conquering Babylonians enslaved Israel and deported the elite, the surrendering of liberty was at root the voluntary turning away from dependence on God. Shackles need not be chains; they can also be like silos constructed of fears or prejudice. These enslavements are by point of view rather than by tyrant, self-created by ascribing absolute qualities to human beings, objects or systems. "Take me out of the net that is hidden for me," pleads the Psalmist.

Our economic net, entangling yet hidden, is for theologian M. Douglas Meeks the one we have knotted from cords of "scarcity, satiation and security."[7] Out of pending scarcity – of resources, jobs or information – we have become more aggressive hoarders, more territorial in silos and more competitive in often ruthless efficiency. The managerial rewards for these efforts are success, meaning we earn the entitlement to control more power or consume more goods, in effect accelerating and accentuating scarcity. However, as we have seen with the growth in stress and consumption, neither success nor satiation fulfills ambition. We go on and on, working harder, working longer, wanting more and more of the privileges for more and more satiation. Meeks notes two consequences of this spiral of scarcity, satiation and security. First is the erasure of "memory and hope." He writes, "We are a society of amnesia. Our everyday modalities of life make us forgetful. It is increasingly difficult to remember not only our public history but also our personal stories."[8] In the tempest of busyness over scarcity, we forget the lessons of our story, including the seminal lessons of freedom from the Exodus of Israel from Egypt, or the emancipation of slaves in the American South. Forgetful of the fragility and moral sacredness of liberty, we do not notice its slow erosions and compromises. Too consumed by choices for consumption to remember, we succumb to "not only amnesia but also anesthesia."[9] This is the second consequence: overproduction and overconsumption, which deaden our sensibility for liberty rather than enrich it, which isolate our dependence and pacify it rather than involve us in the hard, persistent project of creative renewal for human freedom and its mutually fulfilling order.

Freedom is nothing if it is not a practice. It is a claim we make as inheritors of kingly glory, but it is real and experienced only when we practise the high art of kingly judgment. In the calculus of civil liberty we know there is a dynamic equation between rights and obligations. The lesson of Mosaic Law is that we make one another free by our willing commitment to obey the law and share in the search for truth. We are all royalty because we all have indispensable roles in creating and sustaining one another's freedom. This means challenging the autopilot assumptions and everyday pressures that inevitably degrade precious liberty. This means practising freedom not only as choice, but also as judgment, facing ethical quandaries with principle and openness to make our best diagnostic of the threats to human dignity and make our best call about how to protect dignity's claims. Kingly adjudication preserves and promotes the prosperity and integrity of the whole society. Our kingly obligation is to pronounce with vigour and candour on what is right and wrong, on what stakes must be extracted from otherwise numbing complexity, on what principles must be honoured within the otherwise deadening exhaustion of the status quo.

This is perhaps the most important lesson about liberty lost in our amnesia. God's presence among us, God's gift to us, is a sharp blade for cutting the self-made net of our own entrapment. Surprisingly, the knife is time off: to regain perspective; to reacquaint ourselves with beauty or smell the glorious roses; to be and belong in relationships of love, community and nourishing interdependence; to become whole and holy. Sabbath is the antidote to scarcity. It literally suspends consumption and production by one seventh. More importantly, Sabbath consecrates the scarcest resource of all, our time, thereby shifting our perspective from strategies focused on carving up limitation to those leveraging infinities such as creativity, freedom, wisdom and love. Sabbath is also the ultimate resource for satiation, the critical first step of acknowledging dependence and gratitude that is part of the proven twelve-step process for disentangling human lives from addiction. Sabbath finally confers security, situating us in the dignity of God-like rest, and emancipating us from the oppression of work that would otherwise go non-stop 24/7.

God most God

That I know to seek means I have already been shown

That I pray confirms I have already been heard

That I hope at all is from already having been given

That I desist in distraction means I am not yet ready

That I define my needs from commercials confirms I am not yet listening

That I doubt enough to hold back is from gifts not yet opened

God most God

Purify that which keeps me in the compulsion of wanting without doing

Flip the light switch of wisdom to reveal my heart within our heart

And grow in me the sacramental seeds of non-me for loving communion

Amen

We know from history that freedom is preserved by sweat and often blood. This is action, which also requires the usually neglected practice of contemplation. As Dietrich Bonhoeffer wrote in his ethics, capacities for truth and freedom must be learned — wrestled by means of "serious reflection" from the "complex and actual situations" of life.[10] We cannot be free without taking the time to be so, to experience freedom's rush, and to grow its wisdom. We cannot be free without making space for the grace and understanding to grow within and around us. For Bonhoeffer, the essential model of Christ, one whose life was given as a "being for others," which means that the Christian practice of liberty is "being free for others." This is a critical perspective if we are to make real Amartya Sen's vision of an economics that measures development not as the end, but as the means towards dignifying freedom. The job of "value creation" is actually "freedom creation": developing those resources, practices and outcomes that extend and sustain that which is most precious to our human experience and aspirations. How provocative, how right it feels, to regard competition as holy when investments and innovations race to add value by adding to human freedom – by taking away what shackles, by liberating our time for play and reflection, by extending choices that feed our magnificence as souls.

FREEDOM BALANCE SHEET

The Soul's Need for Freedom	The Freedom Managers Need
Oxygen: Inhaling the gracious experience of being; exhaling the choices that particularize identity •	• Gold: Opportunity to select strategy that leverages skills and assets; creating wealth from chosen risks
Dignity derived from not being coerced and being sufficiently loved to decide for oneself •	• Rewards derived from being able to invest from personal competence within a fair competitive environment
The openness to respond to calling and engage in relationship •	• The flexibility to respond to competition or opportunity
Exercises God-given talents to grow meaning and capacities for wisdom •	• Exercises assets to grow results and develop knowledge for smart planning
Words and acts by which the soul is seen, heard and honoured •	• Words and acts by which results earn rewards and reputation for integrity
As the means to love and grow communion within relationships •	• As the means to create and grow wealth that enriches humanity as well as shareholders
Practising deliberation to invite and receive illumination •	• Practising wise judgments to fuse moral with commercial obligations

Gift granted by God and basis for equality within human relationships •	• Charter granted by society and the criteria for moral action within the marketplace, environment and community
Owning and channelling personal power with co-responsibility for the freedom of others •	• Ownership and power channeled by the "invisible hand" that includes the priority of freedom for others
As the reality apart from the enslavement of addiction or idolatry •	• As the reality apart from false dichotomy setting the short-term against long-term
To be "free for others" •	• To be freely accountable to others
Proof of becoming whole •	• Proof of becoming holy
To soar on the uplift of grace, to become that which fulfills the soul's destiny •	• To soar on the momentum of purpose, to find fulfillment in work that is of sacramental significance
To say "no" to what destroys Eucharistic communion •	• To say "enough," so as to not destroy balance in society and nature

Beyond Passive Transparency to Animating Truth

For the soul, truth is both the ground to walk on and the gravity holding it in place. Postmodernism has made us weary about truth, as being too dangerous when applied absolutely or too innocuous when fully burdened with all the appropriate cultural and contextual caveats. Rather than make space for the truth in public discourse and moral development, we have created a growing emptiness – a gap or void between the reductive rationality that confines truth to facts alone and the therapeutic emotionality that aims to "own" some recovered individual truth. This polarization robs truth of integrity, fragmenting its potency and denying the grounding, gravitational mystery. Douglas Porpora notes that our notion of truth has become simplified to the argument that "wins."[11] Not surprisingly, the predominant tactic for truth-making is ever more shrill and competitive monologue that attempts by a hail of facts to destroy the credibility of any alternative. Image, which in Genesis described our human gift that we reflect the glory of God, has become the domain of marketers and public relations. The advertising mantra that "perception is reality" has been one of Jack Welch's oft-quoted motifs for leadership. In this incessant selling of the advantageous truth, discernment becomes the abbreviated one of counterspin. In a hyped-up, sexed-up world, we assume the task is to see through everything, and in the process often see nothing. This has given us truth with a "best before" date, based on facts that wear out or insight that is more the advertising sizzle for persuasion than substance.

Simone Weil wrote that "love is a direction and not a state of the soul."[12] The preciousness of truth for Weil was that it set the aim for love and served as the golden thread that wove through all the needs of the soul. Truth provides the authority and organizing meaning for vital and creative order. It is also the basis of and gives credibility to hierarchy, substantiating our criteria both for honour and justice. Truth inheres in our discernment of fairness. It is at once an attribute of beauty that inspires creative risk and an attribute of belonging that ground our human security. Obedience without truth is coercion. Liberty without truth is enslavement. If the most precious of the soul's needs, it is also the most bedeviling. Throughout human history, we have sought truth, inspiring much of what is great in our religions, art, cultures and intellectual understanding. Yet the power of truth has also been the source of our greatest human anguish, as ideologues or ideologies have competed to gain control of its authenticating certainty. Although we have never been as "informed" as we are today, much of what is true escapes our notice because of chronic busyness. Juxtaposing St. Thomas Aquinas and Marshall McLuhan, we could say that "meanness has become the message." With less attentive hearts and with distracted minds, we settle for the easy ambiguity of Pontius Pilate's question to Jesus: "What is truth?" Wired though we may be, we too seem to be "washing our hands" of truth's accountability, demanding a business case for ethics or more evidence for global warming.

In human, spiritual and managerial terms, we have again mistakenly set up truth as a bottom-line certainty of facts, rather than as a balance-sheet encounter of dynamic factors. We do not understand truth so much as receive it. We do not find it so much as create the personal and social environment for it to emerge. For the soul, truth is a fearful ecstasy because it goes beyond yearning and learning to the actual experience of God. We must make interior space, silencing our monologue of worries, ambitions and distractions to allow this illumination to reveal itself from our depths. We must also make space on the exterior. Jesus told his disciples that his presence would reside "where two or more are gathered in my name." This is truth co-nurtured in relationship. Laws and institutions embody key aspects of truth, which is why Jesus did not presume to abolish these structures for obedience. The distortion, which Jesus threatened, was that structural truths too often become rigid tools for leveraging power and perpetuating oppression. He made truth not the object of spiritual practice, but subject to the human priority of what nourishes and heals body and soul. Knowing what is true may not be quantifiable, but for Jesus the experience of truth is in the action of service towards others.

Much has been made of more scrupulous disclosure. While transparency may be the solution for the problem of concealing, it is still a very passive approach that does not make any promises about the necessity for revealing. After overzealously marketing drugs for secondary benefits or with known potential side effects, pharmaceutical companies responded by putting more of their clinical studies, including contentious ones, on the Internet. This alone is hardly a corrective for misinformation. Transparency may only mean more data, not more honesty. Glaxo Smith Kline went a step further, running ads that placed the blame for high drug prices back on consumers. The copy made the startling comparison between the $1,200 yearly cost for insulin and the $30,000 cost for a limb amputation that would perhaps be necessary should a diabetic not have treatment. The disrespectful implication is that if only the public was smarter about the facts, the controversy over drug prices would evaporate. No one debates the great contribution drugs potentially make to human life, and most people understand that numerous factors affect prices. Rather than engage in a humble conversation about issues, the company chose to deal with perceptions as a cartoon. Rather than admit errors in industry judgment or practice that contributed to suspicions, the company arrogantly assumed that misperceptions were without cause and the public's fault because they did not know the facts.

A balance sheet orientation recognizes that no position has a monopoly on truth and that understanding grows in the relationship between factors. Howard Gardner, Mihaly Csikszentmihalyi and William Damon's research on ethical excellence points to a similar dynamic in which personal values are tested by the consciousness of an expert group and then validated by the conscience of larger society.[13] In the burgeoning industry of biogenetics, we hope that an individual scientist has moral character. With so many potential innovations that have so many far-reaching implications, the ethical challenges are complex. Whatever the integrity of the individual, we can only really be assured of proper deliberation and moral diligence when the individual is also subject to the professional standards and strictures of a peer organization. However, even with confluence, to leave final moral authority to those immersed in the expertise risks dangerous disconnection from the checks and balances of other disciplines and from society at large. Ethical evaluations may take into account personal values or professional principle; however, their impacts – and therefore completion – depend on those who are the recipients of the discernments.

For truth, the test and flowering is not in its personal mastery, but in the relationship that masters us. The truth hurts only when we presume to exclusively control it. The essence of truth is in fact the obverse: truth heals because it holds together different parts, because in the space being made for it within relationship truth unveils the basis for unity and communion. Truth frees when the grace of trust is shared. Truth brings down the walls of silos when the grace of trust creates the mutually enveloping surrender of faith and love. It is from this power to unify that we understand truth to be a blueblood need of the soul.

- Kingly leaders do not spin. They trumpet the truth that ends isolation and creates belonging.
- They do not countenance mere transparency from those entrusted with royal tasks, but instead insist on aggressive honesty towards what unifies and grows communion.

- Kingly strategists know that facts can lie when they are disconnected from context. As much as they revel in the glory of knowledge, kingly strategists draw wisdom more consistently from the humble acknowledgment of what is not known, of Zen-like ignorance.
- Truth is pursued as a treasure, both in beauty, which reveals its universality, and justice, which fulfills its practice.
- Rather than being dispensed, truth is fostered through exchange and dialogue so as to build confidence among persons throughout the kingdom to deal with its ambiguities and paradox.

Again, Jesus adds a reversing dimension that completes the concept. The truth of good news must empower not the average citizen, but the most needy and marginalized. Leaders and managers practise cascading, tumbling the vision and values from the top down, with every layer of the organization receiving a decreasing portion of understanding and reward. As with power, truth is packaged and disseminated to be commensurate with role. Jesus insists that the truth belong to those who usually have least access to it, that their vision and needs cascade upwards to inform the management and leadership class of the real "state of the nation" and criteria for justice.

TRUTH BALANCE SHEET

Truth for the Soul	Truth for Managers
As aim and for sustenance, to pull hope and inspire faith •	• As the obligation for privilege, to account honestly and grow credibility
The glimpse of the eternal that gives scope to the everyday •	• The test of the eternal that gives meaning to the everyday
Wisdom's jewel: the treasure from insight discerned in prayerful contemplation and action •	• Return on knowledge: information raised to understanding that grows responsibilities in parallel to opportunities
How the soul exercises judgment and comes to perceive what is good and what is right •	• How facts and outcomes are synthesized into an accounting that is moral as well as financial

Self-knowledge, seeing anew with compassion to repent for assumptions and behaviours that destroy personal integrity •	• Honest engagement of the moral balance sheet to own the assumptions and behaviours that compound meanness or damage interdependence
Revealed in silence, grown in communion, held in trust •	• Revealed by disclosure, grown in relationship with stakeholders, held as the accountability behind all other accountabilities
What the soul must dare to uphold and love to share •	• What the heart must excavate to ensure balance and justice

Taking Stock – and Options

Disciplines are needed for practising obedience, freedom and truth, but they more closely resemble those of saints than of strategists. In *Christ of the 21st Century*, Ewert Cousins defines these developmental phases with more distinct orientations and implications for practice. The first phase of soul growth is through *purification*, during which we clarify and begin to correct those existing habits and practices that impede conversion or thwart relationship. The second stage involves *illumination*, growing the insights and virtues that align to our deepening commitment to relationship with God. The third and final stage is *unification*, the consummation of self with otherness.[14] For purification we practise repentance; for illumination, wisdom; and for unification, communion.

These are sacramental terms for practical disciplines. Purification sounds like a spiritual enema, so something to be avoided, to get through like an entrance exam, to start with and then move on from. In the soul's context of latent perfection, purity is less a corrective than becoming what is natural and true to us as human beings. There is an aspect of repentance, but also one of reclaiming: acknowledging fault and owning deficiency, but also acknowledging vocation and owning power. More than for penance, practices for purification work at both of these spiritual virtues, helping us see from the heart the damage of unconscious or autopilot habits, and see also how the future depends on the caring and thoughtful investment of the precious talents entrusted to us as a child of God. Organizations and individuals caught in scandal understand only a fraction of this process, which is why we have so many blue-chip repeat offenders. Repentance is now part of the public relations cycle, the admission of fault and the promise not to succumb again. Rarely is there an awakening of the heart. Rarely are the systemic or habitual roots of the transgression brought into contact with the broader human or social consequences. Most rarely of all are the buried talents needed for repair and for holiness unearthed, cleansed and brought into circulation for moral wealth making. As important as it is to face up to wrongdoing, the process of purification is incomplete unless we also assume responsibility to live up to our innate capacity for perfectibility.

Illumination happens when calling, expressing the integrity and integration of head, heart and soul, infuses understanding. Once again this is not an imposition on our humanity, but a natural capability to be realized. Just as artists do, there is a need to discipline talents, mastering basics and progressing towards higher degrees of accomplishment. These foundational practices are forever renewed, a rote of effort and sacrifice that prepares us to receive the creative muse – to be taken over by spiritual grace – to make the art and achieve the glory for which we have been made. All excellence depends on practices performed with the craft and care that derive from both expertise and artistry. All excellence also represents the high practice of memory realized as an achievement that is now also bequeathed to the future. Companies and managers certainly value information. Some also recognize that reflection and analysis are needed to reframe data into knowledge. However, because of our millstone pragmatism, we have usually rushed into process change or training to create what we think we have learned without doing the pragmatic due diligence of reflection and internalization. More and more, out of rush and pressure, we expect illumination to be in PowerPoint when what it demands is a Zen koan (a paradoxical riddle), and what it provides is the poetic yet structured ambiguity of haiku. Just as purification demands that we both repent distortion and reclaim potential, illumination requires that we practise the imagination for reordering what is broken as well as the practical virtues for renewing.

We all have experiences with the joy of investing ourselves in a project or hobby with such passion that we lose sense of both time and self. On teams, there is in those moments of high performance a similar exhilaration from momentum, from the synergy for the whole achieved by the sweat and trust of all that at once heightens our sense of individuality and belonging. These glowing experiences reveal our capacity for unification, which for mystics involves the love endorphins of communion. We do not get illuminated: illumination gets us. We do not own being wise: wisdom instead, like grace, flows through us. The practices for spiritual growth are therefore rehearsals for being taken over, for being more than what we are, which means for being fully ourselves in relationship. Self-interest is not cancelled but fulfilled, which is why Simone Weil insists that our human freedom is an obligation before it is a right. The practice of being the most we can be as humans is to practise being a *we*. With purification we begin inside ourselves. With illumination we stand on the balance of wisdom. And with unification we are appropriated by the power that is external and eternal and yet within and personal.

9
FAQs
Frequently Avoided Questions

I strain for whispers

Ignoring shouts

Searching for clues

While stomping on the evidence

I look for the alignment of miracles

Missing the message in the mess

I hope for grace to illumine

What I refuse my heart to understand

Turning away in the guise of turning within

Denying instruction to protect my ignorance

I clamour to hear

Yet refuse to listen

I insist on questioning

Yet avoid what I am asking

Any dialogue is disruptive, in that we are forced to change in response to our encounter with the other or opposite point of view. More than a survey of difference, dialogue requires us to become immersed in what is unlike us. If our minds are made up or fixed in advance, then we cannot dialogue. If we are striving only to convince others that we are already right, then dialogue is impossible. Only authentic openness prepares us for dialogue. Only being made anew attests that the dialogue has been authentic. Simone Weil's needs of the soul were defined in the harsh but necessary dialogue between the broken reality of France during the Second World War and the country's hope for a more integrated future. Confronting business practices with the needs of the soul has been the dialogue project of this book. Many people regard this as impossible or myopic, yet many others believe the crossing of these disciplines to be imperative. With issues literally involving life and death – with what is at stake, including our natural habitat and human destiny – we cannot presume to create workable solutions without bringing to the exchange with such problems every ounce of our wisdom, enlightenment, technical expertise and strategic imagination. All of our human nature needs to be present in this particular wrestling match, including the experiences, memories and uplifting hopes of our religious traditions.

Like the journey of the soul, our work in this dialogue is unending. That transformation continues throughout our lives, and history should not suggest futility. Quite the opposite: this points to the infinite capacities for perfectibility that we share because we are imprinted with the image and likeness of God. Change is our hope: difficulty our catalyst. While this dialogue between spiritual and managerial practice is startling, there is nothing new in being called to prophetic witness, priestly service and kingly integrity. This is the vocation that marked Israel as chosen, and that signified Christians as baptized into the new kingdom. What is new in every lifetime, generation or society is creation of the response to this holy vocation. Even if we have models and inspiration, the tasks of such transforming discipleship are always particular, with an individual person responding to a specific situation, in the concrete reality of place and in the precise and fleeting moment of time. Each of us will bring unique skills and interior resources to this dialogue, and face our own difficult choices or quandaries in living the transformation and contributing to its coming alive. What we must not do is feign neutrality. What we cannot do is avoid the questions even if we do not like the answers.

One of the strengths of managers is impatience to get to implementation and results. One of the limitations from this orientation to action is that we become circumscribed by plausibility. Some people have critiqued this as going after the low-hanging fruit. I have explained this as "the despair from pragmatism" that keeps us so focused on what is doable that we lose hope and impatience for what is needed. We believe we are asking the tough questions when we challenge idealism. But as history shows, the tougher questions are those challenging us to live up to those ideals. It is far easier to keep faith private and spirituality absent from work. More difficult, and more transformative, are the risks and creativity for integration. When the soul responds to God's call, all that is clear is the response in that moment. Any destination remains opaque, and any roadmap hopelessly incomplete. The clarity comes from taking the first step in what Weil called "the direction of love."[1] Similarly, many of the answers to our questions about the needs of the soul at work become clear only in striving to walk the integration.

1. Can this be done?

The question most avoided relates to doability. Is this living faith at work really practical? Will we not simply be setting ourselves up to be fired if we declare faith's principles so forcefully?

This is a question to answer in stages. First, the movement laid out in this book is a beginning and not a final prescription. The core idea has been to expose the needs of the soul, prove their salience to many of the issues redefining management, and recognize that the ideas agitating magnificence are very much the necessary performance benchmarks for our most pressing economic challenges. To heal the impacts of business, we must heal the people making the decisions and implementing the plans. This fusing of professionalism with profession helps realize the personal integrity that helps uplift company integrity. Many people who are creatively involved in their own wrestling match with principles of faith will, with the support of grace, find other equally imaginative or more effective possibilities for developing practical coherence.

Second, while effectiveness is as important in salvation as it is in business strategy, we cannot presume to constrain God's domain only by practicality. Sometimes, as when addressing global warming or chronic poverty, the practical is trumped by what is necessary. We often hear consultants explain that management is as much art as science. The soul, too, develops from and reaches for both. In this sense, an approach to integrity involving living faith at work may seem as improbable as a Chagall painting, yet the truth still moves us and in some way stretches our perceptions of the grandeur encoded in the everyday.

Third, while we may be more comfortable pursuing integrity in increments, as with corporate social responsibility, the anguish of our natural environment, the pain of our impoverished masses, and the dislocation so many managers experience in their hearts demand a more comprehensive overhaul. If anything, practicality numbs us to the many quantum changes required to achieve the sustainability, justice and human dignity so under threat on so many fronts. I also believe that as managers we have great skills and knowledge to bring to these challenges, but that to attain the fruits of a genuine new economy we must co-fashion a genuine new paradigm for managerial morality.

Fourth, in seeing living faith in business as a threat to our job security, we are admitting two things: that the challenge is difficult, and that, in many ways, our hearts are gagged from speaking out. The implications are that we contest the difficulty but not the validity – and that, for all sorts of reasons, we feel helpless. My experience is that we can always be magnificent by expressing our humanity towards the people we work with and the issues we work through. Like an exercise regimen, we grow the capacities of the soul by lifting small weights first and then adding muscle with repetitions. This, though, may be too rational an expectation. As with Simon of Cyrene, there will be moments when greatness will be thrust upon us regardless of our preparation or courage. Or, as with Dietrich Bonhoeffer, there will be times when we may have to manufacture for ourselves the integration that sustains truly heroic action. In all this work, we must be careful rather than willful – full of care rather than full of demands. We must also be ready to forgive ourselves as well as others for falling short. We must remain open to grace, realizing that God's work has other resources deployed in the project.

2. Is not a more significant obstacle in such a theology for business that it presumes synergy between the incompatible systems of capitalism and Christianity?

One of the reasons I have so relished being a business person, and persist in having hope for a maturing globalization, is that I believe that capitalism is as much about trading ideas as goods and services. We generally understand this from the point of view of the still-emerging information economy that proves that knowledge does indeed create value. I also mean this more foundationally. In only a few short years, we have witnessed the growth and staggering transformation of China. Who could have imagined a successful communist capitalism? Obviously, the Chinese have customized both ideologies, and some would argue that most Chinese businesses are in fact largely divorced from the historical infrastructure of Marxist socialism. My point is that there is no homogenous capitalism, just as there is no homogenous Christianity. Both exist – and have throughout history – as plurals: as dynamic, shifting, tension-inducing, understanding-evolving orientations that have absorbed best practices and critiques from the societies and cultures around them.

For Christians, fusing incompatible properties is at the heart of the mystery of the Incarnation. As fully divine and fully human, Jesus invites us to discipleship premised on uniting what are usually mind-blowing contrasts: ordering earth as if it were heaven; participating in community as if it were holy Eucharist; living in the moment as if it were of eternal significance. In short, incompatibility for Christians is but a starting point, not a stumbling block.

Jesus did not come to abolish the law but to fulfill it. As we work our way through governance and strategy, as we imagine the rules for processes and reporting, we must keep in our hearts this catalytic dimension. Fulfillment is not, from Jesus' perspective, a quality of expertise or adherence, but of relationship. We achieve fullness by filling others; we are filled by the overflowing fullness of grace and love around us. The opportunity in our business world is to bring this relational hope to our expertise, to restore to health the otherwise exhausting system for wealth creation by insisting on the human fulfillments flowing from freedom, dignity, fairness, participation and moral imagination.

In my view, this is not an optional exercise. The great stresses and transformations required to address sustainability and global security demand hyper-sensibilities of compassion, co-operation and co-creation. As noted, for managers and many consumers in the rich world, the imperatives of sustainable development will require effective de-development – fewer excesses such as SUVs to realize fairer distributions of energy and lower emissions of pollutants. Developing such habits for production and consumption may well involve laws, but the efficacy ultimately rests also on some *kenosis* – some emptying of self to serve our shared basic needs and free opportunities for others. The world's problems are so daunting that we need to engage and grow the moral wisdom of all religions and traditions: indeed, we must make whole new theologies by praying together and sharing so as to become genuinely global and co-responsible. In that rich, necessary discourse about global capitalism and consciousness, we need to offer by our example and understanding the wealth of our Christian experience and tradition. These, for me as a manager, represent the terms and challenges of discipleship.

3. Is it not presumptuous to intervene with Christian sensibilities in a secular and diverse workplace?

History shows that missionary work has often tended to heavy-handedness, even brutality. My goal is not to convert or impose, but to heal for myself the reverse presumption that dismisses spirituality as a factor in our human integrity and creativity. As Reinhold Niebuhr has suggested, the contest between good and evil is first inside every one of us because we all share an inalienable equality for doing wrong as well as for having rights.[2] The second contest is between malleability and rigidity. Any profession of faith must include a confession of inadequacy, not because what God has revealed is incomplete, but because as humans we are too limited by our senses, intellect and cultural conditioning ever to presume anything but a partial understanding of the Divine. God is an impenetrable mystery that mystics explain as "unknowing." Our task is to grow our souls in relationship to God, assuming responsibility for what we know, rather than impose exclusions based on what we do not.

The teeth have largely been removed from diversity by political correctness, but diversity remains a subversive premise. By definition, this requires making space for different views, but it is not enough just to hear one another. Just as with any transforming dialogue, the exchange within diversity involves critical thinking. It is within this respectful encounter with others that we must also have the respectful courage to know ourselves. The more spiritual and theological depth we bring to this interaction, the more substantive the potential contribution. From my Catholic perspective, this is precisely the vocation prescribed by the Second Vatican Council, which asks us to embody the Gospel in our everyday careers and duties, while respecting the dignity and wisdom of all other human beings.

Clearly, it will take a lot of experimentation to make spiritual contributions to board deliberations or bring theological insights to tactical business meetings. In an article I was invited to write by the Conference Board of New York exploring the business implications of 9/11, I suggested that companies with international operations would need to radically reconsider the diversity of directors. Most companies already have too many big-company CEOs on their boards.[3] In today's reality, the fiduciary obligation to protect the interests of shareholders may well require inviting Muslim theologians or Confucian scholars to sit as directors, to define the globally responsible terms for governance and approve globally responsible strategic direction for operations. We all need to ask different questions in order to get beyond simplistic bottom lines and to engage the rich ambiguity of balance sheets. Many of these questions are at root moral as well as cultural.

At the same time that our institutions are struggling to learn to think globally while already selling globally, individual managers are increasingly on a spontaneous quest for meaning that again raises the need for theological discourse. As noted already, more and more people are speaking about their faith at work. This hunger to speak about spirituality in hallways, meeting rooms and airport waiting lounges seems to me to have grown in direct relation to our managerial addiction to practicality. The more short term our operating horizons, the more people seem to crave the significance and consolation of what is eternal.

The discourse between secular and spiritual is fraught with tension. Neither side has complete answers or solutions, and these partial answers lose all integrity when they exclude the contribution from the other. The task, as the rabbis teach, is to be human in those circumstances that deny or reduce humanity. In my experience, the split between secularity and faith camouflages a more destructive gap between head and heart. Validating the wisdom of faith as an asset for our social and economic renewal requires that we again honour the value of the human heart. Like Etty Hillesum, we must offer the world our thinking heart and flex that heart by daring to speak the name of God.

4. But I am just one manager, a minnow in a shark-infested sea. What possible difference can I make?

The trajectory of salvation for being restored to health is simultaneously personal and for eternity. In our own way, we are each grappling with the inner reality of our relationship to the Transcendent. In the miraculous mutation that comes from this encounter, each of us in our own way recovers some aspect of sight or has some distortion exorcised so that our participation in creation, history and community is also changed by our heightened sense of communion. Sharks may yet abound, but the fear, which keeps us apart and docile, is greatly lessened because we are no longer alone and are held close in the divine heart of love.

As is true for business, the soul cannot escape taking risks: indeed, it is incomplete or not fully free without risk-taking. Shark bites may be the risk we need to face. This difficult choice, which involves an authentic encounter with our human freedom, brings us again to the significance of the cross. Defeat is an all-too-real possibility, yet the hope is greater. Many saints, such as Francis of Assisi and Ignatius of Loyola, many mystics, such as Teilhard de Chardin and Simone Weil, faced threats and dismissal from their own church as well as their communities or professional associates. The mystery and consolation are that truth prevailed, that the risks taken in troubled uncertainty returned huge wealth in wisdom, compassion and justice.

In diverse studies of power and oppression, cultural historian Hannah Arendt and theologian Walter Wink arrive at similar conclusions. Power is rarely so all-encompassing as to be all-sustaining. Usually, it is held in place by the tacit complicity of a majority. Such power is most vulnerable to truth; hence, the great priority for propaganda. Such power, based as it is on willing or fearful powerlessness, unwinds quickly when individuals confront its falsehoods. This is what happened with apartheid and the Berlin Wall. Crosses must be borne. Individuals of conscience need to take risks. But latent magnificence has its own momentum for undoing even the most tyrannical structures trying to keep it suppressed.

Most of us have possibilities for doing small things with magnificence. A few may find or develop the courage to be like Dietrich Bonhoeffer, offering every word of talent, every insight of intellect and every desire of heart in the cause of truth. While Bonhoeffer's example as the conscience of a culture exemplifies magnificence, it in many ways diminishes his risks and example to too easily consider him exceptional. In his letters and prayers, Bonhoeffer reveals that faith and heroism are in fact founded on fragile humanity very much like our own, with ambitions in a race against doubts, with fear sprinting step by step with conscience. Courage is something we rarely have in advance of the need. Like Bonhoeffer, we must know deep prayer. Like him, we must be intelligent in our critique. Sustained by grace and inspired by truth, we must trust that the courage will be sufficient to what the situation claims.

While we will most likely never confront the life-and-death choices of Bonhoeffer, there will be times in our own lives when the cross bearing freedom, renewal or justice will need our helping hand. This choice is real and the test of character in every human life. Part of our need for prayer is to recognize those Simon of Cyrene moments in our own lives and workplaces, to be open to being seconded by God, to take even a few steps with the burden of the cross to make possible its ascent to healing glory.

Expected One

Expecting me

Holy One

Holding me

Crucified One
Consoling me
Healing One
Touching me
Graceful One
Freeing me
Forgiving One
Uplifting me
Homeless One
Welcoming me
Humble One
Dignifying me
Emptied One
Completing me

5. What will it take from me?

The joy for me of this encounter with the needs of the soul is that we managers have the opportunity to reconsider what we already do well, and from this very structure of disciplines and expertise make possibilities for moral service to humanity and vocational service to God.

The world desperately needs the security and justice from a global order premised on truth and fairness. Managers have great ingenuity and resources to contribute to this pressing need. We have operations that now straddle every time zone and involve communities of suppliers from the far corners of the world. We also have infrastructure and learning protocols for translating floods of information into wealth-creating knowledge and understanding. I am not so naive as to miss that much of what dirties our natural environment and destabilizes our global society comes from the very practices of production and consumption perpetuated by business people like me. Nor, however, am I so idealistic as to assume that the remedies and reforms required for sustainability and justice can be realized without the human and financial capital of our companies. In the mess and stress between what is and what needs to be, we encounter the opportunity for creativity and moral integrity for our profession.

What will it take? The needs of the soul tell us exactly what is needed:

- *Order* that is sustaining of human community and dreams as well as business opportunity, that preserves the operating integrity of the earth's ecosystem and that situates the priorities of commerce within the continuity of God's call and self-communication;
- *Hierarchy* that recognizes truth as a higher value than advertising or public relations, that honours not only the merits of accomplishment but also the inalienable dignity of human beings, including those fired, outsourced or excluded, and that is willing to shoulder the ascent to wisdom, purifying faulty suppositions, gaining illumination from the thinking heart and finally receiving communion, with its gifts of belonging and obligations to include;
- *Responsibility* that admits mistakes, owns consequences and faces restitution, not as an accountability premised on blame, but as an expression of profound carefulness;
- *Fairness* that sees and hears others as human beings, engaging and responding to their needs with the hopefulness that we claim for ourselves;
- *Risk* that thrives on creativity and experimentation, breaking down silos as well as rigid orthodoxies, unleashing the soul to recognize the grace in money and feel the beauty in fashioning enterprises that help people as employees and customers become more than satisfied;
- *Security* that is founded on truth, holding at once the cries of desolation from those suffering or from victims, as well as the hopes of consolation from those savouring freedom and dreams;
- *Obedience* that obliges restraint, not from the perspective of an imposed minimum, but as the kingly governance that enables re-

lationships, forges bonds of community and sponsors the creation of beauty;
- *Freedom* that forgives: forgiving self and others for foibles and also for moral risks taken or missed; forgiving as fore-giving, generosity advanced in response to God's love and as manifest responsibility for the liberation of those, such as AIDS orphans, impoverished single parents, prisoners of conscience or neglect, or the coatless and homeless, who cannot be free without us; and
- *Truth* that instead of an asset is an encounter, a mutual making of meaning that eschews rigidity and embraces the blinding, bonding flash of mystical awakening.

All this and we get to earn a living, too. How blessed are we?

6. If the intervention of faith at work is to happen, how are we even to broach such loaded conversations?

As with the encounter with God, our encounter with each other must be done tenderly, with charity in even greater abundance than clarity and with the humility to know what we do not know. There will be times when stands must be taken, when our view of creation, justice, salvation and hope demand that we stand in opposition to strategies or decisions. This is the action that is the return on contemplation. Most times, however, our contribution will be as voices, eyes and thinking hearts in the context of everyday problems, responsibilities and goals. Here is where faith works, where work becomes grace. Since the issue we are addressing is often the rigidity with which scope and outcome are managed, we must be careful – full of care – not to be rigid in our faith demands or spiritual expectations. Ronald F. Thiemann has developed "norms of publicity" that are helpful in navigating these tricky shoals. He posits three criteria:

1. Public accessibility, which means that principles and concepts are fully transparent and open to scrutiny;
2. Mutual respectfulness, which means that the aim is not necessarily agreement but at least the mutual honouring of differences;
3. Moral integrity, which means consistency not only between ideal and action, but consistency of principle in how we actually engage to solve problems and imagine opportunities.[4]

Thiemann's norms provide a construct and a "to-do" list.
- *To* speak from the thinking heart, *do* contribute to creating a business environment in which others are allowed to speak from theirs.
- *To* expect others to be open to the faith perspective, *do* the disclosure that allows others access to that principle's aims and suppositions.
- *To* hope for respectful encounter, *do* the offering of respect that invites and sustains mutuality.
- *To* keep even conflict respectful, *do* the pattern-setting by respecting the obligations that enable the freedom of others.
- *To* suggest or teach or preach what is moral, *do* what it requires as personal practice.
- *To* discern what lines not to cross as a Christian business person, *do* the contemplation for, with and through the cross of Christ.

7. Where do we start?

Great projects take many hands to come to fruition. Often this entails the work of generations. Whatever the obstacles, someone must start. Whatever the implausibility, someone must dare the future. When, during the Renaissance, Filippo Brunelleschi designed the spectacular dome for the cathedral in Florence, he was not sure it could be built. There was no technology for constructing so high and wide a structure, and no existing materials to handle the weight and stress. With aplomb and faith, Brunelleschi began construction, inventing revolutionary scaffolding as he went, improvising a new herringbone design for the brickwork to disperse the energy in the ascending dome. He died before the building was complete, leaving it to others to provide the craft skills and ingenuity to succeed. Part of Brunelleschi's audacity grew from the spirit and culture of his time. Some grew from his confidence in his creative skills and destiny. Finally, some was inspired by the conviction that it is the nature and vocation of the human soul to reach for what seems impossible. Brunelleschi did not ignore the hard practical or even intractable questions. Rather, he used even those he could not answer as the impetus to start building.[5] Sometimes we need more courage than answers. Sometimes we need to reach for what expertise dismisses as impractical just to learn to grow into our inherent magnificence.

St. Paul defined Christian discipleship as an emphatic "yes" to the invitations and promises of God (2 Corinthians 1:18-20). An ethical orientation involves more than saying no to what is wrong. Integrity is not simply turning down that which compromises principle. In the end, our character and commitments are fulfilled by those projects, claims and callings to which we give assent. Mary's magnificence as the mother of Jesus flourished after she said yes to the annunciation. Her example of faith is to receive the call and go into action, to trust grace and be open to participate in God's will.

As spiritual sustenance for the soul, such work starts with prayer and ends with more prayer. The needs of the soul are for God, not market share; for relationship, not personal development. Through prayer, our being with God overtakes what we do and hope for. This does not make our work less important. On the contrary, the relationship with God consecrates our efforts and uplifts the scope and implications of business. We grow our virtues because we want to grow closer to God. We conform our professionalism to the demands of holiness to discover God's mystery in our productivity and creativity. It is this desire for intimacy with God that compels us to live our faith at work. It is this hunger and thirst for God that makes all of this imaginable, necessary and gracious.

In worship

for a God that we cannot understand

yet makes our understanding possible

In awe

for the precious gift of life,

with untold beauty and unwarranted blessings

In adoration

with bowed head and on bended knee,

for the power and glory that infuses, transcends and does not end

In gratitude

for even being able to have this discussion,

for even wondering in our hearts

how the privilege of management can be consecrated

In contrition

for mistakes made, for obligations denied, for freedoms squandered,

for marketing that promised more than we delivered

In communion

with Teilhard and Simone,

with innumerable teachers and guides,

with animating Word

In shock

at the ongoing, irrevocable scandal of the cross;

at the ongoing, irrevocable hope of Easter

In desolation

pleading for help,

mourning the tragedy of love not yet fulfilled as justice,

lamenting to see for a flash the face of God

In hope

recognizing the healing possibilities of freedom,

giving voice to the creative spirit in our own hearts to also make beauty and

peace

In silence

hearing the poetry in between the words,

experiencing the Other who calls and embraces

In silence

NOTES

INTRODUCTION

[1] Dorothee Soelle, *Theology of Skeptics*, Joyce L. Irwin, trans. (Minneapolis: Augsburg Fortress, 1995), 126.

[2] Peter Drucker, *Managing the Future* (New York: Plume, 1993), 102.

[3] Laura Nash and Scotty McLennan, *Church on Sunday, Work on Monday: The Challenge of Fusing Christian Values with Business Life* (San Francisco: Jossey-Bass, 2001), 110–132.

[4] C.K. Prahalad, "Work of the New Age Manager," in *Management 21 C*, Subir Chowdhury, ed. (London: Financial Times Prentice Hall, 2000), 165–166.

[5] Helen J. Alford OP and Michael J. Naughton, *Managing as if Faith Mattered: Christian Social Principles in the Modern Organization* (Notre Dame, IN: University of Notre Dame Press, 2001), 21.

[6] Simone Weil, *The Need for Roots: Prelude to a Declaration of Duties for Mankind* (London: Routledge, 1996), 6–27.

[7] Alford and Naughton, *Managing as if Faith Mattered*, 270.

[8] Emmanuel Levinas, *Difficult Freedom: Essays on Judaism* (Baltimore: The Johns Hopkins University Press, 1997), 154.

[9] John Paul II, "Crossing the Threshold of Hope," in *Christianity and Plurality: Classic and Contemporary Readings*, Richard Plantinga, ed. (Oxford: Blackwell, 1999), 363.

[10] Cited in John J. English, *Spiritual Freedom* (Chicago: Loyola Press, 1995), 281.

[11] Nash and McLennan, *Church on Sunday, Work on Monday*, 59.

[12] David A. Krueger, Donald W. Shriver and Laura L. Nash, *The Business Corporation and Productive Justice* (Nashville: Abingdon Press, 1997), 129.

[13] Jonathan Sacks, *The Dignity of Difference: How to Avoid the Clash of Civilizations* (London: Continuum, 2002), 88.

[14] Ian I. Mitroff and Elizabeth A. Denton, *A Spiritual Audit of Corporate America: A Hard Look at Spirituality, Religion and Values in the Workplace* (San Francisco: Jossey-Bass, 1998), 11.

[15] Pierre Teilhard de Chardin, *The Divine Milieu* (New York: Perennial Classics, 2001).

PRESENCE

[1] Webster's Electronic Quotebase (edited by Keith Mohler), 1994.

[2] Rosabeth Moss Kanter, "Kaleidoscopic Thinking," *Management 21 C*, 146.

[3] Karl Rahner, *The Trinity*, Joseph Donceel, trans. (New York: The Crossroads Publishing Company, 1998), 35.

[4] David Ford, *Self and Salvation: Being Transformed* (Cambridge: Cambridge University Press, 1999), 210–211.

[5] Louis Lavelle, "Brisk Turnover in CEOs," *BusinessWeek*, March 7, 2005.

[6] John Wall, ed. *Paul Ricoeur and Contemporary Moral Thought*, (London: Routledge. 2002), 47.

[7] Francis Fukuyama, *Our Posthuman Future: Consequences of the Biotechnology Revolution* (New York: Farrar, Straus and Giroux, 2002), 84–93.

[8] Fukuyama, *Our Posthuman Future*, 101.

[9] Fukuyama, *Our Posthuman Future*, 171.

[10] Reinhold Niebuhr, *The Essential Reinhold Niebuhr: Selected Essays and Addresses*, Robert Brown, ed. (New Haven, CT: Yale University Press, 1986), 160.

[11] Centre for Ethical Orientation, *Aiming High: Renewing Trust in a Time of Suspicion*, 2003.

[12] Alford and Naughton, *Managing as if Faith Mattered*, 228.

[13] Soelle, *Theology of Skeptics*, 119.

[14] Centre for Ethical Orientation, *Aiming High*.

[15] Jonathan D. Glater, "Economic Crimes Strike a Third of U.S. Firms," *International Herald Tribune*, July 9, 2003, 13.

[16] Muel Kaptein and Johan Wempe, *A Theory of Corporate Integrity* (Oxford: Oxford University Press, 2002), 164.

[17] Kaptein and Wempe, *A Theory of Corporate Integrity*, 154.

[18] John Macmurray, *Persons in Relation* (London: Humanities Press, 1993), 66.

[19] Harvey Cox, "The Market as God: Living with the New Dispensation," *The Atlantic Monthly*, March 1999.

[20] Douglas V. Porpora, *Landscapes of the Soul: The Loss of Moral Meaning in American Life* (Oxford: Oxford University Press, 2001), 19.

[21] David Rosen, *Caux Roundtable Panel Discussion*, Caux, Switzerland, July 2003.

[22] Jesper Kunde, *Corporate Religion* (London: FT Prentice Hall). 2000.

[23] *Ignatius of Loyola: Spiritual Exercises and Selected Works*. (Edited by George E. Ganss.) Mahwah, NJ: Paulist Press. 1991, p. 263.

[24] Thomas Merton, *New Seeds of Contemplation* (New York: New Directions, 1961), 292.

[25] John Haughey SJ, "The Primacy of Receivement," in *Business as Calling: Interdisciplinary Essays on the Meaning of Business from the Catholic Social Tradition*, Michael Naughton and Stephanie Rumpza, eds. (E-book, St. Paul, MN: Center for Catholic Studies, University of St. Thomas, 2005), 2.

[26] John Paul II, *Christifideles Laici*, Apostolic Exhortation. December, 30, 1988, Section 14.

[27] Walter Wink, *When The Powers Fail: Reconciliation in the Healing of Nations* (Minneapolis: Augsburg Fortress, 1998), 5.

[28] David Specht and Richard Broholm, "One Calling: Three Bottom Lines – A Practical Theology in Support of Organizational Faithfulness," in *Business as Calling*.

[29] Daniel Goleman, *Emotional Intelligence: Why It Can Matter More Than IQ* (London: Bloomsbury, 1996).

[30] Joseph Badaracco, *Leading Quietly: An Unorthodox Guide to Doing the Right Thing* (Cambridge, MA: Harvard Business Press, 2002), 169–188.

[31] Abraham Joshua Heschel, *Moral Grandeur and Spiritual Audacity*, Susannah Heschel, ed. (New York: Farrar, Straus and Giroux, 1996), ix.

BECOMING

[1] J. Krishnamurti, "On God," from *God in All Worlds: An Anthology of Contemporary Spirituality*, Lucinda Vardey, ed. (New York: Pantheon, 1995), 8.

[2] Thomas Aquinas, *Summa Theologiae*, II-II (New York: McGraw Hill, 1966), section 133,2.

[3] Heschel, *Moral Grandeur and Spiritual Audacity*, ix.

[4] Raf Casert, The Associated Press, "EU Checks up on Microsoft's Compliance with Anti-Trust Settlement," *InformationWeek*, February 25, 2005.

[5] St. Thomas Aquinas, *Treatise on the Virtues*, John A. Oesterle, trans. (Notre Dame: University of Notre Dame, 1984), 165.

[6] John Dominic Crossan, *Jesus: A Revolutionary Biography* (San Francisco: Harper Collins, 1994), 65.

[7] Jim Collins, *Good to Great* (New York: Harper Collins, 2001), 198.

[8] Collins, *Good to Great*, 17–40.

[9] Michael Naughton (notes on an earlier draft of this manuscript), May 1, 2004.

[10] Simone Weil, *Waiting on God: Letters and Essays* (Fount: London, 1977), 96.

[11] Thomas Aquinas, *On Virtue*, 141.

[12] John J. English SJ, *Spiritual Freedom* (Chicago: Loyola Press, 1995), 111.

[13] John Elkington, *Cannibals with Forks: The Triple Bottom Line of 21st-Century Business* (Stoney Creek, CT: New Society Publishers, 1998), 109.

[14] Stanley Holmes and Wendy Zellner, "The Costco Way: Higher Wages Mean Higher Profits, But Try Telling Wall Street," *BusinessWeek*, April 12, 2004, 76.

[15] Howard Gardner, Mihaly Csikszentmihalyi and William Damon, *Good Work: When Excellence and Ethics Meet* (New York: Basic Books, 2001), 204–210.

[16] John Schwartz, "Always on the Job, Employees Pay with Health," *New York Times*, September 5, 2004.

[17] Thomas Landen Jr., "Depression: A Frequent Visitor to Wall Street," *The New York Times*, September 12, 2004.

[18] Landen, "Depression."

[19] Keith Glint, *Management: A Sociological Introduction*, (Cambridge: Polity Press, 1995), 2–26.

[20] Bethany McLean and Peter Elkind, *The Smartest Guys in the Room: The Amazing Rise and Scandalous Fall of Enron* (New York: Penguin, 2003), 65.

[21] Naughton, notes.

[22] Paul J. Wadell, "Being Providentially Situated: The Indispensable Vocation of the Corporate Whistleblower," *Business as Calling*, 8.

[23] *The Economist*, "School for Scandal: Is the MBA Responsible for Moral Turpitude at the Top?" February 19, 2005, 13.

[24] T.S. Eliot, from the Introduction to Simone Weil, *The Need for Roots: Prelude to a Declaration of Duties for Mankind*, xii.

[25] Weil, *The Need for Roots*, 6–27.

[26] Weil, *Waiting on God*, 101.

[27] J. Krishnamurti, *On Freedom*, 105.

WRESTLING

[1] Scott Johnson, "The Poor Get Poorer," *Newsweek*, September 29, 2003, 56.

[2] Gustavo Capdevila, "Globalization Leads to Slavery," in *Asia Times*, August 23, 2001.

[3] Michelle Conlin and Aaron Bernstein, "Working and Poor," *BusinessWeek*, May 31, 2004, 58–62.

[4] "Ever Higher Society, Ever Harder to Ascend," *The Economist, Special Report: Meritocracy in America*, January 1, 2005, 22–25.

[5] "Owning Body and Soul: A Lot of Human-Gene Patent Claims May Be Ill Founded," *The Economist*, February 12, 2005.

[6] www.ge.com/sixsigma March 2005.

[7] Drucker, *Managing the Future*, 102.

[8] H.W. Donner, *Introduction to Utopia*, cited in Thomas More, *Utopia* (London: Penguin. 1965), 12.

[9] Steve Brearton, Rob Gross and Kevin Ranney, "2nd Annual Ranking for Corporate Social Responsibility," *Report on Business Magazine*, March 2005, 37–68.

[10] "A Taxing Battle," *The Economist*, January 31, 2004, 71–72.

[11] Walter Wink, *The Powers that Be: The Theology for a New Millennium* (New York: Galilee Doubleday, 1998), 79–81.

[12] Dietrich Bonhoeffer, *The Cost of Discipleship* (London: SCM Press, 1996), 37.

GRACE

[1] Mihaly Csikzentmihalyi, *Creativity: Flow and the Psychology of Discovery and Invention* (New York: Harper Collins, 1996).

[2] John Haughey SJ, *The Holy Use of Money: Personal Finance in Light of Christian Faith* (New York: Doubleday, 1986), viii.

[3] Thomas Merton, *New Seeds of Contemplation*, 206.

[4] Haughey, *The Holy Use of Money*, 18.

[5] Amartya Sen, *On Ethics and Economics* (Oxford: Blackwell Publishers, 1989).

[6] C.K. Prahalad, *the Fortune at the Bottom of the Pyramid: Eradicating Poverty Through Profits* (Upper Saddle River, NJ: Wharton School Publishing, 2004), 5.

[7] Prahalad, *The Fortune at the Bottom of the Pyramid*, 21.

[8] Prahalad, *The Fortune at the Bottom of the Pyramid*, 57.

[9] Haughey, *The Holy Use of Money*, 55.

[10] Amartya Sen, *Development as Freedom* (New York: Random House, 2000), 14–15.

[11] Juliet B. Schor, "Global Equity and Environmental Crisis," in *Creating a New World Economy*, Gerald Epstein, Julie Graham and Jessica Nembhard, eds. (Philadelphia: Temple University Press, 1993).

[12] Sen, *Development as Freedom*, 113–115.

[13] Haughey, *The Holy Use of Money*, 129–131.

[14] Bonhoeffer, *The Cost of Discipleship*, 37.

[15] Bernard Lonergan, *Method in Theology* (Toronto: University of Toronto Press, 1971) 302.

BEAUTY

1. Martin Buber, *Ecstatic Confessions: The Heart of Mysticism* (Syracuse, NY: Syracuse University Press, 1996), 4.
2. Buber, *Ecstatic Confessions*, 38.
3. Hannah Arendt, *Eichmann in Jerusalem: A Report on the Banality of Evil* (London: Faber & Faber, 1963).
4. Thomas Merton, *Contemplative Prayer* (London: Image Books, 1996), 46–47.
5. Zachary Hayes, *Bonaventure: Mystical Writings* (New York: Crossroads Publishing, 1999), 39.
6. *Bonaventure: The Soul's Journey to God, The Tree of Life, The Life of St. Francis*, Ewert Cousins, ed. (Mahwah, NJ: Paulist Press, 1978), 263.
7. Hayes, *Bonaventure*, 51.
8. Cousins, ed., *Bonaventure*, 5.
9. Hayes, *Bonaventure*, 68.
10. Geoffrey Colvin, "Wal-Mart's Growth Will Slow Down – Eventually," *Fortune Magazine*, February 7, 2005, 48.
11. Robert S. Kaplan and David P. Norton, *The Balanced Scorecard: Translating Strategy into Action*. Cambridge MA: Harvard Business School Press. 1996.
12. Edward Fields, *The Essential of Finance and Accounting for Non-Financial Managers* (New York: American Management Association, 2002), 15–43.
13. R. Emmett Taylor, *No Royal Road: Luca Pacioli and His Times* (New York: Arno Press, 1980), 46.
14. Ronald Modras, *Ignatian Humanism* (Chicago: Loyola Press, 2004), 35.

PERSPECTIVE

1. Walter Brueggemann, *The Prophetic Imagination* (Minneapolis: Augsburg Fortress, 2001).
2. John Paul II, *Christifideles Laici*, section 14.
3. Avishai Margalit, *The Ethics of Memory* (Cambridge, MA: Harvard University Press, 2002), 88.
4. Porpora, *Landscapes of the Soul*, 45.
5. Hannah Arendt, *On Violence* (Orlando: Harcourt Brace & Company, 1970), 58.
6. Brueggemann, *The Prophetic Imagination*, 21–59.
7. St. Augustine, *Confessions*, Henry Chadwick, ed. (Oxford: Oxford University Press, 1991), 3.
8. Warren Bennis and Burt Nanus, *Leaders: Strategies for Taking Charge* (New York: Harper Business, 1997), 57–58.
9. James Morris, UN World Food Program, *The Economist*, February 5, 2005, 14.
10. Pierre Teilhard de Chardin, *Christianity and Evolution* (Orlando: Harcourt, 1974), 129.
11. Weil, *The Need for Roots*, 19.
12. Weil, *The Need for Roots*, 19.
13. "Fat Cats Feeding," *The Economist*, October 11, 2003, 73.
14. Collins, *Good to Great*, 65.

[15] Paul Ricoeur, *Memory, History, Forgetting*, Kathleen Blaney and David Pellauer, trans. (Chicago: University of Chicago Press, 2004), 24.

[16] Paul Ricoeur, *Symbolism of Evil* (New York: Harper and Row, 1967), 352–54.

PROPORTION

[1] Dow Marmur, *Walking Towards Elijah* (Burlington, ON: Welch Publishing, 1988), 74.

[2] www.globalsullivanprinciples.org

[3] Collins, *Good to Great*, 1.

[4] Eva Hoffman in "Introduction," Etty Hillesum, *An Interrupted Life and Letters from Westerbork* (New York: Henry Holt and Company, 1996).

[5] Etty Hillesum, *An Interrupted Life and Letters from Westerbork*, 93.

[6] Etty Hillesum, *An Interrupted Life and Letters from Westerbork*, 356.

[7] Etty Hillesum, *An Interrupted Life and Letters from Westerbork*, 74.

[8] Etty Hillesum, *An Interrupted Life and Letters from Westerbork*, 99.

[9] Goleman, *Emotional Intelligence*.

[10] Emmanuel Levinas, *Totality and Infinity: An Essay on Exteriority*, Alfonso Lingis, trans. (Pittsburg: Duquesne University Press, 1969), 79–82.

[11] Marc Gunther, "Money and Morals at GE," *Fortune*, November 15, 2004, 178.

[12] *Aiming High*.

[13] Guntherm, "Money and Morals at GE," 178.

[14] Levinas, *Totality and Infinity*, 152–154.

[15] Howard Gardner, *Creating Minds* (New York: Basic Books, 1994).

[16] Martin Buber, *Ecstatic Confessions*, 5.

[17] Robert Heilbroner, *Twenty-First Century Capitalism* (Toronto: House of Anansi Press, 1992), 95–100.

[18] Sumantra Ghoshal, Christopher A. Bartlett and Peter Moran, "Value Creation: The New Millenium Management Manifesto," in Subir Chowdhury, *Management 21C: Someday We'll All Manage This Way* (London: FT Prentice Hall, 2000), 121–140.

[19] Ghoshal, Bartlett and Moran, "Value Creation: The New Millenium Management Manifesto," 126.

[20] Arie de Geus, *The Living Company* (London: Nicholas Brealey Books, 1997).

[21] Collins, *Good to Great*, 15–22.

PRACTICE

[1] Walter Wink, *Jesus and Nonviolence: A Third Way* (Minneapolis: Augsburg Fortress, 2003), 21.

[2] "The Mind of the Leader," Special Edition, *Harvard Business Review*, January 2004.

[3] Jürgen Moltmann, *The Trinity and the Kingdom* (London: SCM Press, 1981), 154–159.

[4] Felicia R. Lee, "Research Around The World Links Religion to Economic Development," *New York Times*, January 31, 2004.

[5] Lee, "Research Around The World Links Religion to Economic Development."

[6] *The Collected Works of St. Teresa of Avila*, Volume 1, Kieran Kavanaugh OCD and Otilio Rodriguez OCD, trans. (Washington, DC: ICS Publications, 1987).

[7] M. Douglas Meeks, *God the Economist* (Minneapolis: Fortress Press, 1989), 197.

[8] Meeks, *God the Economist*, 197.

[9] Meeks, *God the Economist*, 18.

[10] Dietrich Bonhoeffer, *Ethics* (London: SCM Press, 1993).

[11] Porpora, *Landscapes of the Soul*, 21.

[12] Simone Weil, *Waiting on God*, 81.

[13] Gardner, Csikzentmihalyi and Damon, *Good Work*.

[14] Ewert Cousins, *Christ of the 21st Century* (New York: Continuum, 1994).

FAQs

[1] Simone Weil, *Waiting on God*, 81.

[2] Reinhold Niebuhr, *The Nature and Destiny of Man. Volume 1* (Louisville, KY: Westminster John Knox Press, 1997), 219.

[3] John Dalla Costa, "Meeting a New Reality with Wisdom," in *Across the Board*, January/February 2002, 31.

[4] Ronald F. Thiemann, *Religion in Public Life: A Dilemma for Democracy* (Washington, DC: Georgetown University Press, 1996), 121–178.

[5] Ross King, *Brunelleschi's Dome: How a Renaissance Genius Reinvented Architecture* (New York: Penguin. 2002).

BIBLIOGRAPHY

Alford, Helen J. and Michael J. Naughton. *Managing as if Faith Mattered: Christian Social Principles in the Modern Organization.* Notre Dame, IN: University of Notre Dame Press, 2001.

Aquinas, Thomas. *Summa Theologiae.* II-II. New York: McGraw Hill, 1966.

———. *Treatise on the Virtues.* Translated by John A. Oesterle. Notre Dame, IN: University of Notre Dame, 1984.

Arendt, Hannah. *Eichmann in Jerusalem: A Report on the Banality of Evil.* London: Faber & Faber, 1963.

———. *On Violence.* Orlando, FL: Harcourt Brace & Company, 1970.

Augustine. *Confessions.* Translated by Henry Chadwick. Oxford: Oxford University Press, 1991.

Badaracco, Joseph. *Quiet Leadership: An Unorthodox Guide to Doing the Right Thing.* Cambridge, MA: Harvard Business Press, 2002.

Bennis, Warren and Burt Nanus. *Leaders: Strategies for Taking Charge.* New York: Harper, 1997.

Bonhoeffer, Dietrich. *Ethics.* London: SCM Press, 1993.

———. *The Cost of Discipleship.* London: SCM Press, 1996.

———. *Creation and Fall: A Theological Exposition of Genesis 1–3.* Translated by Douglas Bax. Minneapolis: Fortress Press, 1997.

Brearton, Steve, Rob Gross and Kevin Ranney. "Second Annual Ranking for Corporate Social Responsibility." *Report on Business Magazine.* March 2005.

Brueggemann, Walter. *The Prophetic Imagination.* Minneapolis: Augsburg Fortress, 2001.

Buber, Martin. *Ecstatic Confessions: The Heart of Mysticism.* Syracuse, NY: Syracuse University Press, 1996.

Capdevila, Gustavo. "Globalization leads to slavery." *Asia Times*. August 23, 2001.

Casert, Raf (Associated Press). "EU Checks Up on Microsoft's Compliance with Anti-Trust Settlement." *InformationWeek*. February 25, 2005.

Centre for Ethical Orientation. *Aiming High: Renewing Trust in a Time of Suspicion*. 2003.

Chowdhury, Subir, editor. *Management 21 C*. London: Financial Times/Prentice Hall, 2000.

- Moss Kanter, Rosabeth. "Kaleidoscopic Thinking" in *Management 21 C*.
- Prahalad, C.K. "Work of the New Age Manager" in *Management 21 C*.
- Ghoshal, Sumantra, Christopher A. Bartlett, and Peter Moran. "Value Creation: The New Millennium Management Manifesto" in *Management 21C*.

Collins, Jim. *Good to Great*. New York: Harper Collins, 2001.

Colvin, Geoffrey. "Wal-Mart's Growth Will Slow Down – Eventually." *Fortune*. February 7, 2005.

Conlin, Michelle and Aaron Bernstein. "Working and Poor." *BusinessWeek*. May 31, 2004.

Cousins, Ewert. *Bonaventure: The Soul's Journey to God, The Tree of Life, The Life of St. Francis*. Mahwah, NJ: Paulist Press, 1978.

———. *Christ of the 21st Century*. New York: Continuum, 1994.

Cox, Harvey. "The Market as God: Living with the New Dispensation." *The Atlantic Monthly*. March 1999.

Crossan, John Dominic. *Jesus: A Revolutionary Biography*. San Francisco: Harper Collins, 1994.

Csikszentmihalyi, Mihaly. *Creativity, Flow and the Psychology of Discovery and Invention*. New York: Harper Collins, 1996.

Dalla Costa, John. "Meeting a New Reality with Wisdom." *Across the Board*. January/February 2002.

de Geus, Arie. *The Living Company*. London: Nicholas Brealey, 1997.

Donner, H.W. "Introduction." *Utopia* by Thomas More. London: Penguin, 1965.

Drucker, Peter. *Managing the Future.* New York: Plume, 1993.

Eliot, T.S. "Introduction." *The Need for Roots: Prelude to a Declaration of Duties for Mankind.* London: Routledge, 1996.

Elkington, John. *Cannibals with Forks: The Triple Bottom Line of 21st-Century Business.* Stoney Creek, CT: New Society, 1998.

English, John J. *Spiritual Freedom.* Chicago: Loyola Press, 1995.

Fields, Edward. *The Essential of Finance and Accounting for Non-Financial Managers.* New York: American Management Association, 2002.

Ford, David. *Self and Salvation: Being Transformed.* Cambridge: Cambridge University Press, 1999.

Fukuyama, Francis. *Our Posthuman Future: Consequences of the Biotechnology Revolution.* New York: Farrar, Straus and Giroux, 2002.

Gardner, Howard. *Creating Minds.* New York: Basic Books, 1994.

Gardner, Howard, Mihaly Csikszentmihalyi and William Damon. *Good Work: When Excellence and Ethics Meet.* New York: Basic Books, 2001.

Glater, Jonathan D. "Economic Crimes Strike a Third of U.S. Firms." *International Herald Tribune.* July 9, 2003.

Glint, Keith. *Management: A Sociological Introduction.* Cambridge: Polity Press, 1995.

Goleman, Daniel. *Emotional Intelligence: Why It Can Matter More Than IQ.* London: Bloomsbury, 1996.

Gunther, Marc. "Money and Morals at GE." *Fortune.* November 15, 2004.

Harvard Business Review. Special Edition: The Mind of the Leader. January 2004.

Haughey, John SJ. "The Primacy of Receivement," in *Business as Calling: Interdisciplinary Essays on the Meaning of Business from The Catholic Social Tradition,* Michael Naughton and Stephanie Rumpza, eds. (E-book, St. Paul, MN: Center for Catholic Studies, University of St. Thomas, 2005).

———. *The Holy Use of Money: Personal Finance in Light of Christian Faith*. New York: Doubleday, 1986.

Hayes, Zachary. *Bonaventure: Mystical Writings*. New York: Crossroad, 1999.

Heilbroner, Robert. *Twenty-First Century Capitalism*. Toronto: House of Anansi Press, 1992.

Heschel, Abraham Joshua. *Moral Grandeur and Spiritual Audacity*. Edited by Susannah Heschel. New York: Farrar, Straus and Giroux, 1996.

Hillesum, Etty. *An Interrupted Life and Letters from Westerbork*. New York: Henry Holt and Company, 1996.

Hoffman, Eva. "Introduction." *An Interrupted Life and Letters from Westerbork* by Etty Hillesum. New York: Henry Holt and Company, 1996.

Holmes, Stanley and Wendy Zellner. "The Costco Way: Higher Wages Mean Higher Profits. But Try Telling Wall Street." *BusinessWeek*. April 12, 2004.

Ignatius of Loyola. *Spiritual Exercises and Selected Works*. Edited by George E. Ganss. Mahwah, NJ: Paulist Press, 1991.

John Paul II. *Christifideles Laici*. Apostolic Exhortation. December, 30, 1988. Section 14.

———. "Crossing the Threshold of Hope." *Christianity and Plurality: Classic and Contemporary Readings*. Edited by Richard Plantinga. Oxford: Blackwell, 1999.

Johnson, Scott. "The Poor Get Poorer." *Newsweek*. September 29, 2003.

Kaplan, Robert S. and David P Norton. *The Balanced Scorecard: Translating Strategy into Action*. Cambridge, MA: Harvard Business School, 1996.

Kaptein, Muel and Johan Wempe. *A Theory of Corporate Integrity*. Oxford: Oxford University Press, 2002.

King, Ross. *Brunelleschi's Dome: How a Renaissance Genius Reinvented Architecture*. New York: Penguin, 2002.

Krishnamurti, J. *On Freedom*. San Francisco: Harper Collins, 1991.

Krueger, David A., Donald W. Shriver and Laura L. Nash. *The Business Corporation and Productive Justice*. Nashville: Abingdon, 1997.

Kunde, Jesper. *Corporate Religion*. London: Financial Times/Prentice Hall, 2000.

Lavelle, Louis. "Brisk Turnover in CEOs." *BusinessWeek*. March 7, 2005.

Lee, Felicia R. "Research around the World Links Religion to Economic Development." *New York Times*. January 31, 2004.

Levinas, Emmanuel. *Totality and Infinity: An Essay on Exteriority*. Translated by Alfonso Lingis. Pittsburg: Duquesne University Press, 1969.

———. *Difficult Freedom: Essays on Judaism*. Baltimore: The Johns Hopkins University Press, 1997.

Lonergan, Bernard. *Method in Theology*. Toronto: University of Toronto Press, 1971.

Macmurray, John. *Persons in Relation*. London: Humanities Press, 1993.

Margalit, Avishai. *The Ethics of Memory*. Cambridge, MA: Harvard University Press, 2002.

Marmur, Dow. *Walking towards Elijah*. Burlington, ON: Welch Publishing, 1988.

McLean, Bethany and Peter Elkind. *The Smartest Guys in the Room: The Amazing Rise and Scandalous Fall of Enron*. New York: Penguin, 2003.

Meeks, M. Douglas. *God the Economist*. Minneapolis: Fortress, 1989.

Merton, Thomas. *New Seeds of Contemplation*. New York: New Directions, 1961

———. *Contemplative Prayer*. London: Image, 1996.

Mitroff, Ian I. and Elizabeth A. Denton. *A Spiritual Audit of Corporate America: A Hard Look at Spirituality, Religion and Values in the Workplace*. San Francisco: Jossey-Bass, 1998.

Modras, Ronald. *Ignatian Humanism*. Chicago: Loyola, 2004.

Mohler, Keith, editor. Webster's Electronic Quotebase. 1994.

Moltmann, Jürgen. *The Trinity and the Kingdom*. London: SCM, 1981.

Nash, Laura and Scotty McLennan. *Church on Sunday, Work on Monday: The Challenge of Fusing Christian Values with Business Life.* San Francisco: Jossey-Bass, 2001.

Niebuhr, Reinhold. *The Essential Reinhold Niebuhr: Selected Essays and Addresses.* Edited by Robert Brown. New Haven: Yale University Press, 1986.

———. *The Nature and Destiny of Man.* Volume 1. Louisville, KY: Westminster/John Knox Press, 1997.

Plantinga, Richard, editor. *Christianity and Plurality: Classic and Contemporary Readings.* Oxford: Blackwell, 1999.

Porpora, Douglas V. *Landscapes of the Soul: The Loss of Moral Meaning in American Life.* Oxford: Oxford University Press, 2001.

Prahalad, C.K. *The Fortune at the Bottom of the Pyramid: Eradicating Poverty through Profits.* Upper Saddle River, NJ: Wharton School, 2004.

Rahner, Karl. *The Trinity.* Translated by Joseph Donceel. New York: Crossroad, 1998.

Ricoeur, Paul. *Symbolism of Evil.* New York: Harper and Row, 1967.

———. *Memory, History, Forgetting.* Translated by Kathleen Blaney and David Pellauer. Chicago: University of Chicago Press, 2004.

Rosen, David. *Caux Roundtable Panel Discussion.* Caux, Switzerland. July 2003.

Sacks, Jonathan. *The Dignity of Difference: How to Avoid the Clash of Civilizations.* London: Continuum, 2002.

Schor, Juliet B. "Global Equity and Environmental Crisis." *Creating a New World Economy.* Edited by Gerald Epstein, Julie Graham and Jessica Nembhard. Philadelphia: Temple University Press, 1993.

Schwartz, John. "Always on the Job, Employees Pay with Health." *New York Times.* September 5, 2004.

Sen, Amartya. *On Ethics and Economics.* Oxford: Blackwell, 1989.

———. *Development as Freedom.* New York: Random House, 2000.

Soelle, Dorothee. *Theology of Skeptics.* Translated by Joyce L. Irwin. Minneapolis: Augsburg Fortress, 1995.

Specht, David and Richard Broholm and Ed Mosel. "One Calling: Three Bottom Lines – A Practical Theology in Support of Organizational Faithfulness," in *Business as Calling: Interdisciplinary Essays on the Meaning of Business from The Catholic Social Tradition*, Michael Naughton and Stephanie Rumpza, eds. (E-book, St. Paul, MN: Center for Catholic Studies, University of St. Thomas, 2005).

Taylor, R. Emmett. *No Royal Road: Luca Pacioli and His Times*. New York: Arno, 1980.

Teilhard de Chardin, Pierre. *Christianity and Evolution*. Orlando: Harcourt, 1974.

———. *The Divine Milieu*. New York: Perennial Classics, 2001.

Teresa of Avila. *The Collected Works of St. Teresa of Avila*. Volume 1. Translated by Kieran Kavanaugh OCD and Otilio Rodriguez OCD. Washington, DC: ICS Publications, 1987.

The Economist. Special Report: Meritocracy in America. January 1, 2005.

Thiemann, Ronald F. *Religion in Public Life: A Dilemma for Democracy*. Washington, DC: Georgetown University Press, 1996.

Thomas, Landen, Jr. "Depression, A Frequent Visitor to Wall Street." *New York Times*. September 12, 2004.

Vardey, Lucinda, editor. *God in All Worlds: An Anthology of Contemporary Spirituality*. New York: Pantheon, 1995.

Wadell, Paul J. "Being Providentially Situated: The Indispensable Vocation of the Corporate Whistleblower." *Business as Vocation Symposium*. University of St. Thomas (St. Paul, MN). August 2004.

Wall, John, editor. *Paul Ricoeur and Contemporary Moral Thought*. London: Routledge, 2002.

Weil, Simone. *Waiting on God: Letters and Essays*. Fount: London, 1977.

———. *The Need for Roots: Prelude to a Declaration of Duties for Mankind*. London: Routledge, 1996.

Wink, Walter. *The Powers That Be: The Theology for a New Millennium*. New York: Galilee Doubleday, 1998.

———. *When the Powers Fail: Reconciliation in the Healing of Nations*. Minneapolis: Augsburg Fortress, 1998.

———. *Jesus and Nonviolence: A Third Way*. Minneapolis: Augsburg Fortress, 2003.

INDEX

A

accountability 13, 15, 16, 22, 26, 32, 44, 45, 56, 79, 107, 127, 132, 133, 136, 137, 139, 157–158, 159, 186, 194, 197, 199, 201, 204–205, 209, 222, 241, 247, 253, 259, 263, 276
Adam and Eve 250
addiction 37, 54, 211, 230, 235–236
AIDS 103, 277
AIG 210
Alford, Helen J. 14
ambition 54
apartheid 101, 210, 274
Apple 153
Aquinas, St. Thomas 14, 25, 54, 55, 56, 60–61, 70–71, 81, 147, 158–159, 259
Arendt, Hannah 147, 182, 273
Armstrong, Louis 112
AT&T 157
Attila the Hun 238
Augustine, St. 61, 187
awe 130, 149, 150, 152, 178, 182, 184–185, 190, 191, 204, 239, 242, 244, 248, 279

B

Badaracco, Joseph 52
balance 31, 45, 148–149, 156–166
balance sheet 166–168, 191–192, 195–196, 198–199, 220–221, 226–227, 230–231, 234–235, 246, 252–253, 257–258, 262–263
Barrings Bank 132
Barro, Robert J. 249

Bartlett, Christopher A. 232
Beatitudes, the 50, 102, 132
beauty 143–169
becoming 54–84
Bennis, Warren 189
Biko, Stephen 134
BMW 181
Bonaventure, St. 138, 149–152, 154, 156, 158, 159, 160, 198, 199
Bonhoeffer, Dietrich 107, 136, 256, 269, 274
bottom line 63, 166–169
Broholm, Richard 51
Brueggemann, Walter 173, 183, 184, 198
Brunelleschi, Filippo 278
Buber, Martin 145, 230
Buddhism 103, 250
Buffet, Warren 181
Burke, James 200
Burns, Ken 112
busyness 146–148

C

Cain 85
capitalism 140, 249, 270–271
Cass, Alden M. 67
Caterpillar 95
Catherine of Siena, St. 77
Caux Roundtable 81
Cemmex 124–125
Chagall, Marc 152, 269
Christianity 32, 160, 250, 270
Christians 18, 33, 51, 61, 81–82, 86, 100, 101, 119, 133, 146, 167, 204–205, 248, 267, 270
Christology 50, 116, 167, 204–205

Chrysler 119, 181
CIBC 40, 112, 210
Citibank 73, 136, 210
Collins, Jim 59–60, 71, 81, 150, 197, 213, 236
Colvin, Geoffrey 157
confidence 131–132
contemplation 23, 25, 80, 110, 148, 185, 256, 277
conversion 140–142
Costco 63
Cousins, Ewert 263
Cox, Harvey 46
Csikszentmihalyi, Mihaly 64, 261

D

da Vinci, Leonardo 161
D'Alessandro, Dominic 225
Damon, William 64, 261
Dante 249
Darwin, Charles 85, 120
David 11, 238–239
Davos Economic Forum 81, 231
Day, Dorothy 77
de Chardin, Pierre Teilhard SJ 28, 97, 120, 192, 273
de Gaulle, Charles 77
de Geus, Arie 234
deliverables 179, 230
Dell 109
della Francesca, Piero 160
Deming, W. Edward 93
Denton, Elizabeth 28
devotion 237–265
"double and" 59–66, 80, 84, 91, 96, 116–117, 179–182

Drucker, Peter 12, 15, 63, 197
Dunlop, Al 70

E

Einstein, Albert 162, 228
Eliot, T.S. 77, 228
Elkington, John 63
e-mail 45, 68, 189, 213
emotional intelligence 26, 52, 219, 243
engagement 41, 71, 81, 86, 107, 124, 263
enjoyment 152–155
Enron 40, 42, 68, 73, 132, 210
EQ [emotional quotient] 219
equality 97–99, 134–135
Equator Principles 97
Esau 85
ethics 41–42, 50, 77–78, 101, 154, 156, 164
Eucharist 77, 101, 229, 270
excellence 14, 48, 60, 61–64, 70, 106, 125, 162, 249, 264
Ezekiel 58, 69, 193

F

"Factor X" 36, 43
Fair Labor Association 97
fairness 222–227
faith 24–27, 37, 100–101, 121, 176, 208, 227, 277
FedEx 109, 189
Fiat 181
Ford 72, 181, 211
Ford, David 33
Ford, William III 72
Forest Stewardship Council 97
forgiveness 82, 155, 190, 226

Francis of Assisi, St. 149–150, 158, 273
freedom 131–132, 254–258
Freud, Sigmund 228
Fukayama, Francis 35–36
Fuller, Buckminster 161

G

Galbraith, John Kenneth 232
Galileo 161–162
Gandhi 44, 228, 238
Gardner, Howard 9, 64, 228, 261
Gates, Bill 56
General Electric 68–69, 92–93, 181, 224, 225
General Motors 181, 157
Ghoshal, Sumantra 232
Glaxo Smith Kline 260–261
Glint, Keith 68
Global Crossing 210
Global Sullivan Principles 210
globalization 15, 97–98, 199, 204
Global-we-zation principle 97–99
grace 116–142

H

Haughey, John 50, 119, 120, 125, 133
Hayes, Zachary 151, 164
Heilbroner, Robert 232
Heschel, Abraham Joshua 55
Hewlett-Packard 59
hierarchism 26, 43, 79, 196–199
Hillesum, Etty 215–218, 273
Hochschild, Arlie 67

Home Depot 95
Honda 181

I

IBM 92, 111, 157
ideals 116–143
Ignatius of Loyola, St. 49, 62, 77, 163–164, 184, 240, 244, 273
imbalance 210
Immelt, Jeffery 224–225
implementation 179
Incarnation, the 18, 33, 37, 49, 125, 146, 270
integrity 39–44
Intel 62–63, 94–95
International Declaration of Human Rights 78
International Organization for Migration (Geneva) 88
iPod 128, 153–154
IQ 219
Islam 32, 160, 161, 183, 250

J

Jacob 85–88
Jaguar 181
Jesus Christ 18–21, 23, 28, 30, 33, 37–38, 49–51, 57, 61, 77, 81, 82, 83, 86, 88, 93, 95, 100, 101, 102, 103, 106, 116, 119, 122, 125, 131, 132, 133, 135, 136, 138, 139, 143, 145–146, 148, 151, 167, 173, 176, 189–190, 193, 194, 198, 202, 204-205, 208, 214, 217, 218, 219, 222, 228, 229, 233, 239–240, 247, 248, 249, 251, 256, 259, 260, 262, 270, 279
John of the Cross, St. 119
Johnson & Johnson 59, 199–200
Joseph, Mary 141
Joshua 111
J.P. Morgan-Chase 140

Judaism 32
Julian of Norwich 205
Jung, Carl 247
Juran, Joseph M. 93
Just Time principle 108–111

K

Kanter, Rosabeth Moss 32
Kaplan, Robert 159
Kaptein, Muel 42–43
kenosis 100–101, 229, 248, 271
Kenotic Creativity principle 99–102
Keynes, John Maynard 232
kingliness 240, 242, 247
kingship 247–249
Kolbe, Maximilian, St. 77, 134
Kraft 109–110, 236
Krishnamurti, J. 54, 81

L

leadership 63, 174–175, 236, 238, 243, 244, 247
Levinas, Emmanuel 18, 43, 224, 227
liberty 108–111
Lonergan, Bernard SJ 104, 141, 156, 194
Lord's Prayer 220, 222

M

Macmurray, John 43
Magnification principle 106–108
Manulife 225
Margalit, Avishai 180
Marmur, Rabbi Dow 207, 235
Marsalis, Wynton 112

Marsh McLennan 136
Martha, sister of Mary 148
Marxist socialism 270
Mary, mother of God 106, 107, 108, 145, 279
Mary, sister of Martha 148
Maslow, Abraham 94
McCleary, Rachel M. 249
McCormick, Richard 19
McDonald's 236
McLennan, Scotty 12, 20
McLuhan 259
Meeks, Douglas 254–255
Mercedes 181
Mercier, Ron SJ 42
mercy 214–215
Merrill Lynch 40, 112, 136, 210
Merton, Thomas 49, 119, 148
Microsoft 55–56
Middle Ages 160
Mitroff, Ian 28
Mitsubish 181
Modras, Ronald 164
Moltmann, Jürgen 244
money 117–121
Moore's Law 63, 94
morality 13, 17, 18, 21, 43, 61, 162, 166–167, 180, 209, 235, 239, 249
Moran, Peter 232
More, St. Thomas 37
More/Moore principle 94–97
Mosaic Law 122, 211, 232, 250, 255
Moses 121–122, 133, 138
Mother Teresa 110

Motorola 92
mutuality 129–131
Myriad Genetics 90
mystics 22, 43, 80, 88, 94, 110, 145, 148, 187, 188, 250–251, 265, 271, 273,

N

9/11 109, 154, 272
Nash, Laura 12, 20, 27
Naughton, Michael J. 14, 70
needs 121–129
New York Stock Exchange 112
Niebuhr, Reinhold 38, 215, 271
Nike 63
Norton, David 159

O

obedience 13, 19, 26, 43, 79, 84, 106–108, 132–133, 136, 163, 179, 200, 202, 240–241, 250–253, 259–260, 263, 276
order 129–131, 186–192
Our Father 222
outsourcing 15, 34, 38, 75, 104, 137, 215

P

Pacioli, Fr Luca 160–163
Paoli, Arturo 117–121, 125, 154–155, 167
passion 22, 24, 66, 106, 114, 148, 175, 189, 249
Paul, St. 28, 62, 87, 143, 167, 248, 279
perspective 172–206
Phillip Morris 109
Picasso, Pablo 228
Pio of Pietralcina, St. 77
Plato 121, 247

plurality 19
Pontius Pilate 259
Pope John Paul II 19, 50, 176
Porpora, Douglas 47, 181, 258–259
Porras, Jerry 59
postmodernism 162, 174, 254, 254
poverty 15, 57, 88, 124, 127, 130, 131, 140, 185, 203, 231, 268–269
power 21, 23, 51, 52, 100, 101, 111, 129, 131, 154, 166, 215, 231, 237, 239–240, 244, 247–248, 259, 273–274
powerlessness 99, 219, 239
practicality 51, 72–73, 117, 203, 216, 245, 254, 268–269
practice 237–265
pragmatism 37, 70, 72–76, 78, 125–126, 141, 149, 158, 159, 268
Prahalad, C.K. 12, 123–125
presence 30–53
Pricewaterhouse-Coopers 42
priestly role 208, 214–221
Procter & Gamble 59
proportion 156–158, 207–236
purification 23, 80–81, 34, 263–265

R

Rahner, Karl 32
Renaissance 160–162, 278
Research in Motion 63
responsibility 136–138, 195–196
Ricoeur, Paul 34–35, 204
risk 99–102, 138–139, 227–231
ROI [return on investment] 91, 226
ROI^2 principle 90–92
Rosen, Rabbi David 47

S

Saab 181
Sabbath 71, 108, 146, 208, 235, 241, 244, 251, 255–256
sacrifice 51, 66, 101, 111, 134, 136, 138, 140, 206, 208, 212, 233, 241, 250, 264
St. Victor, Richard 37
saints 23, 25, 73, 76, 77, 80, 110, 120, 148, 174, 249, 263, 273, 277
salvation 85, 86, 100, 103, 162, 166, 173, 192, 252, 268, 273, 277
Saturn 152
Saul 238
Schor, Juliet 132
scriptures
    Christian 17, 183
    Hebrew 17, 122, 129, 201–202, 250
Sears 157
security 231–235
Sen, Amartya 26, 104, 113, 123, 131–132, 228, 256–257
Seven Sigma principle 92–94
Shula, Don 238
Shumpeter, Joseph 232
silos 64, 111, 201–206, 254, 261, 276
Simeon 145
Simon of Cyrene principle 103–105, 269, 274
Six Sigma 92–93, 253
Smith, Adam 46, 232
Soelle, Dorothee 11, 40
Solomon 238
Solomon Smith Barney 210
soul 76–80
Southwest Airlines 63
Specht, David 51

spirituality 11, 14, 17, 19, 21, 22, 31, 32, 43, 47, 48, 56, 61, 71, 74–75, 77, 81, 88, 102–103, 121, 126, 127, 128, 129, 150, 151, 166, 172, 180, 184, 187, 188, 201, 205, 209, 213, 214, 215, 217, 228, 242, 268, 271, 272
stability 103–105
Stravinsky, Igor 228
sublation 125
Sullivan, Leon 210
SWAG analysis 184
SWOT analysis 184

T

talents 57, 62, 65, 82, 100, 102, 112, 130, 131, 147, 180, 188, 228, 230–231, 235, 257, 264
Taylor, R. Emmett 161
Teresa of Avila, St. 180, 251
thankfulness 107
theology 36, 81, 101, 103, 116, 118, 125, 134, 167, 172, 173, 208, 215, 229, 249, 270
Thiemann, Ronald F. 277–278
THQ [thinking heart quotient] 219
TNT 189
Torah 103
Toyota 63, 137, 181
transparency 179, 258–263
Trinity 49, 61, 151, 205–206, 220, 244
Trumpet Blowing principle 111–113
truth 111–113, 139–140, 148–151, 258–263

U

United Nations 78
Upanishads 250

V

vision 178
vocation 13, 18, 25, 30, 87, 112, 114, 151, 157, 242, 167, 272
Volvo 181

W

Wal-Mart 63, 93, 109, 157, 212
Weber, Max 249
Weil, Simone 13–14, 24, 43, 61, 76–79, 89, 92, 117, 128, 133, 134, 135–136, 139, 140, 159, 177, 186, 196–197, 224, 259, 265, 267, 268, 273
Wempe, Johan 42–43
Westinghouse 233
whistle-blowing 32, 111–112, 183, 236, 239
Wilmer, Cuttler & Pickering 42
Wink, Walter 51, 101, 215, 239, 273
Winnie-the-Pooh 238
Wolfe, Tom 67
Wolfensohn, James 203
World Bank 130, 203
WorldCom 132, 210
wrestling 85–114